Please renew/return this item by the last date shown.

So that your telephone call is charged at local rate, please call the numbers as set out below:

	From Area codes 01923 or 020:	From the rest of Herts:
Renewals:	01923 471373	01438 737373
Enquiries:	01923 471333	01438 737333
Textphone:	01923 471599	01438 737599

L32   www.hertsdirect.org/librarycatalogue

Better Than Working

by the same author

Better Than Working

Patrick Skene Catling

Secker & Warburg
LONDON

Published by Secker & Warburg 2004

2 4 6 8 10 9 7 5 3 1

The following photographs are used by permission of Corbis:
the Duke of Windsor, Billie Holiday, Duke Ellington,
Robert Mitchum and Graham Greene.

The author and publishers are grateful for permission to reproduce the lines on p.169
from 'Strange Fruit', music and wordsby Lewis Allan © 1939 – Edward B. Marks
Music Commpany – Copyright renewed; extended term of copyright derived from
Lewis Allan – assigned and effective July 21, 1995 to Music Sales Corporation.
All rights for the world outside of USA controlled by Edward B. Marks Music
Company – All Rights Reserved – Lyric reproduced by kind permission of
Carlin Music Corp., London NW1 8BD

First published in Great Britain in 2004 by
Secker & Warburg
Random House, 20 Vauxhall Bridge Road,
London SW1V 2SA

Random House Australia (Pty) Limited
20 Alfred Street, Milsons Point, Sydney,
New South Wales 2061, Australia

Random House New Zealand Limited
18 Poland Road, Glenfield,
Auckland 10, New Zealand

Random House (Pty) Limited
Endulini, 5A Jubilee Road, Parktown 2193, South Africa

The Random House Group Limited Reg. No. 954009
www.randomhouse.co.uk

A CIP catalogue record for this book
is available from the British Library

ISBN 0 436 20624 2

Papers used by Random House are natural,
recyclable products made from wood grown in sustainable forests;
the manufacturing processes conform to the environmental
regulations of the country of origin

Printed and bound in Great Britain by
Clays Ltd, St Ives PLC

Acknowledgements

Many of the people to whom I owe thanks are mentioned in these memoirs. I would like to add an expression of special gratitude to John Banville, Caroline Walsh, Jonathan Williams, Geoff Mulligan, Mark Amory, James Hegarty, John V. Lennon, Clare Asquith, John McLaughlin, Al Hart and Iris Diana Laing. They have all helped me to achieve publication.

I

The Duke, as usual by tea-time, was drunk. Not very drunk, not yet arrogant and clumsy, but sufficiently soft in the head to have driven his Cadillac convertible along the fairways of Nassau's premier golf club. This was before electric buggies. Evidently, he was not in the mood for long walks between shots; and, after all, he was the Governor. He was HRH the Duke of Windsor, and I was an eighteen-year-old Pilot Officer, still easily impressed. He had given me a friendly wave as he drove the car past me on the sixteenth fairway. He finished his game quickly and was well ahead of me in the bar. In the early stages of drinking, he had a charmingly whimsical, some said boyish, slightly tilted smile. Free for the afternoon from the Duchess's surveillance, he was able to indulge in playful informality.

'Hope you didn't mind my playing through,' he said with an unapologetic smile. 'What'll you have?'

It was gratifying to be recognised by someone so senior, and astonishing to be offered a drink. We were both in civilian clothes, but they did not disguise the disparity of ranks – I in a white shirt and khaki trousers, he in a lime-green shirt and doeskin slacks of Schiaparelli Shocking Pink.

After more than one drink he became quite chatty, asking some of the questions that strangers ask in casual barroom encounters.

What's your name? Where are you from? What do you do?

'A navigator, eh?' he commented. 'That must be jolly interesting. Astronomy and mathematics and so on. Training on Mitchells?'

'No, sir. Ferrying.'

'Ah! Trips to Egypt and India. I envy you.'

Since Churchill had ordered the Duke to assume the governorship – it had taken the threat of a court-martial to move him from Lisbon – he was confined to the Bahamas, not even allowed, at first, to visit the United States. The Prime Minister was determined to prevent the ex-King from attempting to negotiate peace with Germany to help his friends there to fight more effectively against Communism. The Duke's sister-in-law, later to be venerated as Britain's royal grandma, could not abide his wife, but shared his political flexibility. As she told Sir Walter Monckton at the time, she was in favour of a diplomatic deal with the Nazis, provided that they would agree to let her keep her job as Queen. The House of Windsor had had a German name before. She might have been willing to rename it – the House of Berchtesgaden, perhaps. Anything to keep those Russians at a safe distance.

On New Providence Island then, in 1943, there were two separate Royal Air Force establishments. An isolated, underprivileged group were being taught about twin-engined B-25 bombers in an Operational Training Unit on Oakes Field. I had never visited the place and didn't know anyone unlucky enough to be stationed there. Its only distinction was that it was named after a friend of the Governor's, Sir Harry Oakes, the victim of a squalid recent murder. A local playboy was tried and acquitted, and the disappointed authorities, citing courtroom revelations of his unsavoury habits, deported him. Imagine being deported from the Bahamas for bad behaviour!

Yet the colony was anomalously proud of the shenanigans of its British aristocrats in exile. I was quite well placed to observe them, as I was a member of the South Atlantic Wing of the ferry group based in Montreal. At Windsor Field, close to Nassau, a benevolent RAF medical officer had decreed such a low monthly quota of flying hours that we aircrew were compelled between trips to spend as long as two weeks in residence in Nassau's oldest, most distinguished hotel, the Royal Victoria, and lolling on Paradise Beach, on what used to be known as Hog Island and is now called Paradise Island.

Having arrived only a short time earlier, a fresh graduate of navigation school, I was almost entirely innocent. True, I had been welcomed by Lady Maxine Baird, a hospitality committee of one, but that connection had not lasted long, just as it had not lasted long with any of my predecessors. After a midnight swim from the beach near her house, she had insisted, because of sand-flies, on lying on top. She was voracious and bossy, and there was a limit to the allowances that could be made for the fact that her husband had been a prisoner of war since Dunkirk. Anyway, here I was, drinking with the Duke of Windsor.

'Come on,' he said, 'let's go for a ride.'

I left my Jeep at the club. Sitting beside him in the shiny, black convertible, I would have liked to be seen by one of my crew.

'You've been Over the Hill, I suppose,' he said.

'Not yet,' I admitted, as suavely as possible. Over the Hill – the initials were capitalised in everybody's mind – was a district, I had heard, that airmen and others sometimes daringly visited after dark. It was the black ghetto, noted for furtive, all-night revelry in shebeens and shanties. Actually, Bahamians have long been racially more tolerant than most other people. Their ghetto Over the Hill might have been more accurately defined with the title of a Duke Ellington composition, 'Black, Brown and Beige'. Miscegenation did not bother Bahamians. What mattered was money. Over the Hill was where the colony kept poverty, where the haves, for fun, went slumming with the have-nots. In this respect, the ghetto was like Harlem in the distant past.

I knew that the Duke of Windsor had the reputation of a fun-lover, a bit of a sport. He enhanced this reputation by encouraging

Blind Blake, Nassau's foremost calypso singer, to perform as a sort of court jester at parties, even in Government House, accompanying himself on guitar, to sing his popular new song, 'Love Alone':

> Love, love alone,
> Caused King Edward to leave the throne.
> I know King Edward was noble and great,
> But his love caused him to ablicate [*sic*].
> He got the money and he got the talk
> And the fancy walk that would suit New York . . .

The Duke always led the laughter and applause. But now I looked at my watch. Wasn't 4.45 rather early for this expedition?

Part-way down the far side of the hill, I was surprised when the Duke produced an Army cap with the scarlet band of superior rank and jammed it jauntily on his well-groomed fair head. He turned off the main road, along a narrow, unpaved road with a row of dilapidated wooden shacks on each side, and announced his arrival with long blasts on the horn – BAAAAHP! BAAAAHP! BAAAAHP!

I must have looked alarmed.

'It's all right,' he assured me. 'They know me. I come here often.'

Several front doors opened promptly, as if his signal had been expected. Small boys, one by one and in twos and threes, ran out and gathered in the road near the car. There were about fifteen of them, probably ranging in age from, say, eight to twelve. They were dressed in cotton shirts and shorts that looked faded by many launderings, and they were all carrying rifles – that is to say, homemade facsimiles and sticks that represented rifles.

The Duke stood up in the car, a short, upright, slim figure of paradoxical dignity, the authoritative cap transcending the gaudy green shirt and pink slacks. The expression on his face was stern. Without any preliminaries, he commanded the boys, in a high-pitched, military shout, to 'Fall in!' They duly obeyed, forming fairly straight ranks. Then the Duke proceeded to drill them in accordance with the protocol of the Brigade of Guards. When he ordered them to 'Slo-ope . . . *arms!*' they propped their toy rifles on their tiny shoulders very nearly in unison. When he yelled, 'By the left . . . qui-ick *march!*' they quickly marched, and the order 'A-bout . . . *turn!*' soon got them back again. When, at last, he stood them at ease and then easy, the boys were more like boys as they scrambled competitively for the silver coins that their commander scattered in front of them.

How His Excellency laughed! I thought he was an awful shit and a fool, but I was grateful to him, and I am still, for demonstrating so vividly that warfare is absurd.

2

Of course, I am not suggesting that war is a joke. It is an absurdity of the utmost seriousness. Leading politicians and churchmen are never more earnest than when invoking militant patriotism. In the beginning, rival amoebas had to kill or be killed to prove which ones were fit for evolution. Cavemen beat each other to death with stone clubs in the competition for territory, food and women. Pugnacity is an apparently ineradicable element of human nature, the boys-will-be-boys syndrome. Preparing for war, waging war and recovering from war, over and over again, were universally the predominant activities of the twentieth century. They brought about many technological innovations but caused my family great inconvenience.

I sympathise with Holden Caulfield, the narrator of shy J. D. Salinger's novel *The Catcher in the Rye*, who skipped genealogy and 'all that David Copperfield kind of crap', so I'll sketch the background briefly.

My paternal grandfather was an English bank manager who was born early enough to avoid being involved in the twentieth century's most characteristic unpleasantness. Cosseted in Victorian middle-class comfort, with all the traditional labour-saving devices (people below stairs), he was enviably complacent, wishing only to attain his pension while still able to enjoy hybridising roses. My father,

Arthur Donald Skene Catling, was born in 1898 and brought up in Devon. My mother, Sheila Marie Houlihan, was born five years later, in India, where not all the servants suppressed their sense of grievance. One of them murdered her father. She was adopted by her mother's father, one Patrick Blake of Bangalore, an Irish doctor whom Indians liked.

At school in Exeter, Donald did so well in Greek and Latin that he dreamed of reading classics at Oxford. But by the time he was old enough to try to get there, trench warfare urgently required a large supply of young men. In his eighteenth year, he enlisted in the Devon Regiment and was shipped to France.

His ardour for infantry tactics as a subaltern did not last long. The weather was bad, there was a lot of noise, and his best friend, hideously wounded, begged my father to shoot him. My father would not tell me whether or not he complied with the request. I believe that he did.

He distrusted grandiose strategies planned in remote châteaux. He shared the sentiments that Siegfried Sassoon expressed in 'Base Details':

> If I were fierce and bald and short of breath,
> I'd live with scarlet Majors at the Base,
> And speed glum heroes up the line to death.

My father later applauded George Orwell. 'To a surprising extent,' Orwell wrote, 'the war-lords in shining armour, the apostles of the martial virtues, tend not to die fighting when the time comes.'

My father had little respect for Tennyson, none at all for his most celebrated two lines,

> Theirs not to reason why,
> Theirs but to do and die . . .

My father felt that his *was* to reason why. He volunteered for transfer to the Royal Flying Corps, in which there were frequent vacancies. Pilots were awarded their wings after only about ten hours of solo flight, and life expectancy on operations was measured in weeks. But, in the meantime, pilots enjoyed meals in an officers' mess and slept between sheets in beds, not in muddy holes in the ground.

He flew over the Western Front in Sopwith Pups and Bristol Bulldogs (why the canine nomenclature?) – or are those names I remember from adventure stories in the *Boy's Own Paper*, the *Wizard* and *Hotspur*? He certainly did not fly the de Havilland DH-9. He said pilots dreaded flying it. It was notoriously nose-heavy and deserved its nickname, the Flying Coffin.

Having got through service unscathed where it was most hazardous, he almost got himself killed when carrying out a routine air raid, officially called 'punitive', on a village in Mesopotamia. His plane was hit by Arab rifle fire. On landing at his aerodrome, he crashed. The only permanent physical damage to his person was the loss of all his front teeth. At the age of twenty-one, he had to wear a set of false ones, which, in the style of the time, were much too regular and too brilliantly white to look real. Before he obtained a more convincingly realistic set, he used to attempt to amuse me in my infancy by taking his teeth out and replacing them in a protrusive death's-head grin. My mother told me later that the trick never amused me.

In addition to false teeth, my father's only material souvenirs of 'the War to End War' were several Persian carpets, a service revolver, a Sam Browne belt and his wrecked plane's propeller boss. In the centre of that smoothly truncated wooden cone was embedded a single Arab bullet. If it had hit a few inches away, in any direction, it would probably have shattered the propeller. Then, if my father had been unlucky enough to survive an immediate forced landing, he would have fallen into Arab captivity, famous in those days for beginning with castration.

In the hall of a semi-detached house in the London suburb of

Golders Green, the boss was put to civilian use. With holes drilled at intervals around the top, it became an umbrella stand. To my father it was a perennial reminder of death postponed. He accentuated the incongruity of war and peace, abroad and home, as did many others back from faraway countries, by giving the house, the first he owned, an exotic name – Kazvin, a town in Persia. He even went so far as to have the front door painted and annually repainted various fauvist colours, startling the neighbours. He must have derived special pleasure from shocking the householder next door, who, like my father's father, was a bank manager of solemn probity and conservatism.

Involvement in war tends to make one anti-authoritarian.

3

Military service accelerates maturation, or at least creates an illusion of maturity. Who needs university? Royal Flying Corps pilots became the first pilots of the new, independent Royal Air Force. After a short time in the RAF, my father found that he no longer yearned for the life of an Oxford undergraduate. As soon as he got out of uniform, he applied for a job as a reporter in Reuters News Agency, then situated in a small building on the Thames Embankment. Reuters almost immediately sent him to their office in Bombay.

Already feeling an urge to write something less ephemeral than news dispatches, he wrote a letter asking one of his early literary heroes, H. G. Wells, for advice on how to get a book published, though it had not yet been written. A few weeks later, there was a reply, on writing paper engraved *Easton Glebe, Dunmow* and dated Christmas Eve, 1919. Perhaps the great man was in a Christmas mood. In neat, tiny manuscript, he said:

> Dear Mr Catling,
>   I'm really workwrought up to the hilt. Excuse brevity.
>   Few publishers will look at mss. of unknown men. But anyone who has written a few light articles or otherwise made a mark gets prompt attention. Verb. Sap.

Never go to John Lane. Never pay agents for 'advice.' Never pay for publication or 'share expenses.' Never dedicate a first book — it looks self conscious.

Every popular magazine is dying for want of short stories. Price of ten pounds upward & you retain the right to re-publish. A story published in Britain can usually be sold (through an agent) in America.

Curtis Brown is a friendly, honest agent.

Your sincerely,

H. G. WELLS

I won't read any damned mss. nohow.

My father treasured the letter, but allowed enemies of promise (earning a living, starting a family) to postpone creative writing. Twelve years elapsed before he managed to write a publishable novel, *Fever Heat*, about a young English bachelor in love in India. Another ten years went by until he wrote a second novel, *Worldstate Under Women*, a prescient fantasy that publishers rejected. By that time he seemed to be influenced by Aldous Huxley; the subtitle might well have been *Timid New World*. As far as I know, my father then gave up writing, except for newspapers. When I inherited the H. G. Wells letter, I, too, treasured it, but not so much that I resisted sacrificing it at a time of need. In a Sotheby's auction in the 1970s, a collector paid 90 guineas for it, and I paid a bill for electricity.

Donald married my mother in Bombay, when he was twenty-five and she was nineteen. His return to London was her first journey outside the Raj. In a cold flat in Fulham, she learned some of the rudimentary uses of a kitchen. After a number of experiments she succeeded in boiling eggs, though never quite accurately. On grey English days she occasionally put together curries of fervour that brought tears to my father's eyes. She realised reluctantly that clothes dropped on the bedroom floor were not magically gathered and cleaned. However, in a local nursing home on 14 February 1925, without unusual difficulty, she gave birth to me.

I am still astonished by my good fortune. The odds against being born are so large.

Alone with Sheila one day when I was about four, after declaring my affection with customary extravagance ('I love you a million million million!'), I asked her who I would have been if I hadn't been who I was. My memory of the conversation remains vivid. It went along these lines:

'What do you mean?' she asked, after a sleepy sip of tea. She was propped up by pillows in bed. I was sitting by her feet.

'I mean if I wasn't born.'

'Who would you be? Well, I suppose you wouldn't be anyone.'

The notion of non-existence was impossible to grasp. She could see I was upset.

'Perhaps you'd be another boy, just like you.'

'But I wouldn't be me.'

'You'd feel the same. You would be you.'

'You wouldn't be my mother.' I felt pangs of jealousy. 'You'd have had someone else.'

She placed her cup and saucer on a bedside table, leaned forward and put her arms around me.

'But I did have you,' she pointed out. 'So that's all right.'

'Yes,' I eventually conceded, as if saying: 'But only just.'

My mother probably did not mean to make me contemplate perplexing philosophical concepts before I attended kindergarten, but sometimes she inadvertently provoked big questions. One fine evening in my fifth year she allowed me to sleep, or try to sleep, on a mattress outside a small tent in the garden. The July sky was cloudless and the blue twilight faded slowly.

'My eyes won't stay shut,' I complained when she came to check. 'It isn't dark.'

'It's getting dark,' she assured me. 'The stars are beginning to come out. Lie on your back and look up. See how many you can count.' That suggestion, I recognise now, was a variant of the old anaesthetist's trick.

Only a few of the brighter stars were visible.

'Seven,' I announced unenthusiastically. I was a terrific counter.

'Keep on looking. There'll be more. A lot more.'

As the sky became blue-black, the pin-points of light were soon countless. Gazing at the Milky Way, I caught my first glimpse of infinity. I did not like it. Asleep eventually, I was carried into the tent. I can remember the awful buried-alive feeling of awaking in black starlessness.

The next morning, I asked my mother what there was beyond the stars. 'More stars,' she said. And after them? 'More and more.' But in the end? She said she did not know – nobody knew. The awareness that adults did not know everything made me feel exposed to fearful insecurity. Even before knowing the word for the universe, I already knew as much as Galileo and Einstein about its shape and size and destiny – the vaguest and cloudiest of intimations. I suffered from nightmares about space that I could not describe and my parents therefore could not try to explain. Sometimes, quite rarely, I still have the familiar, frighteningly blank dream, and I am bound to say that I have been getting no help from theologians and Stephen Hawking. Contrary to Sartre's opinion that hell is other people, I think it would be eternal consciousness of solitude.

My father and I got on quite well together, though our conversations were not profoundly intimate. Like most other children, I saw my father only briefly on some evenings and intermittently on weekends and holidays. He commuted by bus and Underground to Reuters' headquarters, with only infrequent escapist perquisites, such as Mediterranean cruises with the Home Fleet. He appreciated the Royal Navy's impeccable hospitality. Their presumption of superiority never disturbed him. The Senior Service was obsolescent; airmen have long cherished a confident belief in their avant-garde modernity.

Routine work in the office made him restive. He improved his position there by founding the agency's Mail & Feature Department which sent weekly newsletters to papers all over the world, keeping them up to date on what was happening in London in the theatre, literature and the other arts. Reuters in the beginning had won a reputation for fast communication by sending financial bulletins to and from the Continent by carrier pigeons. My father, in a more leisurely fashion, got tickets to opening nights and invitations to concerts, gallery previews and book launches, and distributed cultural news by air mail. The letters were reproduced in large numbers by mimeograph. He provided me with stacks of super-fluous copies to draw on. Scribbling on the backs conditioned me to believe it was normal to use stationery profligately.

He began teaching me to read when I was very young. Even when it must have been obvious that I had got the hang of reading, my mother let me think she did not know I did not need her to read to me at bedtime. We prolonged this cosy subterfuge as long as possible. But when I was confined to my room with measles at the age of five, I could not refrain from boasting that I had just read all of *The Wind in the Willows*, even the rhapsodic chapters ('The Piper at the Gates of Dawn' and 'Wayfarers All') that interrupted the main narrative, the story of the manic, depressive and finally triumphant adventures of Toad. And next, I added, I was going to learn *The Hunting of the Snark*. Even though I failed to perform that feat, it was impossible to pretend any more that I depended on being read to. The end of an era.

4

Fever Heat was published at last in 1931, to warm acclaim from my mother. The novel was dedicated to her, in spite of H. G. Wells's admonition against the dedication of first books. Reviews and sales were good enough for two reprintings and a cheap edition with a dramatic pictorial jacket. At the age of six, I observed that writing a book was an effective way of attracting attention and possible approval. I vowed to become a writer.

One Sunday afternoon a short time afterwards, my father took me to his office. As there was nobody else in the room, he sat me at a desk with a typewriter and showed me how to operate it. It was a massive, black upright, an Underwood. Striking a key with sufficient force sounded like John Henry's sledgehammer slamming an iron spike, the noise of a he-man at work. After some tentative stabs, I was able to make clear impressions on the off-white copy paper. Using only my forefingers and staring alternately at the keyboard and the paper, I made gradual progress, with only a few x-ings out. It was slower than writing with a pencil; however, in compensation, the letters looked like print in a newspaper, a magazine, a book. My technique has remained the same since that inaugural exercise. Two fingers, vigilantly supervised, can move fast enough, and the product enables me to imagine permanence.

There was another development that made 1931 a pivotal year.

In my second term at a local, amateurish primary school, in a converted manor house beside Golders Green's last dairy farm my father felt something was wrong, though my mother thought the purple cap and blazer were 'sweet'. A teacher was compelling me to write with my right hand, whereas at home, being naturally left-handed, I wrote with my left. I did not object to ambidextrousness — indeed, I have always played ball-games right-handedly — but my father feared that some sort of cerebral wires were being dangerously crossed. I was transferred to King Alfred School, a progressive, co-educational establishment on the northern downward slope from Hampstead, not far below the Whitestone Pond, which, at 437 feet above sea-level, is London's highest point. At KAS the blazers were optional and green, the colour of eco-friendliness. We were allowed to write any ways we chose or not to write at all, for all scholastic activities, even attending classes, were voluntary. Long before permissiveness became a cult idea, Joseph Wicksteed, the benign headmaster, permitted total freedom compatible with the comfort of others.

The art teacher was an amiable, lazy man of elastic aesthetic tolerance. He was favourably impressed when I told him that the mother of a girl I knew had met Max Ernst. The teacher said the way my daubs combined incompatible colours in reckless quantities of liquid poster paints suggested I might have a capacity for Dadaistic anarchism. He was not always that complimentary. However, the longest-lasting benefit of the school's permissiveness was an introduction to jazz. Jocelyn Kelsey, a senior to whom I am still grateful, although his instruction has caused me untold expense, was allowed by the headmaster about ten minutes each week to address us assembled pupils and to play one jazz record. Jocelyn introduced the music with didactic waffle, which, I eventually realised, was an academic disguise contrived to gain permission for brief experiences of sensuous bliss. I recall the first moments of excitement, a Damascene epiphany. He played 'Jubilee Stomp', a 1928 composition by Duke Ellington. I remember every note.

But the most influential event of my eleventh summer was a visit to Germany, when the Olympic Games were played there. My father had already taken us to France on family holidays and once, most delightfully, to the Danish seaside near Hamlet's Kronborg Castle, but this was my first journey alone. I travelled in a small steamer from London to Hamburg and by train to Berlin.

The ticket inspector was a formidable figure, a caricature of Teutonic officiousness. He wore a military-looking cap, high in front with a peak down to his eyebrows, and a Kaiser moustache, upturned and waxed to points at the extremities. He was old enough to have been involved in the Great War. He examined my ticket with an expression of indignation.

'This ticket', he observed, 'is damaged. You have tvisted der ticket.' (That is a sufficient attempt to transcribe his dialect. I could not speak German.)

He was correct. Even then, while thinking of other things, I had a neurotic way of folding and twisting tickets.

'I'm sorry.'

'This is not good enough, "sorry". The ticket is the property of the company.'

'Must I buy another ticket?' I asked, hoping that I would not be compelled to do so, as I had very little money.

'That is not the point. When you are in this country, you should show respect.' He handed back the spoiled ticket with a grimace of distaste and, without another word, moved on to the next passenger.

Welcome to the Third Reich!

My father had been able to persuade the Reuters correspondent, Gordon Young, to put me up in his large apartment. My host's mother, a sweet, grandmotherly lady who seemed ancient (she was probably in her mid-sixties), was in Berlin at the time and assumed the role of cicerone while Mr Young was at work, reporting Germany's disastrous military growth and moral decline. I was an importunate guest, forever asking for more sightseeing, entertainment and other treats. She took me several times to the lake beyond

Sans Souci — far beyond freedom from anxious care, she might well have thought. She sat on the beach while I splashed about, performing a clumsy dog-paddle out of my depth. She was extremely kind. In such circumstances, my mother would not have been as patient as my temporary fairy godmother. I hope my thanks matched her generosity.

The newly constructed Olympic Stadium was architecturally and ideologically daunting. Its concrete grandeur was supposed to be a showcase for the Aryan *Übermensch* of National Socialism. It was odd that the Führer, he of the dangling black forelock and the little black moustache, should extol the alleged superiority of blond young men of Nordic physique. There was delicious irony in the fact that the supreme hero of the games proved to be an African-American who left the imitation Vikings panting in his wake. Hitler refused to shake the hand of Jesse Owens. Admiring him from the stands, I wished I had a chance to congratulate him. Track records have been broken in every subsequent Olympiad but the renown of that 1936 multi-gold-medallist shines as brightly as ever.

I returned to London with two ominous souvenirs. One was a picture-book for children, published by Julius Streicher, one of Dr Goebbels's most virulent anti-Semitic propagandists. A typical illustration depicted a butcher with a bloodstained apron and a grotesque hook nose fondling a pretty maiden with flaxen hair. The text: 'Never trust a fox on a green lawn or a Jew on his oath.' The other present from the Nazis was a Hitler Youth dagger, whose blade was inscribed '*Blut and Ehre*', meaning 'Blood and Honour'. Those two omens alone should have been sufficient warnings of future events. But very soon after I showed my father the book and the knife they disappeared from my room.

5

When my slightly deepening voice betrayed incipient puberty, my father invited me to lunch. He had not ever done that before. We went to Rules, which claims to be the oldest restaurant in London. There is a small-scale Edwardian splendour about it, dark wood, many pictures on red walls, elegant napery, silver and crystal, and a large-scale menu. Rules offered all sorts of game-birds, such as woodcock and snipe, of which, at the age of $11\frac{3}{4}$, I had never heard. I realised that my father considered the occasion to be an important one when he poured me a glass of claret: a first. He told me at length of the establishment's historic literary, theatrical and social associations. I began to wonder when he would get to the point, and he began to seem uncharacteristically nervous.

'Perhaps you've noticed certain . . . er . . . physical *changes*,' he suggested, looking over my shoulder at a distant portrait, perhaps of Lily Langtry.

'Oh!' I exclaimed with blithe aplomb, almost, but not quite, giving him a reassuring pat on the hand. 'I know all about that sort of thing. For biology we read *The Science of Life*.' This declaration enabled us to enjoy the rest of our meal and enabled him to enjoy the tranquillising fragrance of his Romeo y Julieta.

My father returned from Prague in 1938 unconvinced that Chamberlain had secured 'peace in our time'. Perhaps the old prime minister was shrewder than his public utterances. As soon as Chamberlain got back from Munich, Britain spent the last year of interbellum peace arming as swiftly and abundantly as possible, especially building Hurricanes and Spitfires to strengthen Fighter Command for the inevitable war.

During that year of uneasy grace, there were many ostrich heads in the sand and many wishful-thinking conservatives who believed that further appeasement of Hitler would support him as our champion defending civilisation against the red barbarians. However, my father, a suburban Noah, had a miniature fortress, a substantial air-raid shelter, constructed in our back garden. By this time, I had two unexpected but lovable young brothers, Timothy, who was seven years old, and Duncan, five. The shelter, half below ground, with massive walls and a roof designed to withstand any explosion apart from a direct hit, was large enough to accommodate five bunks – no less comfortable than a prison cell. Our immediate neighbours deplored the eyesore in the middle of the small lawn and laughed at my father as Noah's neighbours probably laughed at him and his extravagant ark. The ridicule stopped when rain flooded the flimsy, corrugated-iron Anderson shelters the government provided later.

Journalism enabled my father to enjoy one last peacetime luxury. He sailed on the maiden voyage of Cunard's new *Mauretania* and very much liked New York. I had great expectations of lavish gifts. I forget what he brought the rest of us. Fifth Avenue lingerie for my mother, I imagine. I got an Ellington record ('The Gal from Joe's' and 'I Let a Song Go out of My Heart') and a slab of salt-water taffy.

6

Just as the girls of my age were beginning to burgeon, I was transferred from King Alfred School to University College School, a conventional public school in West Hampstead. Because there were no girls at UCS, the competition in the classrooms was less demanding and the outdoor games were fiercer.

When Germany invaded Poland, my mother and brothers, in accordance with my father's precautionary plan, took up residence in a caravan parked beside a farmhouse near Flaunden, Hertfordshire. I spent only weekends in the country. During the week I lived close to the school in a draughty Victorian house belonging to the parents of a young UCS schoolmaster whose asthma excused him from military service. His disability was a good thing, from his point of view, as he was an evangelistic member of the Peace Pledge Union and kept urging me to become a conscientious objector as soon as I was old enough.

My father, in a uniform splendid with RAF wings and campaign ribbons, went to France as Reuters' correspondent with the British Expeditionary Force. For several months, without much leave, his task was to send back reports of the troops' defensive arrangements, weatherproof billets, wholesome diet and jolly programmes of entertainment and recreation – journalistically as challenging as describing life in a Butlin's holiday camp out of season.

During the 'Phoney War' or 'Sitzkrieg', the major news stories from France were of visits by Very Important Persons. Censorship reduced him to writing about how VIPs were dressed and what they had for lunch. When the King entertained Prime Minister Daladier about thirty miles from 'the front', the royal costume included tweed plus-fours and gaiters as though for grouse-shooting on the moors of Scotland, and the menu offered oysters, duck pâté, roast chicken, salad, ice cream, cheese, coffee, white and red burgundy, champagne and brandy. Reuters informed papers all over the world, apart from Germany, that the King smoked a cigarette. (He survived the war but cigarettes killed him.) On another state occasion not very far from the Western Front, a correspondent complained to Chamberlain that there was not much to write about. The Prime Minister said: 'Personally, I would prefer to be bored rather than bombarded.'

My father's up-beat dispatches were gathered in a book called *Vanguard to Victory*, with a foreword by General Lord Gort, VC, DSO, MC, the BEF's commander-in-chief, and a photograph of the author and the King shaking hands. Publication took place in May 1940, two weeks before the retreat from Dunkirk.

The family were happy to be reunited at home in London. After the exhilaration of the Battle of Britain, in which every enemy plane destroyed was a vicarious triumph, we spent the cold autumn nights in our shelter, which was electrified. After a hot meal, I did my homework and there were games of cards and chess. We did a lot of reading, but the evenings seemed very long. Only once was there any sense of danger. While my father and I were outside the shelter watching searchlight beams swinging across the sky, a pint-size incendiary bomb struck the roof of our house a glancing blow and burnt itself out in a brief, white glare of magnesium, a short distance from where we stood. The next morning, we found that no tile had been broken, but we resolved to stay in the shelter throughout the nightly raids from then on. During the Blitz, every-one had a bomb story, boring to everyone else. When I embel-lished ours as a narrow escape, my friends histrionically yawned.

My father commuted to his office and I commuted to school. A classmate who was having difficulty with Latin persuaded me that we should join the Merchant Navy. Appalling shipping losses in the North Atlantic gave civilian sailors an aura of heroism that fifteen-year-old schoolboys were eligible to try to assume. My father vetoed the proposal, in spite of my ostentatious indignation and to my secret relief.

One evening late in November my father announced a change that radically affected all our lives. Reuters had assigned him to their New York office for an indefinite period and he was taking us with him. It was with an uneasy feeling that I told friends I was going to leave. I had been awarded my house colours for cricket, meaning that I was entitled to wear a flashy crimson and white tie instead of the ordinary dull maroon and black and had looked forward to further glory during the year to come. Fellow cricketers were quite sorry for me. There was no resentful talk of a rat leaving a sinking ship. Well-informed adults were anxious then, but I never heard any of my contemporaries express any doubt that we would eventually win the war. One day, the title of my father's book would no longer seem ironic.

7

We sailed from Liverpool in a Cunarder of medium size, without a convoy, as the ship was said to be faster than any known submarine. Zig-zagging at top speed, the *Samaria* was able to cross the Atlantic in about a week. As the blacked-out ship left the blacked-out port, my father was determinedly cheerful, my mother was nervous, and my brothers and I were oblivious of reality.

Among our fellow passengers was a friend of my father's, René MacColl of the *Daily Express*, who was renowned in Fleet Street for the ingenuity and lavishness of his expense accounts. When not in the ship's first-class bar, he sometimes allowed me to listen with him to records on his portable wind-up gramophone, which, he said, no foreign correspondent should ever be without. His favourite record on the voyage, whose title seemed to forecast his plan for Manhattan, was Fats Waller's 'Loungin' at the Waldorf'. MacColl played it repeatedly, overcoming morbid thoughts of torpedoes. Fats was psychologically more potent than Admiral Doenitz.

My first night in New York was like suddenly playing a walk-on part in a Hollywood musical. My father got a junior colleague to show me around. He took me to Madison Square Garden. We had ringside press seats to watch a boxer, whose name, if not its spelling, was Fritzie Zivik, confirm his primacy at some weight less than heavy. 'Now,' my guide hopefully suggested, 'you must be tired. I suppose you'd like to get back to your hotel.' But there was one thing I longed to do before bedtime.

Fifty-Second Street was still Fifty-Second Street in 1940: the Downbeat, the Apex, the Three Deuces, the Famous Door and other jazz bars were still going strong. I induced my perplexed but hospitable guide to take me by wonderful yellow cab to the Hickory House. That was the Fifty-Second Street box that Duke Ellington said he liked best, partly for the steaks. On that night of my first visit, Joe Marsala, the Chicago clarinettist, was the musician in charge. His brother Marty was on trumpet; Carmen Mastren, guitar; Dave Tough, drums; and Marsala's wife, Adele Girard, harp. She was reputed to be the first jazz harpist. In those days my knowledge of band personnel, music titles and recording dates was encyclopaedic. London boyhood friends and I used to sit around, respectfully tapping our feet in time with records, yet continually talking above them, competing to be the first to identify each player as he began a solo. We liked the music; we were obsessionally dedicated to musical statistics.

As I was tall enough at the age of fifteen, my guide and I were able to sit at the bar, which enclosed the small bandstand. There I was, actually drinking ice-cold Budweiser, only a few feet away from real, live, famous musicians playing 'Tin Roof Blues'. Between sets I took the opportunity to thank Joe Marsala for past and present pleasures. 'Mrs Marsala is in very good form,' I generously commented. 'That was a fine "Four or Five Times".' He was astonished that a mere boy, obviously English, knew who the harpist was. Drawing on the discography I had learned so painstakingly, I was able to drop some names sacred in the annals of Chicago jazz. Marsala became more and more surprised, more and more cordial.

In fact, we became such good friends over the following few months, as friendly as a master and an acolyte can be, that he gave me a couple of studio 12-inch recording out-takes featuring himself and some other heroes, including Chu Berry and Jack Teagarden.

The records were fragile acetates, which I had no means of transcribing, so they soon wore out, even with soft wooden needles, but not before I was able to play them to impress fellow high-school students and convince them that when it came to collecting the esoterica of jazz, British schoolboys were far out, man.

My family spent the first week at the Shelton Hotel on Lexington Avenue. Though not particularly elegant, it was luxurious compared with an air-raid shelter. The establishment's comprehensive amenities included a large, heavily chlorinated swimming pool and a well-stocked library. On the first day of exploration, I found a copy of James Joyce's *Ulysses*, which I had not been able to get my hands on in London. A friend, whose father had bought the book in Paris, had recommended Molly Bloom's stream-of-consciousness erotic soliloquy. He said it was an effective aid to masturbation. He was right.

My father had been advised to consider accommodation in Forest Hills, where they played tennis, and the Village of Bronxville. Fortunately, he chose Bronxville, in Westchester County, only twenty-eight minutes by train to Grand Central Station. He found an unfurnished, four-bedroom, two-bathroom house right next to the school playing field. I noticed a circumferential cinder running track, posts like rugby posts and – exotic novelty! – a baseball diamond. London friends, masters of derision, had consoled me for abandonment of cricket by pointing out that baseball had been modelled on rounders, a game that used to be played by English schoolgirls. Anyway, I was able, cutting across the field, to walk to school in five minutes.

After some easy tests, I was put in the twelfth grade, in which most of the students were two years my seniors. It was pleasant to be in co-educational classes again, though the girls, to my eyes, looked as unattainable as starlets in a campus movie. When they took off their camel-hair coats they revealed tight sweaters (red was the most popular colour), interestingly short skirts, white bobby socks and two-tone saddle shoes. The universal jewellery was a pearl necklace. Their shoulder-length hair, in the style known as page-boy, was shampooed and brushed to a silken gloss. The awful beauty of their lipstick made me feel sick with desire. The boys, in contrast, with greased quiffs or convicts' haircuts, looked immature but laughed with supreme confidence. I was assigned to a desk next to an eighteen-year-old youth who usually began the mornings red-eyed with a beer hangover and always stank of cigarettes. He was the school's star quarterback. Though quadratic equations made him frown, he was assured of free entry into any Ivy League college he chose. His father had given him a Lincoln convertible for his eighteenth birthday. His most casual smile made girls weaken at the knees. He never knew refusal. He made me feel poor.

As a matter of fact, I was poor. Looking back, I realise that my father, too, was financially hard-pressed. Considering the dangers and privations of wartime Britain, he must have hesitated to ask Reuters for a fully adequate housing allowance. But, of course, we had left behind all our furniture, blankets, linen, pots and pans, crockery, cutlery and countless other domestic essentials that are taken for granted in a long-established home, and cost a lot to replace. Our rented house was gradually furnished and equipped as austerely as a Zen monastery. Bronxville was then, and remains, a wealthy community. In many ways, we were materially better off than in London's winter weather; in many other ways, we were much worse off than our new neighbours. Bright lights are dazzling for only a short time. However, my parents' budget was certainly a good deal less stringent than mine. My father was not really mean, but he simply did not understand about American teenagers and American pocket-money, even as they were so long ago. My father gave me one dollar a week, a humiliatingly small fraction of what I needed. Dates were out of the question. Pepsi Cola, as their radio jingle proclaimed, was 'twice as much for a nickel'. But what if I had offered a girl a Pepsi and she asked for a Knickerbocker Glory ice-cream sundae? The horror, the horror!

8

A classmate, Pete Ersdale, whose father had died when Pete was a baby and whose mother made ends meet by working in a not-very-successful dress shop, showed me a way of alleviating poverty. You work. ·

Almost every evening and most weekends, he set up pins in the local bowling alleys. In those days, before automation, pin-setting was a strenuous, low-paid, unskilled job for which there were more volunteers than opportunities. Pete, a veteran, was able to fix me up with the boss. Suddenly I had money. Right away, I bought a record-player and a few records. There were occasional surreptitious trips to Fifty-Second Street. Joe Marsala was still at the Hickory House and Billie Holiday was singing at the Onyx Club. Then one day Pete talked me into saving up so we could hitchhike from coast to coast during the summer vacation.

In 1941, when he was seventeen and I was sixteen, hitchhiking was not dangerous. Our parents did not object to the proposed expedition. Pete's preparations expressed fantastic yearnings: he bought a black Stetson hat and cowboy boots of hand-tooled black leather. He also cultivated a moustache, but that was less convincingly macho. His ancestors were Swedish and the pale-yellow growth was sparse and fluffy. I told our high-school principal of our plan. To us, any woman over the age of forty seemed grandmotherly, but Miss Penney had a gleam in her eye. Far from discouraging us, she provided letters of introduction to whom it might concern, 'proof', she said, 'that you're not bums'. She smiled and added, 'Try not to behave like bums. Think of the reputation of the school.'

Hitchhiking was easy. We soon got beyond the cities that Pete regarded as 'the boring bits' – New York, Philadelphia, Pittsburgh, Chicago, where we stayed overnight in antiseptic YMCAs. Then we were heading 'out West'. It did not take him long to achieve the swaggering, bow-legged gait of a man proud to spend most of his waking hours in the saddle. He even bought a tin of Bull Durham tobacco, which was advertised in giant letters on almost every roadside barn, a packet of cigarette papers and a gadget like a miniature mangle to roll his own cigarettes. Having mastered the mechanical technique, he tried making cigarettes entirely by hand. He had seen a movie cowboy demonstrate that esoteric folk art. As I did not smoke, in spite of his urgings and scornful intimation that non-smokers were cissies, I was able to enjoy his fumbles and all the spillage of tobacco.

We navigated by a series of free Esso maps, staying on the main highways, though Pete, whose sense of adventure was more imaginative than mine, argued more than once, in vain, for taking a small side-road, picked at random, and seeking work – any work – on a ranch, the remoter the better. I was getting my kicks from high speeds, open spaces, far horizons, which I had never known before. A 400-mile day was more exciting than a 200-mile day. I got a bigger thrill from tracing our route on the map, through places with names such as Rapid City and Deadwood, in the Black Hills of South Dakota, than from the actualities of the places themselves. Hamburgers and soda-pop and occasional flapjacks with maple syrup were very much alike everywhere.

Pete got a taste of the romance of the Old West at the side of the road between Sheridan, Wyoming, and the Montana state line. Our thumbs stopped an old jalopy. The driver, a leatherycomplected, thirtyish hombre in faded denims, told us he had come from the Sheridan rodeo, in which he had tamed animals of phenomenal savagery. We listened in awe. The Munchausenesque monologue was interrupted by a sudden sideways lurch of the car. A front tyre had blown out. The ethics of hitchhiking required us to stand by, willing to give assistance, though we could not have been of any use, while our benefactor struggled to install a spare tyre, itself worn down to the canvas. Standing there, dazed by sunshine from a cloudless blue sky, we were startled by a harsh command: 'Reach, boys! Hands on your heads!'

A classic sheriff, in a doughboy's hat and with a silver star on his khaki shirt, pointed a double-barrelled shotgun at us, chest-high. Our driver slowly arose from his crouch by the wheel and turned with his hands up to face the authority of a John Wayne.

'Open up the trunk!' the sheriff ordered.

The back of the car contained a saddle. Its serial number confirmed identification as the property of a rodeo hand still in Sheridan. The sheriff drove us to his office. Pete and I anxiously showed our letters from Miss Penney, which gave the sheriff a laugh. We were released, while the subdued saddle thief was detained. I wondered what his fate would be. Not a public lynching, I supposed. Twelve months' hard labour? This was long before convicted criminals could hope for a course of psychotherapy and hours of community service.

We hitched onwards, past the Custer Battlefield National Monument and the Crow Agency, across the Bighorn River. Until then, since Chicago, the fine summer weather had enabled us to spend the nights in our sleeping bags out in the open. But then clouds formed, enormous heaps of cumulus, towering, dark cumulo-nimbus, discharging an explosive blitz of thunder and light-ning and an apocalyptic deluge. A farmer allowed us to shelter in a warm, dry barn, fragrant with hay, leather and oily machinery.

The following morning, he invited us into the farmhouse kitchen, where his wife fed us a Gargantuan breakfast. Pete and I asked each other why we had not previously availed ourselves of such generous rural hospitality, until a morning spent chopping big logs into small logs answered the question.

Bozeman, Butte, Missoula . . . Allowing fate to determine our route, though we felt free from any compulsion, we found ourselves passing through Coeur d'Alene. We noticed it was not much farther to Spokane, and I got an idea.

'We're almost in Canada,' I pointed out.

'So?' Pete acknowledged, without enthusiasm. Having left the mythical Old West without mounting a single horse, he would have preferred to head southwards to Arizona.

'I have an aunt in Vancouver,' I said. 'We could have showers. Maybe a steak.'

As we crossed the border of British Columbia, I felt a slight twinge in the lower right side of my abdomen. By the time we got to my father's sister's house on English Bay, the twinge had become a sharp pain.

'Oh, you've brought a friend,' Aunt Alys observed. 'Wilfred *will* be surprised.'

I introduced Pete. I had not mentioned him when I telephoned. My aunt managed a welcoming smile, though Wilfred Plowden-Wardlaw, my rich Scottish uncle, was the sort of old-fashioned patriarch who did not like to have his household unexpectedly disturbed. A man of profound unimportance, he was a stickler for protocol in recognition of his domestic status. After idling for three years at Cambridge, he had been banished to distant countries, New Zealand, Chile and finally Canada, and paid handsomely on condition that he stayed far from Edinburgh. His family owned a large share of a Scottish brewery and felt that Wilfred did the least damage when he was farthest away.

While abroad, his only notable activity was collecting rare birds. His skill as a shot and a taxidermist was said to have earned the gratitude of a natural history museum somewhere or other. At the age of thirty-eight he endeavoured to make a favourable impression on the folks back in Scotland by enlisting in the Royal Canadian Air Force. The RCAF appointed him to a junior clerkship with the rank of Aircraftman Second Class (they have no lower rank), in an office and barracks so close to home that he was able to spend every other weekend there. Fellow clerks called him 'Pop'. He had brilliantined yellow hair, a round, red face and watery grey eyes. As soon as he met Pete, he gave him his bus fare to New York, but did not object to my recuperating in Vancouver after my emergency appendectomy. I found Uncle Wilfred charming.

Three years later, I heard that Pete, tired of penury, had joined the US Army, volunteered for an élite ski unit, and was killed on his first foray into snow-covered mountains in Italy.

In Vancouver, my departure was delayed by bureaucratic red tape. My immigration visa had been for only one entry and I had to apply for a new visa to rejoin my family. My uncle's magnanimity proved to be exhaustible and his charm rapidly faded. Snide remarks on my lengthening stay made it embarrassingly apparent that he was finding me burdensome. He had three children; he did not wish to support four. He probably had to put a lot of petrol into his Daimler.

To help pay for my keep, I got a job reading meters for the local electric company. By then we were in September and I trudged along the streets of Vancouver inundated in the city's famous rain. A companion in this inglorious work, who had recently dropped out from undergraduate studies at the University of British Columbia, kindly showed me how to keep dry and to avoid fatigue. Having picked up our meter-reading books, we headed by streetcar to some congenial café, where we spent the morning drinking coffee, playing the juke-box and recording estimates of what the meters *should* have read in accordance with past consumption. We usually had hamburgers and milk shakes for lunch. Our afternoons were free. I saw many films.

'Won't they find out?' I asked nervously.

'Discrepancies won't become apparent till next month,' my

mentor assured me. 'You'll have your visa before then, won't you? Me, I'll be in the Air Force.'

There were many different motives for wartime enlistment in the armed services.

9

It was not long before I, too, was a voluntary fugitive from academe. Safely restored to Bronxville, I soon had to leave it. Many American colleges were offering to admit freshmen in February 1942, to undertake four-year undergraduate courses in three years. Accelerated education was intended to intensify the United States' war effort. Thanks to the benign Miss Penney's mediation, I was able to enter Oberlin College's Class of 1945 at no cost to my parents. They were greatly relieved, and I was glad to receive a high-school diploma without the formality of final exams.

Oberlin's campus, sheltered by old elms, looked like New England on the austere plain of northern Ohio. The liberal arts college was founded early in the nineteenth century with evangelical ideals, pioneering co-educationally and interracially, though not with sufficient ardour to keep me out of social disgrace when I fell in love with a black girl who was studying piano and composition in the Conservatory. An alert fellow student, a white male, saw me kissing her outside our dining hall one spring evening. He told the Dean of Men. The Dean summoned me to his office and said that miscegenation might be tolerated in Europe but it wasn't in Ohio. As a seventeen-year-old, foreign scholarship student, I abjectly kowtowed, and the innocent affair was shamefully terminated. But did I truly love the girl herself or the exoticism of her resemblance to Hazel Scott, the most delicious jazz pianist of all?

In the classrooms, all went well, at first. My favourite professor was one Ralph Singleton, who taught the obligatory freshman course in English composition. He was elegantly precise in his use of words and yet his didactic style was warm with humour; his lectures were useful and entertaining. He enabled me to attain the pinnacle of my scholastic achievement when he set an examination requiring only an analysis of A. E. Housman's poem 'To an Athlete Dying Young'. He distributed exercise books and gave us fifty minutes to write in them. Much frenzied scribbling ensued. After a few minutes, I handed in my work, provoking glances of pity and amusement. I had written only four words, 'Quit while on top.' When the essays were marked, Dr Singleton rewarded my brevity with an A+.

Unfortunately, he then overestimated my intellectual capacity and underestimated my laziness. He invited me to join a senior seminar studying Milton's *Paradise Lost*, an honour I couldn't refuse. The demands of detailed textual exegesis made me feel that oxygen was being withdrawn from the room. Discussing the fine points of seventeenth-century poetry made my head ache. Care sat on my faded cheek. As if to justify his judgment, my sponsor allowed me to finish the semester with a charitable C−.

Academically chastened, I then happened to receive a letter from a London contemporary saying he was in training to fly Swordfish in the Fleet Air Arm of the Royal Navy. As soon as I got home for the summer vacation, I told my parents that I wanted to fly.

'Isn't he rather young?' my mother asked at the dinner table, as if I had not been there.

'I don't think so,' my father emphatically assured her. He checked with the British Embassy in Washington and found that in August I would reach the minimum age for enlistment, seventeen-and-a-half. 'But it's three thousand miles to the RAF,' he pointed out. 'You'd better go up to Canada and try them. It's only a few hours by train.'

10

The Royal Canadian Air Force classified me with the perversity for which armed services are famous. They operated on the theory that no round hole was too small for the insertion of a square peg. I wanted to be a pilot, and mathematics, tests showed, was my weakest subject, so the RCAF decided to make me a navigator. Of course, this was back in the days before technical advances rendered navigators redundant.

The preparation was laborious: after a lot of parade-ground drill and calisthenics, I was enrolled in the University of Toronto for a two-month course to raise my maths to elementary competence. Some of the training was ludicrously irrelevant: an armaments instructor spent wearisome days teaching me how to dismantle and reassemble the Browning machinegun, though it was impossible to imagine how aircrew duties could ever require such expertise. I eventually mastered that quaint old instrument, the sextant, and the arcana of star charts and log tables, though celestial navigation alone was never sufficiently precise for accurate night bombing. The complete course of study exhausted a whole year. It seemed wasteful, but there was still plenty of war to come.

Like my fellow trainees, I was fatalistic about the future. We knew that most of us would be selected for operations in RAF Bomber Command, which lost more than 9,000 aircraft and 50,000 airmen in World War II, but I never heard anyone speculate about the odds against survival. Even with an actuarially unfavourable prognosis, young men do not believe in their own death. In our flight or class of thirty, many were doomed. Our year of training might be their last complete year of life. After that, the man with the top marks would be retained in Canada as an instructor; the next two would ferry planes across the Atlantic and beyond; four would be assigned to Coastal Command, with a good chance of not being shot down, and the other twenty-three to Bomber Command, which demanded the least navigational skill and the greatest stoicism. As in other exams, a certain amount of luck determined whether one was asked the right questions. I was lucky. I learned that I was to be sent not to England but to the Bahamas, for ferrying, the best of all wartime air-force jobs.

The evening after we were ceremonially awarded our wings, some of us gathered for a party at the Royal York Hotel. Canadian Club whiskey flowed in a torrent and drunkenness degenerated from exuberant to maudlin. The next day, walking carefully, I went to a downtown military tailor and bought a ready-made uniform and greatcoat and a peaked cap. Apotheosis! They fitted well and I admired my reflection in the changing-room mirror. The barathea was elegantly smooth in contrast with the abrasive material of the uniform I had been accustomed to. It was gratifying to return salutes in the streets. I walked on air until an RCAF sergeant, by many years my senior, saluted and politely pointed out that the back of my greatcoat still bore its price-tag.

At Christmastime in 1943, on embarkation leave in Bronxville, I impressed Timothy and Duncan, my young brothers, more than my parents. My mother's solicitude reduced me from Pilot Officer to small boy. Remembering India, she advised me on tropical hygiene and diet. My father was strangely unenthusiastic about my splendid new uniform; indeed, in his eyes, apparently, its very newness was a defect. 'The cap-badge will mellow in time,' he said consolingly. He made me feel the bright, regal colours were embarrassing. 'It'll help if you take out the cap's stiffener.' He showed me how to remove the inner wire ring, and the cap drooped around the edges in veteran aircrew style. 'That's better,' he assured me. I now realise that his display of superior air-force knowledge was an expression of envy. I was a fledgling and he was grounded. We were experiencing a rite of passage that is painful for all sons' fathers. My premature claim to manhood made him aware of the early decline of his middle age. Our relationship never quite recovered. He would probably have felt worse if he had known that when I said, almost every evening, that I was meeting school friends, I was actually sneaking around to the apartment of my mother's thirty-six-year-old best friend for Kama Sutra lessons.

I flew down to Miami in a civil airliner and on to Nassau in an RAF Dakota. Past the Gulf Stream, the water changed from dark blue to light blue, turquoise, and, in shallows over coral, pale aquamarine. Although Nassau is in the Atlantic Ocean, the sea around New Providence Island was like a preview of the most beautiful sea in the world, the Caribbean. I fell in love at first sight.

My Bahamian billet was a suite in the Royal Victoria Hotel, overlooking tall palms and scarlet bougainvillaea around the patio where meals were served. Sirloin steak was always available and the sympathetic Bahamian waiters were glad to bring second helpings. The RAF provided the accommodation and meals; my RCAF pay, substantially more than the RAF's, could be splashed about any way I pleased. Suddenly, at the age of eighteen, I seemed very well off, able to luxuriate in habits that have made life expensive and physically challenging ever since.

II

My native land was known, in that far-off era, as Great Britain. The adjective was then apt. The country is seldom called that now, except on some official documents. British cars travelling abroad still bear the initials GB, although their meaning is only historical. Even the title United Kingdom is a misnomer in the present time of incipient devolution. But in the Bahamas when I first arrived at the colony that cloudless afternoon I held the King's commission to fly for the greatest empire the world has ever known. Queen Victoria's statue in Bay Street was a symbol of imperial might, rather than just a background for tourists' photography, and only the incumbent in Government House was a joke.

The adjutant at Windsor Field succinctly set forth my terms of employment. Every morning before breakfast I was to telephone Operations – there was a telephone on my bedside table – to ask whether my services were required. If they were, I had to go to the field to prepare for flight the following day. If there was nothing doing the day was mine to spend as I liked. Aircrew on stand-by usually passed their days swimming and playing tennis and golf, and their nights getting pissed. They bounced with herculean vigour and effervescent morale. The West Indian winter weather was paradisal, the sun and stars were brilliant, and Kinsey was right about the young human male. After nearly two weeks of relentless hedonism, I looked forward to some nice, restful flying.

The pilot I was to navigate for was an Anglo-Canadian flight lieutenant from Saskatchewan. He was raw-boned with a dull-yellow crew-cut like prairie stubble, a chain-smoker whose conversational style was minimalist. At a glance, I could see that he must be at least thirty years old. The radio operator, only a little younger-looking, was an Italian-Canadian sergeant from Montreal. He had suavely Brylcreemed black hair and shrewd, dark-brown eyes, and a tendency to sing fragments of show songs. When first subjected to their appraisal, I doubted that they were pleased to find that their new navigator was absolutely inexperienced. I wondered what had happened to my predecessor in their crew – delirium tremens? a crippling venereal disorder? I dared not ask.

My first plane was an A-30 twin-engined attack bomber, a Baltimore, named after the city in Maryland where the Glen L. Martin Company had manufactured it. It was not a thing of beauty: a belly-tank, added for long-distance ferrying, gave it a clumsy, pregnant look. But it was pristine. There was not a scratch on the beige and brown camouflage for the North African desert. The propellers cleared by inches the small nose compartment, more Perspex than aluminium, in which the navigator, once seated, could hardly move. The pilot sat higher up, amidships, with the radio operator in the rear. This arrangement was not very uncomfortable on short flights. We were about to make long ones.

Early in the morning of our departure, after a bored meteorological officer had told me about the almost invariable weather and I had filed a meticulously checked and rechecked flight plan, I clambered up into my fragile, transparent pod, wincing as its narrow entrance scraped my Paradise Beach sunburn. Fumbling, I stowed my parachute chest-pack behind me, arranged my log, chart, sextant and books of tables on either side and on my lap, and donned my earphones. The pilot, Frank Rothery, exchanged ritual RT jargon with the control tower. They sounded like war movies – 'Do you read me?' 'I read you loud and clear.' 'Roger, over and out.' It was strange to be acting a part in that familiar fantasy. When I had to say a few words to check the intercom, Frank and Tony (named by Central Casting) sounded authentic and I, to my ears, didn't; but apparently they believed that I, too, was real.

After a couple of explosive eructations, each engine settled in a smooth roar, the ground crew got out of the way, and we trundled slowly to the end of the designated runway. I was apprehensive, excited, exuberant as we accelerated, until we were moving faster along the surface of the planet than I had ever moved before. Suddenly, we were airborne, the plane tipped over in a steep bank and levelled out on a south-easterly course, and I was an air navigator, beginning my Grand Tour.

While guns were firing and bombs were dropping thousands of miles away, I was placidly cruising in expensive-holiday sunshine at 9,000 feet, a convenient altitude from which to match islands of the Bahamian archipelago, like small pieces of an easy jigsaw puzzle, with the islands on my topographical map. At about 200 miles an hour, we were moving slowly enough for leisurely observation, fast enough for continuous interest. The world proved to be an accurate, detailed replica of the projection that good old Mercator devised in the sixteenth century. It was ironic that the RAF was making such effective use of the work of Gerhard Kremer, a cartographer whose nationality was German. There may have been truer maps invented since his day, such as the Lambert Azimuthal Equal Area Projection and the Winkel Triple Projection, but I suppose that most older people have always visualised the world as Mercator represented it, stretched increasingly out of shape toward the poles. As a navigator, I was a Mercator man, and, in spite of the technical superiority of all the latest satellite-generated images, I still am.

On the day of my debut, a straight line on the chart led me unerringly a short distance port of Crooked Island and starboard of Mayaguana Island and over Providenciales Island, in the Turks and Caicos. The voyage was as marvellous as collecting previously unimagined, exotic postage stamps. Abeam of Grand Turk, about to cross over Mouchoir Passage (did some French pirate blow his nose there?), I noted the time on my RAF-issue Longines wristwatch, unaware then of the homage due to John Harrison and his 1772 Fourth Marine Chronometer, calculated our ground speed, which differed very little from the speed postulated in the flight plan, revised our ETA and passed it back to Frank. There was a stretch of sea without islands off the north coast of Hispaniola, so I was relieved and gratified – and Frank and Tony congratulated me – when we reached the day's appointed destination precisely on time, the US Air Force Base at Borinquen, on the north-west coast of Puerto Rico.

At the Bachelor Officers' Quarters, we had showers and changed our shirts and got to the Officers' Club – Tony wore no badges of rank – when they began serving frozen daiquiris, pink with grenadine, at the friendly price of 25 cents each. I would have appreciated them even more than I did if the Baltimore's props, spinning close to my head, had not made me totally deaf. However, a flight surgeon, met in the bar, syringed my ears the next morning and gave me earplugs, and I was fit to proceed farther south-east, to Port of Spain, Trinidad, the isle of calypso.

A Royal Navy sub-lieutenant, encountered in the bar of the Queen's Park Hotel, said the Navy had recently raised the price of a tot of rum in the ratings' club from a penny-ha'penny to threepence, to reduce the incidence of drunkenness, but the reform had been a conspicuous failure. Rum permeated the hot, humid atmosphere of Trinidad. The island's most popular song at the time was the Andrews Sisters' 'Rum and Coca-Cola':

> All night long make tropic love
> Next day in hot sun cool off
> Drinking rum and Coca-Cola.

Having been told how much fuel our plane needed, an RAF mechanic asked Frank: 'How many cases of rum?'

'One for you?' Frank asked me. 'It's twelve dollars a case.'

'Why bother? It's the same in Nassau. About a dollar a bottle.'

'We never take liquor aboard in Nassau. On Ascension the Yanks pay ten dollars a bottle.'

Frank was a helpful guide all the way to Cairo.

12

Once we were clear of Nassau, we were autonomous to a remarkable degree, able to alter our itinerary here and there according to whim. We were not entirely irresponsible, but we enjoyed flouting authority up to a point. Our mission supposedly was really quite urgent, yet we were not oppressed by a sense of urgency. We felt no guilt whatever about looking for scenic novelties and the occasional day off; fellow airmen, given our opportunities, would undoubtedly have made the most of them as we did. Though Frank was the captain of our aircraft, the crew in practice was a democracy: at least two of us had to agree to any proposed deviation from the official timetable and route. Our conduct was based on the conviction that war was a nuisance and we must make the best of it.

After Trinidad, our scheduled next stop was Atkinson Field, near Georgetown, in what was British Guiana and is now Guyana. However, after a couple of visits to that unfragrant place, where the sewage evidently flowed imperfectly enclosed, we decided to try Paramaribo, the capital of Dutch Guiana. Being Dutch, it was clean, of course, but lacked charm. On the following trip, we dropped in on Cayenne, French Guiana, which proved more interesting, but sinister. Human heads, shrunk to fist-size, were offered for sale in a bar near the waterfront. Most of the clientele looked as if they had served long terms on Devil's Island; and any of them, possible victims of some baleful lottery, might have been candidates for shrinkage. There was an evil whiff of voodoo in the air.

Continuing south-eastwards from French Guiana, over Brazilian rain-forest and swamp and down across the equator, I would willingly have sacrificed our independence for the security of flying in formation with other planes. The islands in the mouths of the Amazon changed shapes unrecognisably from rain to rain; the local map was a mere approximation. As most of our journeys were over sea and large expanses of unpopulated wastes, it was odd that we were sent to fly alone. It was also odd that our commanders didn't advise us to lay off the booze. Most of us, including me, drank a lot. We almost always stayed up till midnight or later, and had to get out of bed by five o'clock. There can never have been a time on duty when our blood contained no alcohol. If breathalysers had been used, we would have failed and failed and failed again. Perhaps the RAF, with the wise resignation of long experience, refrained in wartime from giving orders impossible to enforce; perhaps – rashly daring! – it treated us as if we were mature adults. Anyway, surprisingly, the South Atlantic Wing achieved an admirable safety record.

Somerset Maugham would have been fascinated by the Canadian station commander of the RAF staging post at Belem, Brazil. Squadron Leader Whitey Dahl had a chequered past. As a freelance mercenary, he had flown against Franco's forces during the Spanish Civil War. He baled out when his plane was hit behind the Insurgents' lines. Because he was a civilian, his captors condemned him to death. However, on the eve of his scheduled execution by firing squad, he gained the sympathy of a priest by showing him a wallet snapshot of a blonde (a Chicago stripper) and saying, 'I'm ready to die, father, but who'll take care of my beloved wife?' Through the good offices of the Church, the execution was stayed and eventually called off when the sentimental Generalissimo himself admired the photograph sufficiently to allow the prisoner to leave the country. That, at any rate, was the story

Whitey told me, and it became increasingly moving as it was washed down by innumerable glasses of Indian quinine water and gin.

'Have you ever been to Rio?' asked this Errol Flynn of squadron-leaders.

'No, sir. It must be a wonderful city. Perhaps after the war . . .'

'How about tomorrow? I have to go down there for a couple of days and I need a navigator.'

I reluctantly demurred, mentioning that I had a prior engagement.

'Let me put it this way,' he said with a brilliant smile. 'You're coming. That's an order. I'll have your plane grounded − a slight bit of engine trouble. It'll be cleared up as soon as you return. I'll explain to your crew. I'm sure they'll enjoy a long weekend in Belem. The girls are terrific.'

Whitey, I discovered, also had a chequered present and a chequered future.

He did not really need my help. He could have navigated from Belem to Rio de Janeiro on his own, by radio compass and the seat of his pants. But he was an extrovert, something of an exhibitionist, so he took me along as an awed spectator.

We flew an RAF Dakota down the coast to Rio, by way of Recife and Bahia, without any difficulty. In Rio, we registered in a grand hotel overlooking Copacabana Beach.

'I have air-force business to attend to,' he said. 'We're doing some liaising with the Brazilians. Very hush-hush, of course. But they'll soon be our allies.'

Whitey was in a festive mood that evening when we met in the hotel bar. After a lavish meal, with champagne, he introduced me to an elegant, private casino, and even supplied chips for me to lose on roulette.

Two days later, a Brazilian crew returned us to Belem. The plane was a Dakota, exactly like the one we had flown down, except that it bore the green, blue and yellow insignia of the air force of Brazil.

I did not attend the court-martial, which was held in discreet confidentiality, as Squadron-Leader Dahl's activities, if publicised, would certainly have embarrassed the RCAF. The gossip was that he had been selling the Brazilian government planes and other valuable RAF property for several months. He had simply had them written off as unserviceable – a sort of Sergeant Bilko operation on a grand scale. Recently overconfident, he had sold an RAF motorbike to a dealer in Belem who had neglected to have it repainted before displaying it in a local garage. Whitey probably persuaded the court to cashier him without any further penalty on condition that he left the service quietly and did not try to sell his story to anyone, anywhere, ever. I wonder whether he did. Of course, in a world at war there were more important episodes than the rise and fall of Whitey Dahl, but surely there were few other leaders of his charisma and sang-froid.

13

The only times I took my sextant out of its case were for the flights from Natal, Brazil, 1,255 nautical miles to Ascension Island – more than halfway across the South Atlantic, between the bulge of South America and the bulge of West Africa. The weather was usually perfectly fine, and Ascension transmitted a radio signal to home on; but an unkind colleague in Nassau had warned me of an incident that occurred when a lazy navigator relied wholly on radio and the pilot reported they were about to ditch, having homed on a powerful counterfeit range that led to a German submarine. In the middle of nowhere, as the saying goes, the plane had run out of fuel. That crew was not heard from again. The dismal tale, whether true or not, stimulated a temporary passion for astro-navigation, even though, flying in daylight as always, the only available celestial aids were the sun and, sometimes, the moon. Only at midday, when the sun seemed to pass over our meridian of longitude, was it possible to fix our position with precision. The rest of the long flight, some six hours of it, was guided mainly by the presumption of probabilities called dead reckoning and by peering down through a simple gadget known as a drift-recorder at the white-caps 9,000 feet below, to measure the difference between the way the plane was pointing and the actual track the wind was making the plane achieve.

And the radio . . . After even the most efficient crossing, we arrived at the tiny volcanic island with only about 30 minutes' fuel remaining in the tanks. Then, safe on the ground, the radio operator, our upbeat music-lover, would tune in the American Forces Network, and there was a good chance of hearing something currently in the Hit Parade. One of our favourite numbers was Xavier Cugat's arrangement of 'Besame Mucho', which, thanks to the similarity of Spanish and Portuguese, we knew meant 'Kiss Me a Lot'.

Cairo was the terminus on several trips. After delivering the planes, I rarely considered what they were going to be used for. I never thought of myself in legal terms as an accessory before the fact. We were too busy having fun in Cairo at night, while awaiting our return flights to Nassau as passengers. We were awarded the highest priority for seats in military aircraft, usually US Air Force C-54 Skymasters, so that more than once I had the pleasure of displacing indignantly Blimpish officers of senior rank.

One night in Cairo I dined especially well at Shepheard's Hotel, celebrating the day's sale of five dozen bottles of Angostura aromatic bitters. Since 1824, when the great benefactor Dr J. G. B. Siegert first blended the elixir's secret ingredients in Angostura in Venezuela, it has been universally esteemed for its soothing stomachic effect, as well as its 44.7 per cent alcoholic content. Every bar in the world with any claim to excellence must have some Angostura. It is painful to imagine a champagne cocktail or an Old-fashioned without it. It is unlikely that Jeeves's morning-after restorative libation for his rash young master could have proved so promptly efficacious had it not contained a dash of the potent flavouring. In Cairo during World War II Angostura became increasingly scarce. I was able to sell easily the sixty bottles that had cost a total of three guineas in Port of Spain for the equivalent in piastres of 240 pounds sterling. Angostura bottles were conveniently much smaller than bottles of rum – almost as compact as the facsimile Omega watches obtainable in Brazil for ten dollars each. Furthermore, though Americans on Ascension did not seem to resent the thousand per cent mark-up on Trinidad rum, I preferred profiteering from trade with profiteers. I thoroughly enjoyed exploiting Egyptians to offset the expense of being exploited by them. My dabbling in black-market enterprises was undertaken only to support an immediate four-star way of life. Alas, I never thought of all the opportunities to make a fortune, which, in retrospect, are so obvious. An ostrich-size nest-egg for after the war was a concept I never contemplated. Indeed, I never regarded after-the-war as anything but the vaguest of hypothetical notions.

Drinking Hine VSOP after dinner in Shepheard's Long Bar (a good opening for a piece by S. J. Perelman), I had one of those chance encounters that sometimes prove more fatally influential than any amount of careful planning. I found myself in conversation with the man on the next stool. He was an affable, middle-aged character with a suntan and a Hemingway moustache whose British Army uniform was emblazoned with what was to me the most magical password, *CORRESPONDENT*. It transpired that he was covering the Middle East for the London *Daily Mail*, and knew my father.

'Next time you see him, say you met Lucas.'

'That'll be in a few days,' I told him. 'I'm due for some leave and I want to see *Oklahoma!*.' (The exclamation mark is part of the title of the musical.) I contrived a casual manner, as if it were quite usual for a junior RCAF officer to be drinking in Shepheard's one evening and in the St Regis in New York the following week.

'Then perhaps you'd do me a favour,' Lucas suggested. 'My daughter's living in New York. There's something I want to give her. Cash, actually. Quite a lot of it.' He chuckled genially. 'I'm sure I can trust you.'

The implication that possibly he couldn't made me consider declining to serve as his courier. But, of course, I did not want to offend a professional acquaintance of my father's. My hesitation was brief.

'She's working for the Admiralty down near the Battery,' Lucas said. His voice became suave with the oleaginousness of cajolery. 'She's also doing some photographic modelling. She's really quite a poppet. Her hotel's at Park and Sixty-Seventh. You could meet there.'

The next day, he handed over a manilla envelope bulging with United States bills of high denominations, and requested that I count them in his presence. The total gave me an early demonstration of the value of an imaginatively concocted expense account.

With the enthusiastic agreement of Frank and Tony, I had already got to a typewriter and replaced our movement orders with better ones. 'On compassionate grounds', they directed our return via New York. The RAF clerk couldn't have cared less. If I had written via Cape Town, he would have sent us via Cape Town. I rationalised that I was not going to hold up the war any longer than if I rested in the officially approved way on Paradise Beach.

With buttons and shoes extra-bright, I strolled as coolly as possible into the bar of the Sulgrave Hotel precisely on ETA. The bartender said Miss Lucas wasn't in yet. He wondered whether, while I was waiting, I would like to try a special new cocktail he had just invented. In honour of the general commanding the US Third Army, then making rapid progress across France, the drink was called 'Patton's Third'.

'I think old Blood and Guts would approve,' said the grizzled, ruddy bartender, an army veteran of the First World War, grinning confidently as he briskly agitated the silver shaker. 'Basically, it's a bourbon sour. It's the Southern Comfort that gives it the added power and speed. Plus the white of an egg for smoothness to please the ladies.'

I was halfway through the second free sample when Marcia Lucas arrived. Knowing which uniform to look for, she came straight over to me.

She was one of those tall, slender, blue-eyed blondes of the refined allure that was so ardently admired by Alfred Hitchcock, a young Princess Grace, in a grateful mood and a simple blue frock in the style of Chanel. Marcia was radiant.

Regrettably, she was also very stupid, almost as stupid as I was. She should have known better: she was twenty-one and I was nineteen. A few days later, with my father's consent in writing, we went to Greenwich, Connecticut, and got married. That was something that many people did then before going to bed together.

We enjoyed *Oklahoma!*.

14

Marriage took some of the fun out of the rest of the war, but it was not without incidents of interest. In a movie, a new bride opened the refrigerator and delightedly exclaimed, 'Look, darling! Our first ice-cubes!' In real life, however, I suddenly knew what it meant to be married when Marcia suggested that she should come down to live in Nassau. I soothingly demurred, then bluntly refused, and we had our first major row. I learned that practical objections to an emotional plea do not foster tranquil marital relations. Logic provokes tears of disappointment and recrimination. 'We can't afford it' is countered by the classic riposte which begins, 'If you loved me . . .' and leads, almost invariably, to stalemate.

As I continued to navigate aircraft from the Bahamas to Egypt and India, by way of Puerto Rico, Trinidad, the Guianas, Brazil, Ascension, the Gold Coast, Nigeria, Chad and the Sudan, Palestine, Iraq and the Persian Gulf states, and to return, usually, via Libya, Morocco, the Azores and Florida (only once more managing the New York detour), Marcia was staying in a guest-room in my parents' Bronxville apartment and commuting by subway from Grand Central Station to Bowling Green at the southern extremity of Manhattan. There were times – for example, when I was sweltering, sleepless, under a slowly revolving ceiling fan in the humid heat of Maiduguri, El Fasher or Manamah – when I would gladly have changed places with her; but those times were rare. I had to admit that she was benefiting very little from the vows we had made before the Greenwich Justice of the Peace. And she was unable to derive any comfort from proof that my reasoning had been correct.

The war evidently having reached its final stage, the RAF transferred many of us ferry crews to Transport Command bases in Britain. Assigned to a new pilot and radio operator, I found myself taking a Dakota from Montreal to Labrador and across the dark-grey North Atlantic beneath oppressive cloud cover to Greenland, Iceland and Scotland, a journey impossible to enjoy as ice formed on the wings and we contemplated the fact that survival time in that cruel sea was said to be a matter of minutes. Our destination near Glasgow was no less dour than the frozen staging-posts en route. Our flight through rain to south-west England was an improvement, but I missed the tropics.

Soon after I checked into a soggy, temporary-looking Somerset encampment amusingly named Merryfield, near Taunton, I telephoned the *Daily Mail* to get the address of their man Lucas. They told me he was no longer in Cairo; he was on the way by Cunarder from New York to Liverpool, and was bringing his daughter with him. They would let him know where I was. Even in wartime, newspapers can transcend security.

I could not meet Marcia's ship, because I had to deliver fresh troops to India and bring back some used ones. When I returned to Somerset, I learned she was ensconced in Taunton's excellent Castle Hotel. There was a festive reunion, but the Dyonisian revels lasted only two nights, with few opportunities for soul-searching conversation. In 46 Group, there were no long rest-and-recreation breaks between trips.

The next time I returned she said she was bored. The time after that she said Taunton was ghastly. And the time after that she was no longer in residence. The hotel concierge gave me a letter. Marcia had written in her charmingly rounded, girlish hand (circles for dots) that Mummy had collected her and she would not be coming back. Ever. There was no forwarding address.

What a tragedy! What a lucky break!

My last operational posting was to the long-established, permanent station at Odiham, Hampshire, quite conveniently close to London. The dignified red-brick buildings looked more like a country club than a concentration camp. I had a comfortable room of my own, immediately adjacent to the mess. My Canadian batman provided cigarettes by the kitbagful, which were distributed free to Canadian airmen and sold eagerly by non-smokers at £1 a carton. They were very valuable in the countries to which my duties then took me, on the briefest of visits: France, Italy, Greece and, eventually, the ruins of the Third Reich.

George, the automatic pilot, was controlling our Dakota carrying passengers destined for Athens, and I was directing George by twiddling a knob on the instrument panel. I was sitting in the co-pilot's seat, while the pilot was resting beside me with his chin on his chest and his eyes closed. We were cruising smoothly at 5,000 feet. The weather was clear and bright over the blue Mediterranean on the way from Marseille to Cagliari, on the south coast of Sardinia, where we had to deposit an unenthusiastic major. I enjoyed map-reading, then navigating by dead reckoning and radio compass across the Tyrrhenian Sea towards Rome. I felt that all was right with the world. However, just before we reached our Italian landfall, there was a sudden, continuous mechanical scream, as if a sheet of metal had been shoved against the blade of a circular saw. The noise alarmed me and awoke the pilot. The port engine had run away: the propeller had slipped spontaneously into fine pitch and could not be brought back to normal or feathered. It was generating great heat and there was an immediate danger of fire.

'Looks like a wheels-up landing,' the pilot calmly yelled at me.

'Got to get down. You'd better tell the passengers to fasten their seat-belts.'

I opened the cabin door and yelled encouragingly while miming the closure of a seat-belt. The thirteen passengers, sitting on long benches on opposite sides of the metal aisle, seemed to recognise the state of emergency. I hurried back to my place at the navigation table — once so substantial, now so flimsy — next to the radio operator at his radio. The plane rapidly, steeply lost height, and the terminally out-of-control prop kept on hysterically screaming.

In less than a minute, I thought, anomalously calmly, we may all be dead. Perhaps that was how Paddy Finucane, the Battle of Britain fighter pilot, felt when his stricken Spitfire (Hurricane?) was about to hit the English Channel, and, according to legend, blithely announced: 'This is it, chaps.'

The radio operator, like me, an expert on military etiquette at times of crisis as depicted in the movies, gave me his hand to shake. Fortunately, the plane's belly, bumping and scraping rocky ground at close to a hundred miles an hour, made too much noise for last words. A brief eternity and nearly three hundred yards later, the starboard wing struck a concrete gun emplacement, and the plane ended its run sliding backwards. We were quite near Anzio.

The sang was not at all froid. We crew members and our passengers jumped from the rear doorway with the manic alacrity of Keystone Kops, fizzing with adrenalin and irrational joy. That was the only time I experienced the sensation of being really intimately involved in the war.

Special effects would have dramatised the situation further, with a huge red and orange explosion, but Douglas had built a hardy machine. The wreckage simply lay there, with a broken wing, a broken tail and a chronically damaged fuselage, grounded for ever.

Nobody was hurt. The pilot and I took turns telling our Very Important Passenger, a lieutenant-general on his way to command land forces in Greece, how well we had managed, with the implication that he was lucky to be alive, thanks to us. We had come down on level ground. It was not till we reached Rome that I learned that the level ground was an uncleared minefield.

We stayed in the Excelsior and did some daily cultural sight-seeing and nightly carousing until a couple of elderly RAF engineering officers (ground staff over the age of thirty) arrived from England. They investigated 'the crash', as they called it, with a grim thoroughness that made us uncomfortable. Eventually, however, they conceded that we were blameless. The general kindly sent our CO a message of thankful commendation, so that on our return to England we were awarded ten days' leave. We would have preferred to have taken it in Rome. The Italians were always so civilised in their attitude to war, so sympathetic, and they were so quick to organise a lavishly accommodating black market. I took a case of Asti Spumante back to London. At high altitude over the Alps, a few bottles popped corks insecurely fastened by rusty wire. The foam made the crew compartment smell like a Roman night-club. In Soho, I gave the rest of the wine to the friendly proprietor of the Jardin des Gourmets. He appreciated the gesture, he said, but, spitting out the first-and-last mouthful, his verdict was brusque: 'Eau de vache!' Cow-piss.

I visited London as often as possible and usually stayed at the Berkeley Hotel in Piccadilly, if Rosa Lewis's Cavendish Hotel in Jermyn Street was full. The Cavendish was by far the best place in London at the time, because she had the style of the madame of an upper-class brothel, both louche and snobbish, and a Robin Hood system of overcharging rich senior guests and undercharging less affluent young favourites. But the Berkeley was a good second choice. The food in the buttery was all right. I liked rabbit.

As soon as I got to the hotel, I changed into civilian clothes. In the bar early one evening, I was wearing a Nassauvian sports jacket of West of England plaid in which the predominant colours were anchovy-brown and lobster-red. A blue-rinsed, Helen Hokinson dowager of formidable indignation demanded an explanation for my presence. My praise of the barman's way with a cocktail only intensified her expression of disapproval. She reached into her reticule and presented me with a white feather. I thought that symbol of cowardice had gone out of fashion several wars ago. Did she think I should have been on the North-West Frontier, doing my bit with the Bengal Lancers? The barman came to my rescue, reminding me not to forget my parachute, as if I had left one in the cloakroom. Collapse of stout party.

Having celebrated D-Day in Brazil with dancing girls squirting perfume, I achieved equal irrelevance drinking in Tel Aviv the day the atom bomb fell on Hiroshima. After V-E and V-J days, in plenty of time for Christmas, I had the more meaningful privilege of carrying to Nuremberg some tea-chests laden with documentary evidence for Hartley Shawcross, the British prosecutor. A Reuters correspondent covering the International Military Tribunal got me a pass to the courtroom press gallery.

Looking down at the twenty-two defendants, I noticed Goering in a military-looking grey tunic, strangely blank without his customary array of ornate decorations. His plump face was smooth-shaven, his dark hair was sleekly groomed and his eyes looked unexpectedly untroubled. Perhaps he already knew about the cyanide capsule that would enable him to cheat the hangman. Next to Goering, in contrast, sat the scruffy, gaunt figure of Rudolph Hess, ruminatively chewing with slack jaws and staring up at the chamber's high ceiling, as if mad or quite convincingly pretending to be – another way of evading execution. Those two and the rest of the conspirators deserved to be put to death millions of times. Eventually, after 216 trial days, the sentences were announced: 3 acquitted, 4 prison for 10–20 years, 3 life in prison, 12 death by hanging. And soon the legal proceedings against criminals lower in the Nazi hierarchy would be concluded prematurely, in order that the Western allies could recruit German support in the new conflict which would be called the Cold War.

As Karl von Clausewitz wrote in the nineteenth century, 'War is not merely a political act, but also a real political instrument, a continuation of policy carried out by other means.' In 1948, General George C. Marshall warned: 'However much any future war starts in the air, as in the past it will end up in the mud.' In Nuremberg at the time of the tribunal, of course, the notion of any future war seemed quite absurd. But, as we found out, the twentieth century and the twenty-first were the Age of the Absurd.

15

Reno, 'The Biggest Little City in the World', early in the summer of 1946 was busy dissolving impetuous wartime marriages. For me, the gambling was an incidental sideshow. I was hoping for a sure thing. An RCAF legal officer in London had recommended the Nevada law firm of McCarran & Kane, so I applied for their help as soon as I got off the train. At the age of twenty-one, I was an apprehensive candidate for divorce.

Not knowing about the legal requirements, I wondered whether I had sufficient grounds. A junior member of the staff chuckled and told me that any grounds were sufficient. The term 'Mental Cruelty' had never proved inadequately elastic. For example, it was possible to divorce a spouse who ate cookies in bed – or refused to eat them. The procedure would be simple: it took six weeks to establish residence in the State of Nevada, and then to obtain a divorce decree took only five minutes. During the wait, I must publicly proclaim my litigious intention, by inserting small advertisements in the classified columns of a Carson City newspaper that the party of the second part was sure not to see. It was important not to allow her to complicate the issue by filing a counter-suit, which might cause unnecessary expense.

'You've got yourself the best lawyer in the business,' I was assured. That was when I learned that Pat McCarran was United States

Senator McCarran, the most influential politician in Nevada, a fearless libertarian, after whom, many years later, the grateful state would name the international airport at Las Vegas. His prestige and power made me consider the contents of my wallet. There was not much more in my bank account in Bronxville, and this was before the illusory security of credit cards. What would such a big-time advocate charge me? I did not dare to ask.

His secretary steered me towards a residence that many previous clients had found satisfactory. The proprietor, the secretary said, was a lady who could be relied on to testify in court that I had stayed in her house for the past six weeks continuously, even if I had sometimes been absent. The secretary gave me a conspiratorial smile.

Peggy's Guest House was more favourably impressive than its name. A taxi delivered me and my suitcase to an extensive building of grey fieldstone and white clapboard in the style known as California Ranch-House, set well back on a green lawn, in a quiet street near the campus of the University of Nevada, a safe distance from the casinos. The grass was irrigated by a sprinkler. Fine droplets in the sunshine created a miniature rainbow. A bellpush sounded chimes behind the blue front door, the first five notes of 'Home on the Range'.

Peggy was middle-aged with a Harpo Marx wig and scarlet lipstick. Her amplitude mocked the confinement of a loose, pink satin-and-lace housecoat, which seemed to promise hospitality of abundant indulgence.

After a warm smile and a few friendly words, she led me into the air-conditioned interior and beyond. Beside her own quarters, there was a large patio, brightened by Mexican tiles of neo-Aztec design, terracotta, yellow and indigo. In the centre of it there was an oval pool, turquoise and glittering, surrounded by a dozen or so women of various ages in sunglasses and casual summer dress, the younger ones in the minimal swim-suits soon to be dubbed bikinis, after an experimentally atomised Pacific atoll, reclining on chaises longues in the attitudes of sun-worshippers with no urgent engagements. Around them, on three sides of the patio, were rows of bedroom doors, uniform but of different pastel colours. And on the fourth side, visible behind sliding glass doors, there were a communal bar and dining room and what Peggy called 'the games area', with upholstered bamboo sofas and chairs, card tables and a one-armed bandit. In Nevada, all establishments, even dentists' waiting rooms, provided at least one slot machine. There, in the games area, in the pre-television age, people were actually able and willing to sit around and *talk*.

When Peggy and I entered the patio, conversation stopped. All those whose eyes were open looked at us with frank curiosity. In those days, divorce proceedings were customarily initiated by wives. *The Women*, a witty yet sentimental play/film written by Clare Boothe Luce, was a realistic depiction of a Reno dude ranch, where all the guests were divorcées-in-waiting and the only males were the paid-for pseudo-cowboy gigolos and some of the horses. Peggy introduced me, and the sunbathers gave me their names.

'Want a Tom Collins?' asked a neatly constructed blonde in a playful little green dress, raising her eyebrows and a tall glass. 'It's almost noon. We're rehearsing for the happy hour.'

'Happy hours plural,' a brunette in red roguishly corrected her. I imagined there was a lot of laughing through the tears in that place. People in our situation had to try to convince themselves and each other that divorce was a welcome escape rather than a failure. It was time for a party, a continuous wake, revelry beside a corpse. Peggy may have noticed a certain uneasiness in my demeanour as I confronted six weeks in a harem of Dorothy Parkers.

'There's another man,' she consolingly informed me. Turning to the women, she enquired, 'Where's Charles?'

'Charlie's still in bed,' said a blonde with a deep tan, which signified that she was close to term. 'Resting. He needs his rest.'

There was general laughter.

'He sure will be glad to see you,' the brunette predicted.

'We're all glad,' said the redhead.

'OK,' Peggy briskly interjected. 'Come on. I'll show you your suite.'

The bedroom was beige and cream. The bed was queen-size.

I had just finished putting my clothes away when the telephone rang. It was the other man. His name was something like C. Cabot Griswold III. He spoke in the not displeasing flat drawl I would learn to recognise as the sound of old New England. He wondered whether I would care to join him for lunch.

We walked. Not far away, in what looked at first glance like a private house, there was an excellent small French restaurant. Six weeks might not seem too bad, I thought. But what was there to do?

'It's really quite simple,' Griswold said. 'One fucks one's brains out.' He sighed philosophically. 'It makes everyone feel less unwanted.'

16

The court proceedings were not at all embarrassing. The judge did not wear one of those antique, long, grey wigs that intimidate the laity in some British courts. He looked like a prosperous businessman, which, I suppose, is what he was, and he greeted me with a friendly smile. The McCarran effect? All I had to do was confirm my identity. Peggy testified that I had resided in Reno for the required six weeks. My counsel read out a routine complaint without any unpleasantness. The judge ruled that a divorce was granted. It had taken very little longer than the boiling of an egg. The fees totalled $120 – $100 for McCarran & Kane and $20 for Peggy. Of course, that was when $120 were $120.

In keeping with tradition, I should then have walked to the parapet of the bridge over the Truckee River and thrown my wedding ring into it. However, I had never worn a ring, so the formalities were over. That day, the first of the happy hours began even earlier than usual. There were shrill cries of congratulation. The woman who had been most demonstratively sympathetic during my stay and I exchanged addresses, like passengers at the end of a romantic cruise. Like cruise passengers, neither of us heard from the other ever again.

During the days in the eastbound train, I spent a lot of time in the club car wondering about the future. I was in exuberant health, with a little money, no liabilities and no sense of vocation. I concluded, over the umpteenth bourbon, that I might as well go back to school and hope for divine guidance. I was certainly in no mood to look for a job. Like many others after military service, I was luxuriating in the the-world-owes-me-a-living syndrome.

The Canadian government had passed legislation like America's GI Bill, offering veterans funds for tuition and subsistence. It was no longer necessary for me to maintain a B+ average to keep a scholarship. I adjusted my curriculum accordingly, signing up only for courses for which classes met late in the morning and did not threaten to burden me with information difficult to grasp. As I languidly toyed with Modern English Poetry, Roman Daily Life, Astronomy and Charcoal Drawing, I recognised that I was goofing off and failing to prepare myself for the practical demands of the 'real world', but frankly, like Rhett Butler, I didn't give a damn.

The holiday lasted until the summer of 1947. Having spent more than my income, I was beginning to feel pressure to do something. Mastery of the subjects I had been playfully studying did not seem to constitute an ideal preparation for journalism, but what else were they a preparation for? The combination of an education that could be described most charitably as motley and a temperament that moved me usually to feel nostalgia for the places left behind, optimism for places that lay ahead, and a restless discontent with immediate circumstances virtually forced me to become a newspaper reporter. In no other occupation is the present more fleeting. Somehow at home, I don't know how, it was understood that I would eventually drift into newspapers. My father's encouragement, without ever reaching great heights of lyricism, was expressed at times in terms I found irresistible: 'You may not get rich, but at least you'll get free tickets for first nights, or possibly second nights, and plenty of paper and typewriter ribbons.' Stationery supplies in bulk have always powerfully attracted me. He never tried to persuade me to apply to Wall Street or Madison Avenue. The only professional advice he gave me was quite fervent. 'There are two important things you must remember,' he said. 'For heaven's sake, never write for a news agency; and always spend as much time as possible away from the home office. I think you'll like it. It's better than working.'

17

A Baltimore & Ohio Railroad train took me from New York to Baltimore in September 1947, at the age of twenty-two, for an interview with Charles H. Dorsey, Jr, who had recently been appointed managing editor of the *Sun*. The meeting had been arranged by means of a brief, non-committal exchange of letters. There was no way of knowing what to expect. In spite of all the travel and worldly experiences of the past few years, I was strangely naive, and I was nervous.

Walking down Charles Street toward the old Sunpapers' office, I felt a spasm of dread. I had brought with me a scrapbook, bound in imitation red leather, containing cuttings of everything I had ever written or drawn for publication: a parody of 'Hiawatha' and an essay on 'Homecoming' for the *Gower*, the magazine of University College School; a grotesque ink drawing for the (English) *Mickey Mouse Weekly*; articles and cartoons for the Bronxville High School *Mirror*; a one-shot guest column for the Oberlin *Review*, and news and feature articles, with emphasis on the activities of local advertisers, for the Pelham, New York, *Sun*. At the time of publication, each piece had been read and reread with pride. Now, as I carried the suddenly pathetic, intimate scraps up to Mr Dorsey's office, I was sweating. But they were my only credentials. What if Mr Dorsey should turn first to the drawing from the *Mickey Mouse Weekly*?

Mr Dorsey was not in his office when I arrived, one minute before the time of our appointment.

'He suggested that you go and have some lunch and come back in about an hour,' his secretary said. I tried not to show how appalled I was by the thought of further suspense.

'Could you recommend a nearby restaurant?' I asked lightly. 'A reasonable one.'

'The Lord Baltimore's just across the street. Your lunch will go on your expense account,' she added encouragingly.

With a dry mouth I chewed what might as well have been hardtack, and rehearsed silently the clever remarks that might save me from humiliation. I tried to convince myself that I did not need the job, that I would not mind going home to announce that I had failed. By the time the interview took place, not in the managing editor's private office but exposed at a desk in the newsroom, I was in such a state of mental paralysis that I could say hardly anything. Mr Dorsey himself was not noted for garrulousness. We sat opposite each other murmuring occasional monosyllables. Now and then he uttered a muffled snort. Then he posed the classic job-interviewers' question, for which I had composed no appropriate answer.

'Well, just what makes you want a job in *Baltimore*?'

At that time, I knew nothing worth mentioning about H. L. Mencken's coverage of the Scopes trial in the controversy between Darwinians and creationists, nothing about the Naval Academy, soft-shelled crabs, the Johns Hopkins University, the Maryland Club and Pimlico, or even the Baltimore *Sun*, except that it was reputed to be a good paper. My father had said that members of its staff kept being awarded the Pulitzer Prize. I merely gulped and said: 'New York's so big . . .'

'Humph,' Mr Dorsey snorted. 'Things move pretty fast around here sometimes.'

He looked up at the clock and frowned.

'Have you done any writing?' he asked. I hesitantly lifted the scrapbook from my lap, opened it as though by chance at the carefully marked page of a signed article on a Westchester phono-graph-record factory, and handed the book over. He riffled through it in the brisk manner of a Customs inspector.

'Mm,' he said, handing it back. 'Yes. Thank you.'

'Don't you want to read any of it?' I asked, temporarily forget-ting that, a few moments before, the last thing in the world I had wanted was a reading. 'I could leave it with you, if you like.'

'No, that's all right,' he emphatically assured me. 'Look, er, Mr . . . – as I told you in my letter, as you may recall, there is no immediate opening on the paper. But if one should come up, I'll let you know. Tell Mrs Johnston how much today has cost you. She'll take you to the cashier.' He stood up and I stood up and we shook hands and I thanked him and walked away. It was over.

When I got back to Bronxville, my mother said there was a telegram for me. I could not have been more surprised by its contents.

'Can offer you forty-five to start,' it said. 'If interested wire when you can come. Other details can be talked about later. Anxious to have you. Regards – Dorsey.'

That telegram after that interview still baffles me. Having telegraphed my acceptance I did some joyful arithmetic. During the few weeks I had spent that summer writing for the Pelham *Sun* I had been paid $25 a week. Now the Baltimore *Sun* was going to pay me $45! That would be over $180 a month – $2,340 a year!

But what were the other details? So far there had been no mention of any details. What would they expect me to do for that kind of money?

I went back to Baltimore a week later, and gradually I found out.

18

The main room of the police station at Pennsylvania Avenue and Dolphin Street, in a black section of north-western Baltimore, was like an underendowed charitable institution. White fluorescent lights emphasised its bareness and the darkness of the paint. The excessive steam heat, rumbling and rattling through the pipes and hissing from the radiators, intensified the thick, sweet smell of floor wax, the chemical smell of antiseptic, the faint, musty smell of decay, and, when the door to the cell block was opened, the whiffs of ammoniacal pungency. It was a poor room with a high gloss. While the turnkey, an inferior policeman with an indoor complexion and a dark grey cardigan, mopped and polished the linoleum, I imagined rats and termites gnawing below.

This room was animated with the harsh jollity of a barracks three times a day when shifts were changing and patrolmen assembled to receive their orders, and some, laboriously, with much slow licking of lips, wrote out their reports.

Now, a wet evening in autumn, the room was almost empty and almost silent. It was separated into two parts by a high counter across one end. A sergeant in uniform was writing in the docket. Behind him, in a corner, a radio operator in shirtsleeves sat reading a book while his radios hummed and crackled as though irritable. Against the wall at the opposite end of the room there was a small table bearing a telephone that belonged to the Baltimore *Sun*. I was sitting at this table drawing triangles and cylinders and cones on folded copy paper and waiting for something to happen.

'Here's a good one,' said the radio operator his book in his hand.

'Huh?' said the sergeant. He swivelled heavily around in his chair, peered over his steel spectacles at the book and read aloud: '"Homicidal Investigation: autopsies – what can be deduced from gunshot wounds."'

'Ain't that a dilly though?' the radio operator asked. He showed the sergeant a colour photograph of what had been a man's face. Half the portrait was a mass of blood; the rest was animal alarm.

'This illustrates when fired at close range the effects of a shotgun may be devastating,' the radio operator said with a proprietary smile. 'Look – there's a worse one than that.' His eyes were shining as he licked a finger and flicked over the pages to a photograph of a man who had suffered 'direct violence'. The sergeant leaned closer.

'"Strange to say,"' he read, '"the victim was alive and perfectly conscious for several hours after receiving this injury." Well, how about that? Wonder what he thought must of happened to him.' The sergeant sounded faintly awed. He looked up and saw the radio operator's expression of satisfaction. 'What are you trying to do?' the sergeant asked, belligerently jocular. 'Learn how to be a detective?'

The city editor had said that police reporting was the foundation upon which all journalism was based. 'Succeed as a police reporter,' he had said, 'and you'll be able to do anything. The first thing a police reporter must do is to get to know the cops. Humour them. Listen to all they have to say. They can help you a lot – or make things very difficult.'

There were sounds of scuffling on the station steps. Two patrolmen appeared, breathing hard, dragging a black man by the arms. He was leaning back, his head forward, and he was kicking at the shiny floor, but his shoes were slipping. I noticed the turnkey's look of fury as long, dull streaks were scraped on the linoleum.

The man failed to check his progress to the desk. He was elderly – his close-cropped hair looked like steel wool – but he seemed very strong. His shabby coat was taut against his back, and a vein in one temple was distended with the effort of resistance. One of the patrolmen was holding the prisoner by something resembling a single handcuff with a handle. There were new smells in the room: sweat and wine.

The black's eyes were closed. When he raised his head and blinked in the direction of the nearest fluorescent tubes, it was possible to see that his eyes were rheumy white blanks. It was strange to see a blind man under arrest. I had always assumed that blind men were helpless, virtuous, patient philosophers, even on rainy nights when nobody bought their matches.

At last the police had him pressed securely against the brass rail that extended along the top of the counter, and the black, holding on to it, suddenly seemed acquiescent.

'Jeez,' said one of the patrolmen, speaking over the bowed head. 'I thought we'd never get him here. Mean son-of-a-bitch, huh?'

The other patrolman was holding the handcuff with one hand and wiping the back of his neck with a handkerchief. His face was red and moist. He put the handkerchief in his pocket. He raised his cap by its shiny black peak and with a couple of free fingers scratched his scalp.

'Really didn't like to hit him,' he said. 'Real stupid, he is. What you going to do?'

The sergeant carefully blotted what he had written in the docket and looked mildly over his glasses.

'What's he here for?'

'Disorderly conduct, sergeant. Creating a disturbance outside a shoeshine parlour. He's loaded.'

There was a sudden ripple of energy through the black's body. It was with difficulty that the patrolmen restrained him. Something that one of them did made him wince and shudder and clench his teeth and then he was still and meek.

'All right,' the sergeant said severely. 'Name?' There was no reply. The black's forehead was resting on the brass rail, a sweaty forehead on the turnkey's polished brass.

'Hey, you!' one of the patrolmen yelled into the prisoner's ear. 'What's your name?'

'OK, let him sleep it off,' said the sergeant. 'Look him over good, Ed,' he told the turnkey. 'I don't want him cutting his throat.'

The turnkey frisked the prisoner with malevolent vigour. The search produced a pink celluloid comb with some broken teeth, a small harmonica and about $1.50 in silver.

When the patrolmen returned from the cells, one of them was adjusting his necktie and the other was fastidiously picking small pieces of skin from the inside of the handcuff. He saw that I was watching.

'I'm going to have to wash the goddamn thing,' he said. 'I wonder how many times I've told them? "If you don't struggle, you won't get hurt."' He raised his eyebrows at a sudden inhuman bellow from a concrete echo-chamber behind closed doors. 'Ed's really pissed off about something tonight,' he commented, then returned his attention to the handcuff. 'Look,' he said to me, as patiently as a father explains a toy to a child. 'See what happens when you pull against this thing?' He squeezed the steel ring and there were sharp clicks as teeth sprang, locking the handcuff at the reduced diameter. 'The more you pull, the tighter it gets. You understand?'

A short time later, there was another demonstration. The man under arrest was white. There was no discrimination to speak of.

It was quiet in the police station, except for the creaking tread of policemen off duty walking around the pool table upstairs. My telephone rang. It was the city desk. A rewrite man said unreproachfully that I hadn't called for several hours. Didn't I have anything for him? I told him about the men that had been brought in and about the terrible cry I had heard. Could that sort of thing be reported?

'We don't bother about drunks,' the rewrite man said, 'except now and then when there are good quotes in a magistrate's court.' Some of the magistrates were comedians.

'But would you go down to South Baltimore General? Russ is having dinner. A private plane crashed and the casualties should be arriving about now. Get names and where they're from and all that.'

At the hospital it was difficult to get information. I badgered a nurse in the accident ward until she was rude. Then, walking along a corridor toward the ambulance entrance, I happened to see the room that the casualties had been wheeled into.

On a table lay two men. There was something wrong with their necks, and their feet hung heavily over the end of the table like the leaden feet of marionettes.

'Are they badly injured?' I asked a man in a white coat who was leaning over the table. The doctor gave a short, humourless laugh. 'They're dead,' he said.

They were the first dead bodies I had ever seen. We hadn't gone in for that sort of thing much in my part of the Air Force. My inexperience must have been apparent: the doctor became helpful, giving me the names and even supplying facts that I failed to ask for.

'There's a pay-phone in the reception room,' he said. But the city desk was not very interested.

'Just give us enough for a four-head,' an assistant city editor said. 'We've got a good murder in the Eastern District.' The rewrite man came back on the line. 'Russ is back,' he said. 'You can go eat.'

19

My aptitude for police reporting was limited, no doubt, by a number of factors; however, I like to think that not the least of these was a rapidly diminishing sympathy with the police. I came to welcome the ringing of the police stations' automatic electric bells signalling fire alarms. There was a refreshing moral clarity about fire-fighting, an elemental conflict between water and fire, between good and evil; and, though the conflict was occasionally a fierce one, victory was assured. Compared with sitting in a police station, sometimes, willy-nilly, ingratiatingly pretending camaraderie in an exchange of scatological repartee, it was not at all unpleasant to stand in a suburban street at night, sipping coffee from a cardboard cup, watching a Niagara of diamonds fall through the searchlights' beams while men in black oilskins and smoke masks axed holes in the roof of a Baltimore colonial mansionette. It was especially gratifying to watch the forces of righteousness blasting away when I learned that the building being saved was fully insured.

The most loathsome assignments inflicted on us police reporters were intrusions into the homes of the next of kin of criminals or their victims. Generally, the *Sun* was less offensive than its downmarket Hearst rival, the *News-Post*; but overzealous junior editors, sitting beyond embarrassment in the security of the newsroom, sometimes violated the temperate spirit of the *Sun* by ordering a reporter to interview the mother of a youth condemned to death, say (Maryland still believed in hanging), or the mother of a girl who had been raped and murdered. Mothers were always preferred for this ghoulish enterprise; they wept more gently than fathers and talked more. After having gone to a bereaved family for a portrait of a murdered child, which, incidentally, they gave me as meekly as if I had been invested with the authority of a priest, I resolved never to do so again. On each of the few subsequent occasions when similar requests were made, I responded with pessimistic mumbles over the telephone and retired to the nearest tavern for an hour or so of beer and juke-box music.

What with one thing and another, not many weeks elapsed before the city editor of that era, who had the anguished look of a displaced sports writer, informed me that I was no longer a police reporter. I was to 'come inside' to join the pool of general assignment reporters, from which I could expect to be selected to cover anything from the weekly tea of a ladies' sewing circle to the first flight to the moon – anything at all, except, as a rule, the activities of the Police Department. That I would have nothing more to do with the Police Department sounded too good to be true, and it was.

During the ensuing months I wrote weather stories, obituaries and accounts of speeches delivered at luncheons of Rotarians and Lions and Veterans of Foreign Wars, and met Susan Watson, an ambitious Vassar graduate on the teaching staff of the Baltimore Museum of Art. I toured New England with the Baltimore Symphony Orchestra (the article given most prominence was a report that a gunman had held up the orchestra's business manager in his hotel in Boston, taken several hundred dollars and temporarily immobilised him by making him remove his trousers). I attended the coronation of Queen Shenandoah XXII in the Apple Blossom Festival in Winchester, Virginia; accompanied Mayor Thomas

D'Alesandro of Baltimore to Hagerstown, Maryland, where, on a bicycle, he raced against and defeated the local mayor riding a mule; learned how John A. Cypulski, caretaker of the Haunted House at Carlin's Park, felt about pressing the button that activated jets of air to blow up women's skirts ('OK'); celebrated National Cage Bird Week; went on a Maryland House & Garden Pilgrimage; witnessed the meeting of Robert E. Lee IV and Major General Ulysses S. Grant III at Appomattox Court House (they were coldly polite, as was noted also by a promising young reporter on the *Washington Post*, Ben Bradlee); mourned the passing of Baltimore's last burlesque theatre (it reopened); described a dog's funeral; attended annual banquets of the Maryland Wine and Food Society and Alcoholics Anonymous; tested the handicapping system of Thomas Justin White, Jr, a distinguished Baltimore horse-player, at Laurel Park, and found it wanting; and reported a Johns Hopkins poetry reading by e. e. cummings.

The e. e. cummings piece was written in free verse and printed entirely in lower-case type. A Hopkins acquaintance told me the poet was amused. Then I heard that the publisher of the paper, a remote figure, was sufficiently entertained to commend the city desk. I wrote him a thank-you letter and suggested a raise in pay. Mr Dorsey, naturally, was very unamused by my having gone over his head. However, after he had made his displeasure abundantly apparent, his own sense of humour fortunately prevailed. He increased my salary to sixty dollars a week.

So Susan Watson and I got married.

20

A few of us young reporters, as soon as we got off, at about half past eleven in the evening, used to get together at the Calvert, the bar closest to our office. We drank there, we used to say, 'to unwind', which meant to get more or less drunk. Most times we drank National Bohemian beer, a local brew usually within the meanest budget; now and then the beer was supplemented with shots of blended Maryland rye, which we flattered by calling it Old Overshoes.

Our conversation, ardent yet protectively cynical, was mainly about the stories we had just covered, how we were going to quit to earn more in public relations, and our plans to write the Great American Novel. I doubt that even the most talented and ambitious of my contemporaries, Russell Baker, who ended his professional career as a columnist on the *New York Times*, squeezing wry satire out of sociological trivia, did much creative writing after we returned to our homes long after midnight. I certainly did not do any, although I felt continuously guilty about not trying. Journalism is believed to be the best possible apprenticeship for other, supposedly superior sorts of writing, but often turns out to be an interminable substitute for them. The vital ability is to recognise when, if ever, to switch.

Our early mornings, what was left of them, were devoted largely to sleep, Zen trances under the shower, large mugs of black coffee and other detoxifying therapies to get ready for another day of reporting.

By the spring of 1951 I had been on the *Sun* for three and a half years, my duties remained unchanged, and my salary seemed to have got stuck at $75 a week, which was barely enough for subsistence, and left next to nothing for the little niceties of life, such as paying the doctor's bills. Even apart from economic limitations, normal social activities were impossible because of my hours, from 2.30 to 11.30 p.m. There were two days off a week, but, because the paper was published every day, the holidays were as likely to occur in the middle of the week as at the end.

There was one welcome, brief aberration from the norm. Reporters, before writers such as Ken Kesey and Tom Wolfe introduced the subjective licence of the New Journalism, were instructed to act only as recorders of verifiable objective facts, without any colourful embroidery and guesses about what people might be thinking. The first person singular, such a prominent feature of modern journalism, was taboo. But then the *Sun's* drama critic, having seen *Oklahoma!* several times, had me assigned to review a revival of the show at Ford's Theatre. Thus, for once, I was free to express my own opinions undisguised, in prose as purple as I could contrive. News stories were unsigned, except on the highest level, from Washington and abroad, but reviews of all sorts were always signed. I got my first by-line. It was a major achievement, I thought. I have noticed ever since that no writer tires of seeing his name in print.

Next I spent most of the time writing feature articles. One of them appeared almost every day, between society news, drama criticism, the knitting pattern, the crossword puzzle and answers to questions about etiquette and affairs of the heart, on the women's page. This occupation was not arduous. Frivolity was encouraged. There were countless interviews with all sorts of women, women librarians, women teachers, women strippers, even a woman pilot.

In retrospect, the whole period is a blur. Yet somehow Susan managed to become pregnant. Newspapermen's wives have to be ingenious.

Then, writing for an hour or two every morning for a week, I managed to write a book for children. *The Chocolate Touch*, a variation on the legend of King Midas, is about a greedy boy by the name of John Midas whose lips turn everything they touch into chocolate. Generation after generation of children on both sides of the Atlantic have written letters, sometimes compulsorily, to tell me they have enjoyed the story, especially the bit when John inadvertently turns his mother into a chocolate statue. The year 2002 was the book's fiftieth anniversary. It has earned more money than anything else I've ever written. If only I had written a children's book every year . . .

Euphoria eluded my wife and me. I found it more and more difficult to assume that air of insouciance and amiability that is a *sine qua non* for reporters whose task is to stimulate ordinary men and women to chatter entertainingly about their ordinary lives. I was beginning to comprehend that wasting time is slow suicide.

Against this background of near-poverty, frustration and self-pity, at a time when the front-page news was being made by soldiers in Korea, one of the assistant city editors, with a nudge, a wink and a click of tongue against palate, informed me that I was a lucky guy: Jane Russell was about to visit Baltimore, and I was to interview her. Now, looking back, I can imagine Nathanael West's sadistic Shrike leeringly inflicting such a tease on the wretched hero of *Miss Lonelyhearts*.

The interview took place the following morning, in the actress's hotel suite. Two RKO Radio Pictures publicity men and two photographers were already there when I arrived. Scotch and soda and the official studio biography were handed out while we waited for Miss Russell. The biography consisted of three mimeographed pages that told the story of her life from birth in Minnesota to discovery by Howard Hughes and stardom in *The Outlaw*, the story of Billy the Kid. Jane, the studio said, was essentially a sensitive, introverted person, much given to critical self-examination.

A door opened and in came the famous breasts. Jane was wearing a shiny black blouse, black velvet pedal-pushers and a black scowl. She was snarling like a black panther with a migraine. She had not had enough sleep, she complained; she needed nine hours and had only had seven. And didn't the goddamn hotel know how to make goddamn coffee?

After coffee, the conversation was neither better nor worse than usual in this sort of interview. She talked about a movie she'd like to make next, Vincent Price's art collection, and a new brand of nail-polish. While the photographers pleaded for a little more cleavage, I looked through my few chaotic notes, inwardly groaned, and drank whiskey.

Jane put on a long mink coat and was driven to a hospital to pose with a small boy on crutches, to help sell Easter Seals for medical research.

She changed into a tight, dark blue satin dress to meet a lot more newspapermen and a member of some organisation of motion picture censors at a cocktail party in her hotel. A great variety of people gave parties for the press — shipbuilders and aircraft manufacturers, art museums and publishers, jockey clubs and professional ball teams, building contractors, restaurant associations and any number of patriotic, fraternal, philanthropic and political organisations. But for ease of admission and plenitude of refreshments there were no parties that surpassed the press parties given by the motion-picture industry.

At the *Sun*, I soon finished writing a long and objective eulogy. As five o'clock drew near, I was one of the first to leave for the hotel. Typewriter after typewriter fell silent. Desk after desk was stealthily abandoned. Even a couple of editors glanced furtively at the clock and reached for their hats. In the homes of newspapermen, in run-down town-house apartments and in the bright, shoddy bungalows of jerry-built new suburban developments, prematurely haggard young women in aprons broke dishes and slapped babies, in hasty preparation to join their husbands for recreation at somebody else's expense.

Most of the men and women were intelligent enough to resent both the paper and their benefactors. The usual results were fierce rapacity at the bar, savagely cynical conversation and as much sourness in reporting as the paper would tolerate. The paper had a condescending attitude toward show business, especially movies, so that the most lavish, prolonged parties often resulted in the most insulting publicity. Printed insults were declarations of personal integrity: reporters insisted they could not be bought. But still the studios, distributors and exhibitors persisted, operating on the long-validated theory that any publicity is good publicity. Their representatives extended glad hands and bared their teeth in big smiles, though they knew they were disliked, and though they, in turn, disliked almost all their guests.

'Jane's fabulous,' said one of the hosts, as he welcomed the invited and the uninvited impartially, with unshakeable bonhomie. 'Isn't Jane fabulous? Isn't she a living doll? Wait till you meet Jane. You're gonna love her. Go get a drink, then let me introduce you to her. Believe me, this Jane is really special. No kidding, Jane's something else . . .'

But the great majority of the guests, those who were not compelled to write anything, were impervious to all appeals. They went to the long bar and stayed there in small groups, men and women asking each other whether they had ever heard such bull-shit.

The censor put his hand on Miss Russell's naked shoulder and said: 'Between you and I, Jane, as far as I'm concerned personally, there's nothing objectionable about photos of . . . a healthy young woman like you. If we were considering only men of maturity and high intelligence, I'd say: "Show *The Outlaw* just the way it was originally made!" But the thing is: dare we expose the youth of our state to such . . . ?' His glance fell, lingered for an instant and returned to her impassive face. 'Censorship,' he explained solemnly, 'is a heavy responsibility.'

'Uh-huh,' Miss Russell said.

When he invited her to dinner she said she wished she could make it but she couldn't. She had promised a journalist an interview. She turned and pointed at me, who was eavesdropping nearby. I was the only reporter whose name she remembered.

So I was permitted to take her to hear tenor sax virtuoso Johnnie Sparrow and his Golden Arrows play jazz at a little black club called the Frolic. 'When I can pat my foot to the music,' Sparrow used to say, 'I know other folk can pat theirs.' He certainly could that evening. The joint was really jumping. Nobody asked Jane for her autograph, but she had not been unnoticed. There was no check.

I took her to a restaurant in Little Italy, in East Baltimore, where the call-girls, the Mafia and the Mayor lived. I knew that the owner of the restaurant, who looked like a Neapolitan Sophie Tucker, was susceptible to celebrities. Fortunately, the gamble paid off. Maria's photographer took a few pictures, and dinner was on the house. When I delivered Jane to her suite, she kissed me so effectively that she felt she had to get down on her knees to pray for detumescent peace.

Saying goodbye, she told me she had had a ball. My night on the town was for her a nostalgic glimpse of the simple life.

21

On a leave of absence from the *Sun*, one fine day the following winter, Susan and I were being cosseted by attentive stewardesses in a Trans World Airlines Constellation high above the Rockies on the way to The Coast. In the motion-picture industry, known as The Industry, one never flew to Los Angeles; one might sometimes fly to LA, but usually to The Coast. The very phrase seemed permeated with the seductive smell of money, as in Gold Coast.

All our expenses to, in and back from Hollywood were being paid by Howard Hughes, who owned TWA, RKO and Jane Russell's contract. He had her in thrall for twenty years, at $1,000 a week, which seemed a lot when she signed. We were to spend a couple of months in Hollywood – the agreement was open-ended – while I gathered material for a Jane Russell biography. So there we were, at Los Angeles International Airport, like F. Scott Fitzgerald, William Faulkner, Christopher Isherwood and any number of other writers who should have known better, being met by a man in California non-athletic sports clothes with an immaculate California smile, and checking into a villa at the Garden of Allah, on Sunset Boulevard. 'RKO have brought Pat Catlin [*sic*] to write the Jane Russell bio,' noted the *Hollywood Reporter*. 'They're paying him a thousand a week.' Not quite accurate, but the item gave me a certain necessary status. *Everyone* read the *Hollywood Reporter*, while nobody cared about what anyone did east of the Sierra Nevada.

The villa consisted of a bedroom, a bathroom, a drawing room with a dining alcove, and a kitchen. There were two telephones. Immediately after the bellboy left, we called some friends 'back East' to describe our surroundings, to tell them there was a desk but I did not intend to do any writing for several weeks, there was a kitchen but Susan was not going to cook, and when we looked outside we could see moonlight through palm fronds. I rang a local number that had been given to me, and Perry Lieber, the RKO publicity director, welcomed us to California.

'You're going to need an automobile,' he said. 'Why don't you pick one up tomorrow morning?'

'Oh, I don't know,' I said, the extent of my allowances having been left unclear in New York. 'I thought we'd probably use taxis.'

'When the sun's out – like every day – it's kind of nice to ride in a convertible,' he coaxed me. I conceded the point. He gave me the name of a garage a few blocks away where I could choose a car of a colour scheme that pleased us, and, 'of course', charge it to the RKO account. We chose on Oldsmobile, with a Rocket engine – pistachio-green exterior, red leather inside. Its miles-per-gallon performance was impractical, but, for us, gasoline was free.

We walked along a meandering pathway through what the Garden of Allah management said was like 'a garden in Old Spain', past the swimming pool – which the original owner, a homesick Russian ballerina, had built in the shape of the Black Sea – across a small terrace, into the main hotel building, through the dining room to the bar. It was with a reverent sense of the history of the place, when Robert Benchley and companions did their best to make it Algonquin West, that we ordered two martinis.

'How do you like them?' enquired Rocky, the bartender, who had the appearance of a superannuated prize-fighter and the gravely concerned manner of a Savile Row tailor. 'Quite dry?'

'Very.'

He poured chilled gin into chilled, outsize glasses and murmured over them, softly, in turn, 'Martini and Rossi.'

I had read *The Day of the Locust* by Nathanael West, and other works on Hollywood by writers who had professed to despise it and themselves for being there, yet had succumbed to its lotus charms. The drinks were strong, so it was not surprising to see a big blonde in besequinned sunglasses, ermine stole, cyclamen matador's trousers and high-heeled shoes mince hippily into the room, leading by the hand a very short dwarf with a very large head. She sat on a high stool at the bar; he climbed up the cross-bars of an adjacent stool as nimbly as a sailor climbing up rigging, took his place beside her and demanded, in an authoritative bass voice: 'The usual, baby? Two vodkas on the rocks. Or how about two vodkas on Rocky?' The dwarf laughed until he coughed and choked, and his companion kindly shook him until he could breathe again.

At mid-morning we had breakfast on the terrace by the pool. Two unemployed extras were playing chess and sipping Bloody Marys. The dwarf, in a big Mexican straw sombrero and a tiny bikini, was lying on his stomach on the warm tiles reading the *Hollywood Reporter* while the blonde sat leaning over him and fondly anointed his muscular shoulders with lotion. A waiter told me that the dwarf currently was a smash-hit as a Teddy bear in TV commercials for California orange juice. The commercials were important, because there was fierce competition with Florida. The commercials lasted only thirty seconds, once a week, but they were live, and the performances were so stressful that he was developing a vodka problem. The blonde said they were considering electro-convulsive treatment and hypnosis. 'He's doing so great it'd be tragic to throw it all away.'

We drove fifty miles up the coast, just for fun, and inland between vineyards, and back at high speed, with the top down and the radio loud. As there was hardly any money in my pocket, we returned to the Garden of Allah, our magical oasis, lunched on lobster salad and Chablis, and signed the check, tipping lavishly. After a nap, we drove over to RKO, to shake hands with everyone in the publicity department and to be introduced to the cashier.

'Give Pat a couple hundred, a little spending money over the weekend,' Lieber said. 'He'll be coming in to see you the first of the week.' I tried to look casual as I stuffed uncounted cash into my jacket.

'Good,' I said. 'Now, if you'll excuse me, I promised Jane I'd get in touch.'

West along Sunset; north at the Beverly Hills Hotel; up along a gently inclined avenue of palm trees, green lawns and extensive white houses; up a steeper, winding road between the cool rock walls of a canyon; still climbing, across the peaks of broken hills, over, down, up again, and around a cliffside road called Round Valley Drive – one couldn't miss it, as Jane had promised: the mailbox was adorned with a golden cutout of a quarterback about to throw a pass, identified in neat letters as R. S. Waterfield, 'Robert the Rifle', her husband.

From the road, the house was invisible, set back on a ledge that fell away precipitously on three sides. The steep, narrow drive, like the first ascent of a roller coaster, tilted the car back alarmingly. Above the sulphurous haze and the clamour of Los Angeles, Jane had attained the secure sequestration of a mountain fortress. Everyone to whom she gave her frequently changed telephone number was under oath to guard it with his life.

Two Dobermann pinschers the size of ponies reared high against a steel mesh fence and barked in deep, angry voices, then turned aside and ran in circles, ululating plaintively because they were not being allowed to strip the flesh from my bones.

The wide, two-storey house was lightened by vast sheets of green-tinted plate glass and softened at the edges by bougainvillaea, scarlet, magenta and mauve. The upper-floor expanse of picture windows overlooked Van Nuys, her childhood home, in a broad valley, where her mother still lived, and, beyond that, a range of mountains, pale blue-grey in the distance. Jane's house was a mirador, an eyrie.

A fat, brown Buddha with complacent eyelids and a reticent smile sat next to a large gong between a stairway and a three-car garage. I was tempted to seize the padded mallet hanging beside the gong to announce my arrival. Instead, however, I walked around one end of the house and up a ramp to the only door I could find. Feeling like a delivery boy, I made an effort, tightening the knot of my tie, to look like a biographer. I rang the bell.

'All right! All right!' screamed a voice, female, harsh and impatient. Jane before coffee.

I found myself in a sewing room, a nursery, an all-purpose room adjoining the kitchen. Jane Russell, a national symbol of glamour and affluence, was in a white shirt and blue jeans, arranging a baby's diaper. She appeared to be having some difficulty, as though trying to force a large bundle of laundry into a small bag. Her hair was hanging all over her face and the tip of her tongue protruded as she bent forward and took great care to insert a safetypin through the diaper, not the baby.

'Oh, *you*,' she said when she looked up. 'I'd forgotten. Why come in the back way, for heaven's sake?'

'I thought –'

'Here, watch Tracy. I'll fix some coffee. Don't let her fall on the floor and bust her head.' Jane hoisted her adopted daughter's rubber shorts and pulled down her dress, and left her lying on a table. I put a hand on each side of the roly-poly body to keep it from moving. A grandmotherly woman, the baby's nurse, came in.

'Who has my little Tracy?' she demanded in a mock-scolding manner. 'She has been changed, I suppose?' I said she had, and Tracy was carried away in the nurse's strong, possessive arms. It isn't easy to ask a woman romantic questions about her life when she seems so preoccupied with domesticity. Jane was having trouble with a percolator.

'I detest gadgets,' she said. 'Do you know anything about electricity?'

Once it was plugged in, the percolator began to work all right. I made a furtive note: 'detests gadgets'. The information was exclusive. Soon the potion was concocted that transformed her from female Hyde to Jekyll. We moved to the living room, so expansive that it suggested rollerskates.

'What do you want to know?' she asked.

'Well, everything. First of all, could you tell me . . .?' My voice faded anxiously as I heard heavy paws drumming in crescendo across the kitchen floor. The two giant dogs burst into the room.

'Lie down, you idiots!' Jane told them. 'They're quite insane,' she said tolerantly as they raced around the chairs. One of the dogs suddenly ran straight at me. Unashamedly, I raised a protective forearm across my face. But the dog only collapsed at my feet, all four of its legs wriggling feebly in the air, in the manner of a capsized insect.

'She wants to be petted night and day,' Jane explained sympathetically.

We talked about dogs.

'Would you like to see the rest of the house?' she asked, already leading the way.

I wrote down the titles of some of the books in the library: *The Hunter's Encyclopaedia*, *The Dickens Digest*, *Success in Letter Writing*, *Chinese Household Furniture*, *Handbook of Athletic Games*, *How to Tie Flies*, *Fun in Bed*, *The Fireside Book of Dog Stories*, *Living the Creative Life*, *The Predicament of Evolution*, *The Greatest Story Ever Told* and *The Law of Faith*.

The library was also Waterfield's den or lair. Here was his biggest television set, a rack of rifles and shotguns and boxes of ammunition, the stuffed pelts of a couple of animals he had killed, and trophies of his success as the star of the Los Angeles Rams.

Jane showed me their facilities for fine-weather entertaining, a harp-shaped pool, which could be illuminated from within, so that it glowed at night like a giant aquamarine; a stone terrace with a barbecue fireplace and, behind sliding doors, a bar and the swimmers' changing rooms, with Jane Russell murals – nude Hawaiian girls on the walls of the men's room, and almost nude men on the walls of the women's room. She showed me her purple dressing room, its walk-in closets, her sixty pairs of shoes, her collections of slacks, bathing suits and shorts, her evening gowns, her fifteen jackets and coats, her innumerable sweaters, her thirty-five pairs of earrings.

We were leaving her bedroom as Waterfield entered the living room from the opposite end. He was a hard, suntanned man in tee-shirt and jeans. His head looked as if it had been carved in teak with a blunt chisel. A bottle of beer protruded from his mouth. A rifle was slung over his left shoulder. He looked as though at every indolent step he was ready to leap, dive, somersault or otherwise go into violent action, hurling the bottle from his right hand while simultaneously firing from the left hip. His powerful, wide neck and short-cropped hair gave the impression that he would never have to walk around anything he preferred to tunnel through. I hoped that if the worst came to the worst his taxidermist would do a neat job on me. Perhaps I might be arranged in note-taking pose and identified with a small metal plaque as 'Reporter'.

But Waterfield was friendly, if not articulate.

'Hi, lovie,' Jane said.

''lo, dear.'

After a few minutes, in which he and I desultorily discussed our shared belief that sunny days were better than smoggy ones, Waterfield retired to watch television and Jane made tuna sandwiches for lunch.

'Now, what is it you really want to know?' she asked, when she and I had settled again.

'Well,' I said, 'suppose you start by –'

There were cries from the baby's room. Jane looked around. The nurse came in bearing Tracy.

'She wants to play,' said the nurse with twinkly eyes.

'OK. Put her down here.'

'Why not just start with the first things you can remember,' I eventually suggested.

'Dianetics took me back all the way. I can remember being in the womb. In the womb I was perfectly happy. I just lay there in the warmth and darkness. It was all mine. Nobody bothered me. I didn't have to do a thing. But then suddenly I felt sick to my stomach. I felt as though I was standing on my head. I had to push, push, push, until I felt like my head was pushing my neck right into my body. I was born with a splitting headache. I was surrounded by all these *people*. They bored the hell out of me. I felt like saying, "All right, you guys – leave me alone, will you?" But I knew they wouldn't.

'Tracy!' Jane yelled, snatching from the baby a copy of *Silver Screen*, a movie fan magazine with a cover picture of Jane Russell. 'Don't tear that, damn it! Here –' she handed Tracy a copy of *Screenland* – 'tear Betty Grable!'

22

Russell Birdwell, a public relations consultant, did more than anybody else, except, perhaps, Howard Hughes himself, to make Jane Russell a star. I took Birdwell to lunch at a restaurant on Sunset Boulevard. It was the first time I had bought lunch for a publicity man. The reversal of the accustomed relationship was refreshing. All newspapers should fortify their reporters by enabling them to pick up at least their share of the checks. Reporters enabled to pay their own way don't sell out so readily; nor otherwise do they feel they must prove their resistance to blandishments by writing hypercritically.

'Building Jane Russell was three years of day and night work,' Birdwell said. 'We set up a thousand stunts. We caused things to happen in Paris, France. We caused things to happen in London, England. All over the world things were erupting about this girl. There were heartaches, problems, difficulties to overcome. There were complaints we were showing too much breast. We took that to court. We employed mathematics to figure out the skin area revealed by Jane in proportion to her overall size. We had 60-by40-inch photos of Jane and other stars prepared. We were able to prove that Jane wasn't showing any more in proportion to what she had than other stars were. Why should she be persecuted because she was better developed? We won the case.'

Birdwell did not take all the credit for the success of the publicity campaign. He acknowledged one of Howard Hughes's outstanding contributions.

'You know,' Birdwell said, 'Howard designed the brassière Jane wore in *The Outlaw*, after other designers had tried and failed. Howard knows what he wants. He won't settle for less. He's a perfectionist. Nobody else seemed to be able to get exactly the right uplift, the ideal separation we were striving for. So he went to his drawing board and got to work. He applied the principles of aeronautical engineering and made the best damn set of blueprints for a bra the world has ever known.'

By the end of his campaign for *The Outlaw*, Birdwell claimed, the public were so conditioned 'they couldn't see any pairs of round things – doughnuts, melons, cymbals, smoke rings – without reacting: "Jane Russell!" It was the greatest!'

I interviewed writers who had written scripts for Jane, directors who had directed her, her dress designer, hairdresser, make-up man, a cameraman and still photographer, her personal publicity woman, Jane's friends and her mother. Whenever I got a chance, I questioned Jane exhaustively, and learned her opinions on many subjects. The French Riviera: 'Fabulous! – just like Southern California!'; Lucille Ball: 'A living doll!'; Gainsborough: 'He stinks!'; an Armenian dish consisting of mincemeat wrapped in grape leaves: 'Heaven!'; Robert Mitchum: 'A living doll!' When I reviewed my notes at the end of every day, I felt deeply depressed.

Jane spoke so admiringly, so often, of Mitchum that I went with her to the studio early one morning to meet him. When we arrived at the hangarlike building marked 'Stage 11', Mitchum was standing outside, getting some air between scenes. A tall, hefty man wearing combat boots and olive-green combat fatigues with silver eagles on the shoulders, he looked forlorn until he saw Jane. This was their first meeting since his return from several weeks on location in

Colorado and her return from a month in Europe. She ran across the studio street squealing with joy.

'Mother!' he shouted, as they embraced. Animatedly chatting, they ambled through the stage door, across dusty concrete beneath a Piranesi complexity of scaffolding and catwalks, beyond the mobile dressing cubicles to the bright centre of things, part of a United Nations briefing room in Korea. Several UN infantry and Air Force officers, all American, all smartly shaved and combed and starched and pressed and polished, were sitting alertly at a long table near brilliantly illuminated wall maps. Their faces had the smooth, healthy, confident, inhuman glow of faces in a recruiting poster. The director was making annotations on his script. A cameraman was tape-measuring the distance from a window to the camera. A couple of electricians were adjusting spotlights and wire-mesh screens diffusing the illumination of a photographic panorama of a Korean village, the view from the window.

'OK!' an assistant director shouted, clapping his hands imperiously. He had seen Mitchum come in. 'Here he is. Let's have some quiet now! Let's get on the ball! Let's go!' In Hollywood there were a lot of exclamations.

'I've got to go and recite,' Mitchum apologetically told Jane. 'Put it down here a minute.' He patted a camp stool at the periphery of a tangle of electrical cables. 'This won't take long.'

A man with blue stubble on his beefy jowls and an unlighted cigar between his teeth hurried over to Mitchum and touched his forehead and cheeks with an orange powder puff. This cosmetician, the head make-up man on the lot, known as Shotgun, was shared by Mitchum and Jane. Shotgun produced a comb and deftly arranged Mitchum's forelock in romantic disarray. In this movie, as usual, Mitchum was one macho hombre; but now, for a moment, he pressed his hands between his knees and pivoted coyly away, like the shy young girl bather in 'September Morn'. Shotgun patiently chewed his cigar and dulled Mitchum's nose with more powder.

'Well, suh,' Mitchum said, assuming a hardy Kentucky drawl, 'I reckon it's time we-all got back to war.' Turning to Jane, he added: 'There's a jug of *sake* a-bubblin' on the hot-plate in my dressing room, in case you-all are in the mood for a libation.'

Jane shook her head and clicked her tongue in mock despair. 'Isn't he hopeless?' she asked me. 'Isn't he divine?'

Mitchum was earnestly singing 'Mammy's Little Baby Loves Short'nin' Bread', while his fellow players desperately muttered their lines to themselves before the call for action.

An electric bell rang. There was dead silence, except for the last few words of 'Mammy's Little Baby'. The assistant director hissed, 'Shh! Please!' and cried, 'Quiet now, everybody!' The director said, 'All right, roll 'em!' And the cameras were running.

'The South Koreans have come a long way since the Commies first jumped,' Mitchum said in a bored monotone. 'They're really armed and trained now.' He walked with his characteristic, easy, slow swagger through the other officers, and led them to the window to look out.

'Cut!' the director shouted. 'Bob,' he said in a low, unnaturally calm voice, 'you put your hand through the window again.' The panes had to be imaginary to avoid reflections.

'I did do it again, didn't I?' Mitchum agreed. In a loud, hoarse aside, he added: 'Better had I been a producer.'

Jane explained that Mitchum often sabotaged filming because he was trying to break his contract with Howard Hughes. Since Mitchum had become a box-office hit, Hughes often hired him out to other studios at a great profit.

The brief passage of monologue and the simple action were performed again and again until Mitchum enabled the director to accept them.

'Do you realise, gentlemen,' another officer said ardently, 'this'll definitely put us on the offensive?' There was authentic grimness in Mitchum's voice when he responded: 'Don't you think it's about time?'

Mitchum was feeling rather embarrassed about playing the part of a war hero in a second-rate movie, *The Korean Story*, while other men of lesser physiques were involved in the real thing. On a later occasion, drinking brandy and white crème de menthe from tumblers and listening to Joe Bushkin playing the blues at the Hangover Club, in an after-hours special concert for Mitchum and me at three o'clock in the morning, he said he was deeply pissed off with his work; but, whether I believed it or not, he needed the money; he had got into hock during his brief imprisonment on the Los Angeles 'honour farm' for possession of marijuana. But the scandal had vastly enhanced his popularity.

'But, hell, what are *you* doing?' he asked me unreproachfully. I was a reporter, and I wasn't in Korea either.

During another break in the shooting, Mitchum rejoined Jane. 'Tell me what happened in Colorado,' she said. 'I hear you've been brawling in bars again.'

'Yes, Jane,' he replied with dignity. 'There was an incident. It occurred in a public place of refreshment. The guy was shwacked. I am standing talking with a colonel — a *real* colonel — when I notice this character, this private, giving me dirty looks. "I can lick that son of a bitch," he says.' Mitchum shrugged his massive shoulders. 'OK, OK. This can be ignored. The joint is crowded. I don't want to make any trouble. Somebody says this guy is the heavyweight champion of somewhere. So what am I supposed to say? Then he comes up too close, and the colonel says: "Fix your necktie, soldier." He is a very sloppy soldier. He gives the colonel a shove in the chest. You can see the colonel doesn't like this. Already the private can be put under arrest. The colonel is more patient than I am.

'I grab the guy and shake him a little and say, "Now listen, Jack: straighten up, will you?" I bang his head against the wall a bit, to show I'm serious. He won't listen to reason. He starts swinging.' Mitchum rolled his eyes upward in sham horror, drew in his receding but solid, cleft chin, turned his head to one side and raised his hands, palms fore. 'Gee, don't strike the fair princess! I grab him by the lapels and bang his head on a table for a while. "Cut it out, Jack," I say, trying to soothe him, "or else someone may get hurt." There's a call to have me pulled off.' Mitchum looked aghast; reformers are so often misunderstood. He reminiscently felt the back of his thick neck. 'This can become serious. Now I have a thumb in his eye, but he is getting hysterical. A very excitable character. So a couple of guys pull me, and I pull back, harder. I notice that my opponent is no longer fighting. He is lying on the floor. Some champion! So I raise my foot, a slow back-swing. Some prude says, "Now don't you kick him!" He says this to me, the protector of the peace. Well, I do just bounce a little one off his bonnet, for luck. They take him to hospital: nothing broken. Then all the newspapers . . . Sometimes reporters make me feel like throwing up. Did I or did I not hit the guy? Sure I hit him. But he was the one who was out of line. I had to talk to the colonel, so the soldier didn't get thrown in the stockade.'

'Everybody wants to slug Tarzan,' Jane commented. 'Everybody wants to beat up Bogie and Vic Mature and Kirk Douglas. Everybody wants to prove he's tougher than Mitch.'

'It ain't fair,' Mitchum equably agreed. 'So let's get loaded.'

The next morning, when I went to see Mitchum alone, to ask him about Jane, he was in his dressing room in a tropical dress uniform decorated with the *Croix de Guerre*.

'Today, according to the continuity girl, I'm on leave. In Japan? I don't know. Japan, Korea – what's the diff? Anyway, you're in time for breakfast.'

A beaker was fuming sweetly on the hot-plate.

'Have some *sake*,' he suggested.

He was eating sardines and Limburger cheese that was shockingly pungent.

'This morning, I'm scheduled to make love to Jennifer Jones.' She was a producer's wife whose acting career reached its zenith in the title role in *The Song of Bernadette*. 'If there's anything I hate it's making love to a saint on an empty stomach.'

After winning his leading lady's hand in matrimony, Mitchum came back to his dressing room and complained to his secretary that it smelled like the burning ghats of the Ganges.

'When you're in Beverly Hills, get some incense, for God's sake.'

'Incense,' she acknowledged.

'Make it jasmine.'

'Right. There's Scotch in the cupboard and plenty of ice.'

'That girl's a genius,' he said to me. 'How did she know I want to get good and *dronk*?' As his secretary left the room, he began pouring drinks with a heavy hand. 'She's a good kid,' he said. 'I like her. But you want to talk about Jane. Here is a living legend in the tradition of Lillian Russell and Mae West. They have in Jane a great hunk of beautiful, healthy protoplasm. And what do they do with her? They have her behave like a block of wood. And yet Jane is really an intelligent dame. Ain't everything ridiculous, though? You say you're going to write a book about Jane. I don't see how it can be done. She's usually in hiding, and not only when she's in public. I wrote a book once, a novel. I don't know what happened to it. Before that, I drove trucks. Writing, driving, acting – what's the diff? I'll tell you one thing though: playing colonel out there is the easiest way I know to get the dough to pay for Scotch like this. It's twenty years old, man.'

After a certain time, he began softly singing bebop and drumming expertly with his fingertips on a coffee table.

'Did you hear the one about the two bopsters walking past the church? The huge bell falls out of the belfry, just misses them and shatters by their feet. "*Jesus!*" screams one of the cats. "What was *that*?" The other cat answers: "C sharp." Have another drink, then let's cut out. We only have a few hours to get in the mood to go listen to some jazz.'

23

The Hollywood Mortuary was across Sunset from LaRue, a restaurant that had attracted national attention as the scene of a celebrated underworld shooting.

Considering mortality and remembering *The Loved One* by Evelyn Waugh, I visited Forest Lawn Memorial Park and heard a recorded lecture on 'the world's largest religious painting', a mural by Jan Styka depicting Calvary. Hollywood's Jerusalem in oils measured 195 by 45 feet. After the lecture, I sat in the Mystery of Life Garden, reading a brochure that said: 'Beauty costs money and the general development of Forest Lawn is no exception. But truly the dollar has greater purchasing value at Forest Lawn than anywhere else.' That day I came to realise that Waugh was a less fanciful satirist, a more literal reporter, than I had previously believed. It was worth having gone to Hollywood to learn that: it made reporting seem more important.

Jane recommended the Sportsmen's Restaurant, which provided guests with fishing tackle. I stood on a small, hump-backed bridge and fished for trout in a floodlit artificial lake. The water was full of fish, flopping about, gasping as if desperate to get into a frying pan, but I failed to catch one. Was my luck running out?

Over eggs Benedict at the Brown Derby Jane told me what would happen after death. She believed in eternal consciousness, fixed for ever at one's favourite age, 'in perfect physical shape'. I imagined Jane looking for all time, all timelessness, as she looked that day, radiantly optimistic, breathing deeply in a violet cashmere sweater. She expected to spend eternity practising interior decoration in some ideal, outer-galactic, maximum-security, California-style housing estate. It was advisable to clarify one's vision of life after death, she said, because she was sure the end of the world we knew would come in our lifetimes, perhaps quite soon. The final holocaust was plainly foretold in the Old Testament. 'Why don't you come to the Chapel tonight?' she suggested. 'We always have a ball.' It seemed fitting that I saw Aldous Huxley browsing in the Beverly Hills Bookshop, probably contemplating apocalyptic disaster, when I paused there on the way back to the Garden of Allah. To my account of the day's expenditures I added: 'Holy Bible – $7.50.' It was only a paperback. I looked over my shoulder, wondering when the first punitive thunderbolt would come crashing in through the thin stucco.

The Chapel had been built by Jane and her brothers beside their mother's house in the San Fernando Valley. Mrs Russell regularly preached a fundamentalist doctrine of her own at informal evening services. Jane managed to get there two or three times a week. She often brought friends and new acquaintances from Hollywood. Some of them were inclined to go there the first time when suffering from alcoholic and/or postmatrimonial remorse. A few of them returned again and again.

That night, after the hearty singing of some old-fashioned hymns and the exposition of a comforting homily from the pulpit, the small congregation, about a dozen young men and women, settled on cushions on the floor, while Mrs Russell vehemently exhorted them to allow the holy spirit to use their voices. As Jane explained, if one could relax in humility, one might be able to serve as God's medium; one might receive the gift of tongues. I achieved no more success than I had at the Sportsmen's Restaurant.

However, Jane, after only a few minutes of concentration, became blissfully rapt. When she spoke, her voice was still what Mitchum had affectionately described as 'that Van Nuys whine', but the words were strange. An incomprehensible babble evolved into an Oriental sing-song that was equally incomprehensible to me but suggested an actual language. Afterward, Jane told me about it. 'When I get tongues', she said, 'it's usually medieval Chinese.'

On the way to the Chapel kitchen to fix coffee and cookies, Jane laid a kind hand on a novice, a pretty little blonde who very much wanted to break into the motion-picture industry. She was writhing about on a rug and sobbing: 'It won't come! I can't! I can't! I can't . . . !'

'Take it easy,' Jane said. 'You'll make it.'

If I had taken it easy, I suppose I might have been able to write a biography that honestly recorded all I had learned in Hollywood. The trouble was that the New York publisher wanted something scathing, like Lillian Roth's *New Yorker* profile of John Huston and the filming of *The Red Badge of Courage*. But I did not feel willing to scathe. I liked Jane Russell.

I spent a few days in Palm Springs and met a Texas oil man whose wife's poodle was having difficulty with psychoanalysis. In Baltimore, Susan gave birth to Sheila. She was normal. Normality was reassuring.

The Hollywood tan faded away. There was no book. Jane and we exchanged Christmas cards for three years.

24

'There's an Air Force junket to some new base in northern Greenland,' Dorsey said, no longer Mr, but not yet Buck. 'You may as well go along.' In these few casual words, he awarded me my first foreign assignment.

It was his policy to leave foreign assignments nebulous, without instructions on where exactly one was to go, how one was to get there, what one was to do, how long one was to stay, the amount of one's budget, and what sort of stuff one was to write. The policy was sound, because it was practically impossible to foresee the way a story or series of stories might develop; but such unconfined freedom, suddenly conferred, could give a beginner sleepless nights.

With fellow reporters I had often scoffed at what we regarded as shortcomings of the paper's correspondents abroad. In the home office, it was easy to decide how a correspondent might have been more usefully employed in the field the previous day. But now, about to go out myself, I wondered how I would know what to write about. For that matter, how did one compose a cable? What was cablese? Did one have to know a *lot* of Latin? How could one think about style while thinking about the cost of semicolons? Nobody had said how long the dispatches should be or how they were to be conveyed from Greenland to Baltimore.

It is wonderful how the secret lore of journalism, the practical knowledge beyond journalism schools, is transferred from generation to generation. During the next few days, I learned it was essential to take a Hermes portable typewriter, pencils, a penknife (with a device for opening bottles), *Roget's Thesaurus*, *Webster's Dictionary*, bilingual dictionaries and phrase books of the countries through which I would be travelling, Fowler's *English Usage*, Mencken's *American Language*, relevant issues of the *National Geographic Magazine* and maps, a dinner jacket, golf shoes and swimming trunks for infiltrating diplomatic society, a tape recorder (vital for authenticating quotations in defence against law suits), a miniature camera for photographing secret documents, letters of credit and letters of introduction to government leaders, an international medical certificate bearing up-to-date stamps proving the receipt of shots for smallpox, diphtheria, yellow fever, beriberi, sleeping sickness, blackwater fever and yaws, a first-aid kit, including sleeping tablets, stay-awake pills, morphine, prophylactic rubbers (condoms) and ointments, and lethal capsules for use when threatened with torture by secret police, an automatic pistol, a compass, an American flag, an assortment of gaudy trinkets with which to appease aboriginal savages, a box of Kleenex and a bottle of *good* Maryland rye.

I had not as yet had the privilege of meeting Fred Sparks, an itinerant columnist whose rules of foreign correspondence would have done much to allay my qualms. 'As long as you know what country you're in and what day it is,' he used to say, 'you've got it made. It's the date-line that counts.' I had to take what advice I could get.

One of the *Sun*'s Pulitzer Prize correspondents, Price Day, said: 'Take plenty of money, in tens and twenties, and don't change too much of it into any foreign currencies at one time. By the way, where are you going?'

'Greenland,' I said, as modestly as possible.

'Oh,' he said, turning back to his typewriter.

'To see the new air base at Thule.'

'Yes,' Day said, without looking back. 'Well,' he concluded kindly, 'I don't suppose you'll need much of anything there.'

25

There were twenty-four of us, representing the major American and Danish news services, newspapers, magazines, radio and television. The Danes had been invited because Greenland, after all, was still a Danish possession. American bases had been established as an early warning system and a first line of defence against the Soviet Union. We were Cold War correspondents. I had promoted myself from reporter to correspondent on leaving the city limits of Baltimore. Most of my colleagues were disappointing at first sight, middle-aged men, most of them, many with spectacles and bald spots and an air of suburban mortgages; no Hemingways. And not one woman, for this was before women began to play an equal, often dominant, role in international journalism.

We took off from an airport near Washington in an Air Force VIP aircraft with comfortable seats, landed in Massachusetts for Arctic clothing and at Goose Bay, Labrador, for a briefing. A major introduced a colonel, who introduced a general, who stood at a microphone on a podium, addressed us solemnly as 'gentlemen' and read aloud what the major's staff had written for him. He told us that Air Force cargo planes in all seasons of the past seventeen months had flown 2,100 round trips to Thule, delivering 12,500 tons of matériel and service and civilian personnel. The major then brightly announced that we were invited to attend a reception in the officers' club.

The next morning, with headaches, we left Labrador and flew over Davis Strait and up the coast of Greenland. Below us were the deeply crevassed edges of the great Greenland ice-cap. The map showed that there were villages down there, Akunaq, Ujarasugssuk and Tuqtoqortoq, to mention but three, but I did not see any. I saw nothing human, nothing animal, nothing vegetable. I saw nothing but the sea and bay after bay, fjord after fjord, icebergs and glaciers, the mountains and the sky. We cut across Melville Bay, passed Cape York, rounded a hill and some red-light-bearing masts, and the wheels squawked on a runway. Like the end of most other spectacular flights, arriving at Thule was anticlimactically ordinary. On just another vast military airport, though the wind was like ice-cold razor blades, it was difficult to realise we were only 900 miles from the North Pole and about 1,500 miles from a similar base, where, I supposed, briefing officers were feeding journalists information to tranquillise readers of *Pravda* and *Izvestia*.

In the Thule Air Base officers' club the sense of familiarity was almost stupefying. Marilyn Monroe, nude, was spreadeagled on the wall behind the bar.

'There's one thing real special here,' a local lieutenant said. 'The ice in these drinks is thousands of years old. It's been under tremendous glacial pressure.' He held forward his glass. 'Listen to that!' Snap, crackle, pop! After that exciting experience we were taken to a large office where there were typewriters on a row of desks. There we were encouraged to write summaries of all that we had been told in Labrador. We might not have been able to write much more than we could have written in our own offices (an Air Force censor who had flown up with us made sure of that), but we wrote with more enthusiasm than if we hadn't made the trip. We had vested interests in the importance of the story. We had flown all that way; it had to be important.

The work having been done, we were escorted to the Eskimo

village of Thule, the northernmost settlement in the world. This visit was a rare privilege. The Danes usually kept people away, for fear that the inhabitants might be contaminated by the diseases of civilisation.

Colonel Bernt Balchen, a merry, plump, ruddy-cheeked Norwegian-American who looked like a smooth-shaven Santa Claus, was our guide. Wolstenholme Fjord was misty. Blue ice-islands floated near us in the smooth, dark-green sea. The putt-putt of the small boat was the only sound. Nobody talked. The enormous silence of the Arctic inhibits chatter.

The Eskimo village was situated on mossy turf sloping down to the water's edge. 'This is the garden spot of the Arctic,' Colonel Balchen said without irony.

We had expected igloos. But the Eskimos – Inuits now by politically correct *diktat* – constructed ice-block shelters only on hunting trips. The huts at Thule were made of imported wood, fortified and insulated with layers of sod. Seen from outside, they resembled compost heaps.

We visited the village patriarch, of unknown age, one of Commander Peary's guides to what he claimed to be the Pole in 1909. Some counter-claimed that Peary never really reached 90 degrees North. The guide's name was Odaq, which, he said through the good colonel, means 'the seal lying on the ice'. There must be another Inuit word meaning 'rich foreign lady's seal fur coat'. Odaq's long hair was still black and shiny, cut in a neat fringe. His round, leathery face was intricately wrinkled. His eyes were slits and his nose was short and flat. When we bent our heads down and entered his low-ceilinged, over-heated, ammoniacal single room, a few of us at a time, he was sitting on the side of the bed, dressed in his best clothes, a blue woollen cap, a white pullover, polar-bearskin trousers and sealskin boots. From his chest dangled the red and white ribbon and Distinguished Service Medal he had recently received from the King of Denmark in person.

By local standards, Odaq was wealthy. The Danish government

gave him an income of $150 a year. The Explorers Club of New York had built his hut and gave him another $150 a year. The Danes paid an Eskimo woman to call on him every day to cook and clean up. The villagers gave him fish and sometimes meat. He spent most of the time sitting by the stove, snuffling and wheezing and coughing. Our guide tried to make conversation in Odaq's language. Odaq said little. But he pointed, more than once, at a framed, dim photograph of himself as a strong, young hunter, standing at the (alleged) Pole with Peary.

The Thule Eskimos were reticent but cordial. When we said goodbye, they kept nodding and saying 'Thank you, thank you, thank you.' The US Air Force, in appreciation of our interest, gave us a farewell treat, a flight to the actual Pole, low enough to see it. It was a bright, pale-grey blank. A young escort, a public-relations captain, encouragingly said: 'You'll be able to say you've been there.'

At the *Sun*, unsurprisingly, nobody thanked me. However, a few weeks later, Dorsey said: 'There's some sort of junket to Alaska. You seem to be the Arctic expert, so you may as well go along.'

I suspect even the hardest-boiled newspapermen of sentimentality, but, of course, they never show it.

26

Defence against possible Russian attack was again the theme. A score of us correspondents landed at Anchorage. 'If the Russians come across the Bering Strait, we'll bump them, and bump them hard,' a general jovially assured us. We watched six hundred army airborne infantry from Georgia tumble out of Flying Boxcars onto frozen tundra and among birch trees near Big Delta, in central Alaska. Expert observers said the drop was very successful: only seven men were injured; the casualty rate was often higher.

After the official tour of Alaska was over and the main party returned to Washington, I flew in a chartered plane to the Arctic Research Laboratory at Barrow, the territory's northernmost point. That was before statehood. Under the auspices of the Navy and the Johns Hopkins University (the *Sun*'s local angle), the scientists at Barrow lived in Quonset huts beside the Arctic Ocean. They were working on the coldest aspects of the Cold War. It was hoped that their research would help United States forces in cold countries. Some of the subjects being studied were 'Fat Metabolism in Arctic Animals', 'The Role of Lipids in the Adaptation of Animals to Cold', 'The Blood Chemistry of Eskimos', 'A Survey of the Fishes of Northern Alaska' and 'Respiratory Exchange in Man During Intensive Muscular Activity'.

The scientists, all men, sometimes tired of their labours and looked for other things to do. Some of them invited me to accompany them to a dance in the nearby Eskimo village of Barrow. 'It won't be like a *nelakatuk*,' I was warned by a man who was measuring the effects of permafrost on building foundations. A *nelakatuk*, he explained, was the all-night fiesta held each spring in celebration of the successes of the past whaling season. During a *nelakatuk* the Eskimos and their guests gorged themselves on *muk-tuk*, strips of raw whaleskin with thick chunks of blubber attached, which, he said, tasted like walnuts and castor oil. Another favourite springtime delicacy was 'Eskimo ice-cream', whale or walrus blood and oil, beaten to a froth, frozen and served in lumps. No, he apologetically repeated, the dance wouldn't be like a *nelakatuk*.

The Weasels' motors chugged explosively and their tracks crunched the crisp snow south-west along the coast to the Eskimo village. We were wearing olive-green parkas with wolf fur around the hoods and cumbersome 'bunny boots', like divers' boots, but made of canvas and white felt. The temperature was 35 degrees Fahrenheit below freezing, and falling.

The village dance hall was a big Quonset hut. A group of young Eskimo men and women were shuffling about outside on the hard, squeaky snow. They were reluctant to go in. My informant said they were always shy at the beginning of a dance. Inside the hall men and women were voluntary wallflowers, standing around the edges of the room, whispering and softly giggling. The women were wearing loose, fur-trimmed long cotton dresses. The men's parkas were of dull colours. Both men and women wore *muk-luks*, heavy fur boots of seal or caribou, ornately embroidered in bright colours. Their Mongoloid faces were orange with red cheeks, flushed by the cold wind and the excitement of the occasion. An hour after the dance was supposed to have begun, the floor was still empty.

Near an iron stove, six musicians, men of late middle age, sat side by side in a row on the floor, with their legs stretched out before them. Each man held a long drumstick and a hoop covered with tightly stretched skin from the liver of a whale. Without any announcement, the leader began beating the rim of his drum. The rhythm closely approximated the normal rhythm of the human pulse. One by one, the other drummers joined in. The leader began singing and the others sang with him. Their nasal chanting reminded me of Scottish bagpipes.

The leader himself eventually got the dancing started. He put down his drum, stood facing the band, donned a pair of white gloves, stamped his right foot, and gesticulated with his arms as though signalling in semaphore without flags. It was a traditional point of etiquette that an Eskimo man must put on gloves before dancing, though all the dancing was solo, without any contact with any other dancer. At last, men and women of all ages took to the floor. The expressions on the women's faces suggested intense, introverted concentration. The men held their heads higher and jerked them back and forth in pecking motions. After each dance, the dancers returned separately, silently, to their places, ostensibly unconcerned by any interest they might have aroused in each other.

'Do you ever dance with them?' I asked the permafrost man. 'God, no!' he exclaimed. We left at about 2 o'clock. As we gloomily rode away, it occurred to me that scientists and reporters had something in common. We were all non-participating observers. The dance was to continue all night.

The next morning I attended a service in Barrow Presbyterian Church. It was half filled, mostly by women. Some of them had babies at their breasts. There were no young men. They had put on uniforms, taken their skis and rifles, and had been flown away to practise defending the Arctic against the Russians.

When I got back to Baltimore, a fellow reporter said: 'What kept you so long up there? Are those Eskimo women hot stuff?'

27

Dorsey sent me to Korea in January 1953, when the war had reached stalemate. The prospect of a long separation from my family was not a pleasant one, but we agreed that the assignment represented professional progress. Every newspaperman sooner or later ought to cover a war, even a stagnant one. Thus began the end of my second marriage.

On my way to the Far East, I paused in Hollywood for a couple of days. I found Jane Russell doing a song and dance number, 'When Love Goes Wrong, Nothing Goes Right', with Marilyn Monroe in a Paris café at Twentieth Century-Fox. They were doing a re-take to finish *Gentlemen Prefer Blondes*. While waiting to accompany both of them to the studio commissary for lunch (an historic double, I thought), I sat and was talked to by a studio press agent. It was a quiet lunch. The blonde and brunette rivals said little to each other.

'Korea', said the press agent, when he learned I was on my way there, 'is a real nothing now. It's cold mashed potatoes. Nah, if I was you I'd tell them to shove it. What's wrong with those editors?'

'President Eisenhower has committed himself –' I began.

'I'm not saying *nobody* cares,' the press agent conceded. 'But for the public as a whole, it's nothing. Oh, sure, Keenan Wynn and a few of the other kids have been out there recently on personal appearance tours. But, frankly, they were wasting their time. Let's face it: Korea ain't what it used to be. It's lost its impact. Why should anyone that's anyone go *there* any more?'

At Pearl Harbor, the admiral's barge took me with a public affairs officer to see the wreckage of USS *Arizona*, a relic of the 'day of infamy'. The Chief of Staff of Pacific Command, US Navy, told me the Pacific Fleet had already used more bombs and shells in the Korean War than the entire Navy expended in all of World War II. 'Most of the ordnance goes to interdict enemy supplies on the north–south roads near the coasts. The Gooks carry matériel on A-frames on their goddamn *backs*. When we take some out more come along to replace them. They don't seem to care how many of them get killed.'

In Tokyo I checked into the Press Club, in Shimbun Alley. Shimbun means newspaper. I was sitting in the lounge drinking gimlets, with nothing to do but wait for Far East Command, US Army, to issue me military uniforms and a Noncombatant's Certificate of Identity, with a 'simulated rank of major through colonel', for the privileges of a senior officer in case of capture, when I encountered Patrick O'Donovan, the star correspondent of the *Observer*, which was then London's best-written paper. He was a striking figure, a tall, lanky man with long, dark, disorderly Irish hair and a luxuriantly livid face, dressed in a dark-grey flannel suit with Edwardian cuffs and narrow legs, a loosely knotted tie of pale-peach silk, cream socks and sand-coloured suede shoes. He looked elegantly decadent. I was later to discover that he had commanded tanks in France and Germany as a major in the Irish Guards. Reporters should try not to jump to conclusions. I asked him what he was doing in Japan while waiting to go to Korea.

'Really!' he protested. 'I'm not merely waiting in Japan. I'm arranging to enter a Zen Buddhist monastery. I shall write a most significant article.'

'But aren't you going to Korea?' I persisted. At the moment, I could think of nothing else.

'All in good time. There's some important jade in Kyoto that I must see. And they haven't finished renovating my Korean screen. It is very beautiful. You haven't been to Korea yet, I gather.' I admitted that I hadn't.

'Well, there's nothing going on there, so I wouldn't hurry, if I were you.' He asked me where I was staying. When I said the Press Club he looked aghast.

'You *can't*,' he said. 'It's *ghastly*. Loutish photographers and Australians and their *squalid* friends. The midnight crash of furniture through windows. The most adolescent sexual boasting. No, not the Press Club.'

A young Japanese with solemn glasses, neatly combed black hair and the respectable attire of a Western bank clerk came up to O'Donovan and inclined his head in salutation.

'Ah, Juzo!' O'Donovan said. 'This is Juzo Fukunaka. Mr Catling-san. Juzo, you're late.'

'Yes, Mr O'Donovan. I had difficulty obtaining the best Kabuki tickets.'

'That is no excuse.'

'The *yukatas* and fans, Mr O'Donovan. They had not been properly packed before my arrival at the shop.'

'You should have instructed them better. It's just not good enough, Juzo. You really are a very naughty interpreter.'

'Yes, Mr O'Donovan. I am sorry.'

'Well, please at least be sure to call up and order dinner. Remember: master wants thrush.'

'Yes, Mr O'Donovan. Thrush.'

O'Donovan had travelled extensively in Africa. Though in fact humane and liberal, he enjoyed assuming the mode of address of a severe district commissioner scolding a lazy houseboy. Juzo, a graduate of Waseda University, did not get the joke, but he seemed to know there was one, for his smile did not appear to be a symptom of Oriental chagrin.

Having handed Juzo a wad of banknotes and dismissed him, O'Donovan asked: 'Do you like thrush? Perhaps you would care to join me for dinner. I am staying in a Japanese hotel. There are no other Europeans or Americans staying there. If you like it, I'm sure you could get a room. It would certainly be a lot better for you than this place. Juzo is an excellent interpreter. He did terribly well at university. Waseda is probably the most distinguished university in Tokyo. You've got an interpreter, I suppose? No? No wonder you haven't ventured out of the Press Club. Some correspondents stay here for months and never go anywhere but the Foreign Office and Tachikawa Airport. I know what: you can share Juzo if you pay half his salary.'

'Here we are,' O'Donovan said, as the small Japanese taxi came to a halt. 'It's not a bad place, really.' The driver gave sibilant thanks. The taxi rattled away. We were left in darkness, on a deserted street between a faintly gleaming canal and a large building with wings embracing an obscure little garden. As we walked along the stone pathway to the building's unadorned front entrance, O'Donovan said, in the confidential manner one might adopt when warning a friend about the quirks of one's eccentric relations: 'Don't walk on their woodwork with your shoes on. They get most frightfully offended if you do. They're easily offended.'

The foyer was not like the foyer of a Western hotel. There were no uniformed porters and bellboys, no marble and plush, no newsstand, no registration desk, no lifts. We were in a bare room of polished dark wood. There were two wooden receptacles for umbrellas, a wall of open pigeonholes for shoes and a cupboard for coats. And that was all. O'Donovan removed his shoes and thrust his feet into flat, open, leather slippers. I did likewise. In order to keep the slippers from falling off, it was necessary to shuffle; the Japanese gait came naturally.

We walked up bare wooden stairs to the upper floor. O'Donovan opened a sliding door. His suite was in three parts: an antechamber, a square room measuring about 25 feet each way, and a small balcony looking out in daylight, he said, on stunted trees and raked pebbles. The partition between the room and the balcony consisted of delicate wooden windows with translucent white paper panes. The windows, the antechamber partitions and the hall doors could all slide in sections in various combinations, giving the impression of a magician's cabinet. The furnishings were simple and few, built close to the fine rice-straw mats that completely covered and partly insulated the cold floor. The dressing table rose only a foot above the matting. The narrow mirror, about a yard tall, was modestly concealed in an embroidered, pale brown cotton bag. The telephone table was about 9 inches high. The square dining table, about 18 inches high, was made of a dark wood that looked like walnut. Fat pillows had been arranged around the table. There were hard-upholstered elbow rests. The decorations were watercolours of a scowling Chinese devil and two squirrels on a bough. There was a miniature flowering shrub in a ceramic bowl in the prayer niche. Heat was provided in moderation by glowing charcoal on a bed of sand in a heavy, squat, carved wooden bowl with a copper lining.

Two Japanese serving girls twittered prettily outside the door. O'Donovan summoned them in. They prostrated themselves in the open doorway, crossed the room with bowed heads and crawled around the table with our hors d'oeuvres. Their attitudes and gestures of humility were so formal and graceful that they achieved a peculiar dignity. Celery, asparagus, young cucumber and pickles were succeeded by almost colourless, almost tasteless consommé, and this was succeeded by golden-brown, plump, soft little birds, which had been decapitated but had retained their tiny claws, now curled up together in a pitiable supplicatory plea. 'The feet are delicious,' O'Donovan said. They were as tenderly crisp as the extremities of fried softshell crabs.

Halfway through this dainty meal there was a crescendo of uneven thuds in the hall. A maid scuttled into the room, perfunctorily touched her forehead to the matting and urgently babbled what we guessed was a warning that there was an unmanageable intruder. There was a snarl of rage nearby, and a torrent of Chaucerian epithets.

'It's all right,' O'Donovan resignedly told the maid. 'My friend.' She looked uncomprehending. 'Friendo,' he explained. 'Friendo!' the maid exclaimed. 'Ah-so!' She quickly slid open a door and a British Army captain, who looked grotesquely clumsy beside her – who was, in fact, grotesquely clumsy – lurched into the room. He had the face of an albino rabbit with an unsuitably heavy straw-coloured moustache and glazed pale-blue eyes.

'On leave,' he muttered.

'Do come in,' O'Donovan said with wasted sarcasm. 'There will be a third for dinner.' He held up three fingers, pointing to each of us in turn. 'Chop for this bwana. Food. *My*,' he said to the captain, 'you *are* drunk. I have never been able to understand why the Eighth Army speaks of "Rest and Recreation"; quite obviously, there isn't time for both on a brief visit from Korea. Buzz, you've got your shoes on.' The captain took his shoes off. They fell off his long, khaki feet in different directions. He sat heavily on a cushion beside the table and began tearing with his hands one of the remaining thrushes.

'The Japanese are extraordinarily kind to men who are drunk,' O'Donovan said. 'They are considered to be in a condition of special privilege, requiring special care.'

Later, after bottles of cool Asahi beer, we changed into kimonos and shuffled down the hall to a tiled room where an outsize wooden bathtub was set into the floor. A wall panel slid open and the custodian of the bathroom climbed through with soap and towels.

The cleaning was done outside the bath. As we sat on miniature stools, the attendant scrubbed our backs and poured innumerable wooden buckets of scented hot water over our heads. Then we descended into the tub. The water was nearly chest-deep, faintly redolent of sandalwood and almost boiling. A lobster's death in the kitchen may not be so bad. After the first shock, I felt pleasantly faint and disembodied, weightless and devoid of thought . . .

During our absence, maids had arranged sleeping-bags made of soft, thick eiderdown quilts on the floor. They contained earthenware hot-water bottles. I experienced the most delightful lassitude, an awareness of the softening of the bones of the spine and the toes, as I lay back, acquiescently listening to the captain and, surprisingly, O'Donovan singing 'Rule, Britannia!' out of tune, very loud. I was happy. I was a war correspondent, allowed to write about anything I experienced.

It was morning. The windows were partly open. Birdsong. A distant muted cacophony of motorcar horns. The foliage of an evergreen was silhouetted against white sky. There was an aroma of herbal tea beside my pillow. I had slept well.

'What's this place?' asked an unenthusiastic voice.

'Oh, shut up, Buzz,' another voice replied.

'Fukunaka-san comes,' announced a maid.

'Mr O'Donovan, I have brought you the newspapers,' Juzo said.

'Oh, God!' O'Donovan complained, burrowing deeper beneath his quilt. 'Nag, nag, nag . . . Is there no end to it?'

Juzo had a cup of tea and translated some of the Tokyo front-page stories and editorial articles for me. He was especially interested himself in an account of the annual poetry recital at the Imperial Palace. Royal poetry readings were instituted in 1483, he said. Each year thousands of Japanese submitted poems on a theme announced by the Palace. The theme for 1953 was 'Outgoing Ship'. I wrote down some of them.

The next day, I gathered my military identity cards. At liberty, we retained our civilian exemption from army classification. We were theoretically the equals of the top-ranking generals. I collected my 'invitational travel orders', tickets for unlimited free flights in air-force aircraft between Japan and Korea. I had a duffle bag full of khaki clothing, and my Olivetti portable and cameras.

I took a taxi to Tachikawa and committed myself to the most dreadful plane of all, a double-decker transport like a tin whale, a Globemaster, bound for Seoul. There were 109 other passengers, all soldiers. As I sat strapped to a canvas bench, I read the Japanese Crown Prince's poem for 1953:

> Across the surging seas
> To new and wondrous worlds
> I sail.

28

The battle scenario was a handsome public-relations production, bearing the insignia of the US Army's Seventh Division in red, blue and black and the admonition 'Secret – Security Information – Operation Smack'. Copies of these detailed programme notes were distributed to UN correspondents of several nationalities in the press billets, in good time for spectators to assemble in comfortably heated observation bunkers overlooking the proposed scene of battle. The purpose of the operation, the notes explained, was to demonstrate 'the manner in which the infantry can take maximum advantage of shock action'.

'Operation Smack' was preceded by ballyhoo that would surely have interested any enemy agent. It was impossible to believe that the North Koreans had failed to place one in the native civilian staff who served us press. On the eve of the attack, the US Air Force dropped a lot of bombs on a small Chinese sector of the western front. More air raids and a heavy artillery barrage began early the following morning. At 1 o'clock in the afternoon tanks led the infantry advance. Their proclaimed mission was to destroy Chinese bunkers, kill Chinese soldiers, take Chinese prisoners, search for weaknesses in the Chinese line, prevent the Chinese from burrowing closer to UN territory, 'improve UN battle techniques' and return to base.

The operation lasted for four and a half hours, even longer than the most extravagant war movie, and was an awful flop. The infantry failed to reach the top of their main objective, which public relations called 'Spud Hill'. Chinese mortar fire, machinegun fire and hand grenades drove the Americans back. No Chinese prisoners were taken. Three Americans were killed and sixty-one were wounded.

The cable I sent the *Sun* on my first day in Korea said nothing about the possibility of a security leak, though I believed then and still believe that almost certainly there was one. I reported the preparations for the raid, the curious innovation of the printed timetable, the invitations to spectators, the raid's lamentable results, and the Army's final communiqué.

In the United States, after my article appeared, all hell broke loose. A Congressional inquiry was demanded. The Chicago *Tribune* called the raid 'a specimen slaughter'. The New York *Daily News* blamed it on 'a criminal lapse of judgment'. Representative Clare E. Hoffman (R., Mich.) recalled gladiators who died for the amusement of Roman emperors. Some commentators who endorsed my report's implications were not allies I would have sought. My own paper's editorial comment did not seem to offer unambiguous support: 'Operation Smack', said the *Sun*, 'left a decidedly bad taste in the mouth.'

Fellow journalists accredited to the UN in Korea who were accustomed to being spoon-fed information resented a newcomer's critical attitude to the local establishment. Some of them had received angry demands from their editors, cables known in the trade as 'rockets'. Why hadn't they been sent the low-down on Smack? *Newsweek* described me as 'a thirtyish writer of children's books'. If the magazine had said more accurately that I was the twenty-seven-year-old author of only one book for children, they might have suggested I was even less capable of writing maturely about grown-ups killing each other. I cabled Ottawa and very soon received the insignia of an RCAF navigator and a short row of service ribbons, which a Korean maid sewed on one of my khaki shirts. In Washington, General J. Lawton Collins, the Army Chief of Staff, issued a public statement in which he said, 'I offer no brief whatsoever for the eager beaver' who distributed the plans for Operation Smack. 'That was a mistake. The Army accepts it as a mistake and regrets it.'

The atmosphere in the press billets became friendlier. Almost everyone soon forgets even the most sensational stories in last week's newspapers.

29

'One can be a foreign correspondent,' John Ridley of the *Daily Telegraph* always used to say, 'and still be a gentleman.' While some other correspondents, merely pausing in transit, lived in casual disorder in rooms furnished with only a GI camp bed, a rickety desk and a straight-backed wooden chair, Ridley, the senior occupant of the press billets, presided over an establishment that was a marvel of acquisition, efficiency and comfort.

He had two rooms, one of them for his Korean houseboy, Kim, who was a vain, petulant young man of whom Ridley was indulgently fond. The larger room was Ridley's bedroom, sitting room, office and bar. It was all arranged as meticulously as a master mariner's stateroom. Ridley's beds were remarkably like the American hospital beds that had somehow found their way onto the Korean black market. His desk was as substantial as a bank manager's. Ridley had carpets, chairs with cushions, and vases of flowers. There was a liquor cabinet crowded with all sorts of bottles. He kept up-to-date files of newspapers and official announcements. He had a powerful short-wave radio. He supported a cat he had 'found starving in the mountains near Seoul' and 'nursed to health'. The cat's name was Yao of the Imjin. The Imjin River was one of the UN's principal natural defence lines north of Seoul. The cat was addressed as Yao, pronounced like the noise made by cats of all nationalities late at night. His diet consisted largely of beef stew from the mess. His favourite sport was retrieving a ball made of the Army press releases of the day.

In addition to his houseboy and Yao, Ridley's pets included a parrot and a goldfish. Because of his concern for their well-being, it was only after lengthy consideration that he felt he could leave the building. Unless something very special was happening at British Commonwealth Division HQ, he usually restricted his excursions to weekly Jeep drives with his houseboy to the Seoul NAAFI, a British shop that sold duty-free alcohol of all flavours.

From time to time he divulged fragments of his personal mythology. For instance, he would look sombrely into his pink gin and say: 'It's a terrible thing to have to cut a man's throat while he's alseep. [Long pause.] But [sigh] that was the sort of thing one simply had to do if one wanted to serve with the Maquis in Occupied France.' With modest hesitations, coughs and stammers, he intimated that he was the scion of an aristocratic family with vast estates in Northumberland, went to Spain during the Civil War to volunteer for one army or another, married a Spanish lady of flawless beauty who was killed by aerial bombardment, vowed to spend the rest of his life in exile, and, ever since then, had been fighting in wars or covering them as a correspondent. In the course of that heroic, nomadic existence, he had maintained certain charming social rituals. His houseboy daily delivered invitations to sherry and biscuits at 11 a.m.

Ridley was a man of about forty years of age and of unimposing stature, but he had *presence* and a rich voice, strained, more often than not, through clenched teeth. Wearing a Paisley silk scarf inside the open collar of stiffly pressed British tropical khakis, his shoes gleaming like old mahogany, he would punctiliously greet his guests, enquire after their health, usher them to their places and relay their drink orders to the houseboy. 'Sherry' on the invitations was mainly symbolic; whisky, gin and brandy flowed more freely. By lunchtime his room resembled the cabin scene in the Marx

Brothers' *A Night at the Opera*. Ridley's hospitality brought him a great deal of information. Putting it all together, he was able to concoct dispatches that were often more complete and always more vivid than those written by correspondents who did the tiring legwork.

When President Eisenhower withdrew the US Seventh Fleet from what is now called the Taiwan Strait, some Western commentators said Chiang Kai-shek could 'unleash' the Nationalist troops on Formosa to invade China. As long as the United States continued to send dollars, he would keep proclaiming his slogan 'Back to the Mainland'. I took the opportunity to visit Formosa, by way of Hong Kong and Macao.

In Hong Kong, I stayed in the Foreign Press Club on Victoria Peak. A tailor, vouched for in writing by Cary Grant, made me one of those overnight suits for which the Crown Colony was justly renowned, and a waistcoat of Burgundy-red brocade embroidered with multicoloured Pegasuses, for good luck on racecourses.

My only other useful achievement there was to visit the Tiger Balm Gardens, the colossal hillside shrine that Aw Boon Haw, a Chinese multimillionaire, constructed in honour of himself and Tiger Balm, the aromatic pink ointment panacea that made his fortune. In the gardens, the spirits of Hieronymus Bosch, Barnum & Bailey and George Washington Hill (the Madison Avenue genius who proclaimed that Lucky Strike Means Fine Tobacco) were embodied in hundreds of weirdly imaginative, garishly painted statues, tableaux and frescoes in bas relief.

Stone serpents, gorgons, hippogriffs, dragons and other accidents of evolution and fantasy were dimly recognisable as horrors from the dark corners of the subconscious. Chinese parents used them to teach their children cautionary tales of hell. Images showed in ghastly detail how punishments fitted crimes. A man who had been a gossip on earth was having his tongue torn out with red-hot pincers; a mortal glutton was suffering eternal disembowelment; a sexual libertine was being sterilised with a knife. Children loved everything. They ran along the maze of narrow pathways, up and down steep, twisting stairs, and, wherever they suddenly confronted monsters, yelped and squealed with tremulous delight. Another multimillionaire, I told readers of the *Sun*, should acquire a remote island and build a Garden of Warfare, in which all the world's military commanders and most of its politicians would be permanently confined, to discover terrible new secret weapons, made of painted concrete.

Serendipity, rather than methodical planning, sometimes enables the free-ranging journalist to come upon interesting off-beat stories. Nationalist Chinese visas were not available in Hong Kong, because Britain had recognised the Peiping regime, so I had to apply for a visa in Macao, which was still Portuguese. How else would I have encountered Patrick O'Brien, alias Robert Stephens, alias Stephen Stanley Ragan?

We met in the saloon of the *Lee Hong*, a ferry that plied continually between Hong Kong and Macao. O'Brien, his favourite name, was sitting alone in the otherwise unoccupied saloon, so I asked him whether I might sit at his table. He was a Bogart type but not unfriendly. He became friendlier when I obtained a bottle of King George No. 1 Scotch Whisky: Guaranteed First Class Edinburgh Grapes, and two glasses. I had had worse, in a shebeen in Chad, and soon conversation flowed.

He had got aboard the *Lee Hong* in Macao, he related, and after more than three hundred crossings to Hong Kong and back, he still had not been allowed to disembark at either terminal. He was stateless, without any cards of identity. He told me a lurid hard-luck story of orphanages, reformatories, jails and military stockades, of various legal imbroglios and contretemps in the United States, his native land, and some trouble in a Shanghai night-club. It was alleged that a sudden death there had been his fault. Persons without fixed abodes were often blamed when things went wrong. Humphrey Bogart would have been just right for the part.

Without further ado, I wrote a letter, which he signed, asking Mrs Eleanor Roosevelt to intercede on his behalf. She had recently been engaged in drafting the United Nations' Bill of Human Rights. It seemed to O'Brien and me that one basic human right was to get off the *Lee Hong*. The ferry company was obliged to provide a bunk and to feed him, but the accommodation was cramped and the cuisine was not up to much and the long days were boring. O'Brien was not an ideal candidate for citizenship anywhere, as he ruefully acknowledged, but surely Mrs Roosevelt could persuade some country to take him.

Much later, I learned that the Dominican Republic had accepted him. I never found out how he got there or how he made a living. But I imagined that he and President Trujillo understood each other, deservedly.

Wasn't it Sir John Bowring who wrote that charming little poem that begins, 'Gem of the Orient earth and open sea, Macao! . . .'? How nice it was in the evenings, sitting on the terrace of the Bella Vista Hotel, high on a hillside, overlooking junks with sails like bats' wings, and the hills of Taipa darkening between the pink and silver water and the pink and grey sky. Macao rose steeply from the cluttered wharves to peaks, the Old Fortress of Mong Ha, the Guia Lighthouse, Old Monte Fortress, the Cathedral and the Bishop's Palace. In the European sections of the small colony, which was founded in the sixteenth century, there were Portuguese buildings with wrought-iron railings, terracotta tiles and stucco façades washed in pastel colours, crumbling like the icing of stale cakes. There were avenues shaded by wide-spreading trees, and a bronze bust of Vasco da Gama on a plinth in the Avenida Dr Oliviera Salazar. 'Mr Macao,' Dr P. J. Lobo, the Eurasian Director of Economic Affairs, owned a Catalina flying boat that brought a load of gold ingots once a week from India for transshipment into the People's Republic of China. Like Nero and Al Capone, Dr Lobo had his tender moments. He wrote sentimental semi-classical music, conducted orchestral recordings of it, and broadcast the records over his own radio station. Before Macao was absorbed by Kwantung Province, the colony was picturesque, quaint and corrupt.

In the hotel bar I met three RAF officers in mufti. They had come over from Hong Kong for the weekend. They invited me to accompany them to a local casino.

'You like playing the games?' asked a woman of advanced years who looked like a Hogarthian warning. She had soot-black hair, a chalk-white complexion, false eyelashes like spiders, a crimson mouth and gold and black teeth. Her fat, naked arms were blue-white and as flaccid and wrinkled as balloons long after a party.

'I am Russian lady,' she said. 'White Russian.'

'A countess in distress,' one of us unkindly suggested – I, as a matter of fact.

'You are clever man,' she said. 'You have heard of me? Yes, I am countess. But all that', she added tragically, 'has gone. I have been in China many years.'

'Many, many,' said the medical officer.

'Which gentleman will marry me and take me to England?' she wanted to know, chuckling when we recoiled. 'What's a matter,' she scolded, 'you no like jig-a-jig?'

'We like jig-a-jig, yes,' someone said.

'You like to see?' she asked. 'I show films. I show South Sea island film – very pretty man, pretty girl, make jig-a-jig on the beach, best you ever saw. Also Paris film – two girls, one man, very naughty, do everything.'

The synopses were not unappealing. I had not been receiving many letters from Baltimore, fewer and fewer as time went by. Marital celibacy does not weaken the libido.

'Do you think we'll have our throats cut?' I asked.

'You're safer walking the back streets of Macao at night than the streets of Soho,' one of the pilots promised.

'I've heard that the authorities here are very strict about the murder of Europeans,' the doctor said. 'Informers are well rewarded; there's no way of escaping from the colony; culprits are punished with exemplary speed and severity.'

'What are we waiting for?'

'What indeed?'

The old hag led the way, along cobbled alleys foul with sewage and the garlic steam from cooking pots, through an obscure doorway, up a flight of stairs, through a beaded string curtain and into a dingy dining room. We sat on chairs lumpy with broken springs. A boy brought beer at about five times the normal price. A Chinese man in a shabby brown suit looked up to appraise us, then threaded film through a projector aimed at a sheet on the wall. The lights went out. There was a whirring. A flickering beam of dusty yellow light cast forth the images of two women undressing a man in the frenetic, jerky movements of Keystone Kops. The scene was a Western living room furnished in Department Store Modern, circa 1925.

'It's very sexy,' the Russian procuress assured us apprehensively. Our comments were frivolous.

'I think you like South Sea island better,' she said, secreting our money in her crêpe bosom as a precaution against requests for refunds. 'You wait and see. It's more pretty people. This is more naughty, but that is more pretty.'

'But this one's very funny,' I politely conceded.

'You can buy a copy of this film,' the hostess said, as the three twitching contortionists on the wall achieved their terminal entanglement. 'You take it home, you never have to work again.'

'Reminds me rather of rugger, this bit,' the second pilot murmured. 'A scrum, you know.'

'One hundred pounds sterling,' she said.

'Shut up about money and show us the second one,' the first pilot irritably requested.

The second film was a bit highbrow in the beginning: there were surf and palm trees. Then a plump Polynesian fisherman, or perhaps a Hawaiian cook, or just possibly a Turkish weightlifter, and a girl with long hair with a red flower in it stood face to face, holding hands, smiling.

'It's OK,' the old White Russian countess said. 'Only wait and see. Soon they begin. Very nice film, very dirty, everyone like it.'

After the initial romantic suspense, the director had focused on extreme close-ups.

'Good God!' the doctor exclaimed. 'If I'd seen this in medical school I'd have gone into something sensible, like plumbing.'

The Nationalist Ministry of Public Enlightenment in Taipei strongly recommended that I stay in the Friends of China Club. I was glad to find that I would not be without companionship during the possibly trying days ahead. In the bar before lunch, I encountered John Ridley, in a ginger tweed hacking jacket and cavalry twill trousers, sipping a pink gin. I was surprised.

'What are *you* doing here?' I asked.

He evidently knew what I meant. He replied rather pettishly. 'The same as you, I imagine. You mustn't believe the slanderers who say I spend all my time in the Seoul press billets. I get about. As a matter of fact, I have come to talk to George Yeh, a dear friend.' Dr Yeh was the Foreign Minister. 'He read history at Cambridge, you know. I'll introduce you to him. But first shall we have just one more tiny drink before lunch? The food is abominable.'

While we were picking disconsolately at cold meat, a messenger came to our table, presented Ridley with an envelope, and waited, apparently expecting a reply.

'Oh, dear,' Ridley said wearily. 'How they do go on! This boy keeps coming over all day with these tiresome chits. This one's an invitation to an interview with an agronomist. Really! Young man, please tell the director of the Ministry of Public Enlightenment that Mr Ridley is most appreciative but he really doesn't want another talk about the rice yield.' To me Ridley said, 'If I hear another word about tons of rice per hectare I think I'll go right off my rocker. I don't even know what a hectare is, do you? It isn't in the back of *my* diary. Why can't they tell us these things in acres, if they must tell us at all? What are they trying to prove? Why must they be so *inscrutable?*'

'Mr Lee said the interview is arranged,' the messenger insisted. 'He said it is important. He said you should bring Mr Catling too. Mr Lee said that afterwards he will arrange an interview with Dr Yeh.'

'You see,' Ridley said. 'They've got us where they want us. No agronomy, no foreign affairs. That's the way it works. If we don't go now they'll make us go another day before they give us anything we really want.'

So we went and heard a long lecture on chemical fertilisers and rice yields, with two-year-old statistics.

The Ministry of Public Enlightenment sent many press releases to the Friends of China Club. One bulletin announced that secret agents in Hong Kong had learned that the Communist administration of Chungshan, a Cantonese provincial subdivision, had ordered compulsory marriage for widows between the ages of twenty and fifty-five, and for women whose husbands had been overseas for three years or more.

'What's the point of this release?' I asked Ridley.

'The bit about women whose husbands have been overseas for three years – that means wives of Nationalists who are now on Formosa, for example.'

'That'll be rather hard on Nationalist Army morale, won't it?'

'I should think so, yes, very,' Ridley agreed.

'Wouldn't it have been wiser for the Nationalists to have kept this bit of news dark?'

'Inscrutability,' Ridley explained.

As a further precondition to an audience with the Foreign

Minister, we had to travel by train to the distant military base at Tso Ying to witness the invasion training of 6,000 Chinese marines. A seventy-two-man US Marine Corps amphibious warfare instruction team demonstrated invasion techniques with toys on an outdoor basketball court. The audience included Nationalist senior officers.

'Ah,' sighed a Nationalist naval captain, 'if only we had battleships and aircraft carriers.'

'I can see that our artillery is obsolete,' a Nationalist infantry colonel remarked.

'What can we hope to achieve before we receive sufficient bombs of modern potency?' asked a Nationalist air-force general.

Two forces of Nationalist marines, each 3,000 strong, took part in realistic battle manoeuvres on rough terrain. There was much barbed wire and heavy machinegun fire using live ammunition. Several men died.

In Taipei, we were granted an audience with Dr Yeh. Glasses of green tea were served.

'The basic requirements for retaking the mainland are not yet in sight,' he told us. There was obviously a need for substantial additional financial aid from the United States.

The Ministry of Public Enlightenment sent Ridley and me invitations to a reception in the Government Guest House for Martin Artajo, the Foreign Minister of Spain, who was visiting Formosa to proclaim the solidarity of the governments of Madrid and Taipei.

Several American priests, refugees from the mainland, had been invited to the party, presumably to give it a Catholic appearance. One by one, they approached us to ask if we could do anything to bring world opinion to bear against Chiang Ching-kuo, the Generalissimo's Moscow-trained son. They said his commissars were campaigning against Christian teaching in the Nationalist armed services and civilian schools. Citizens could not be loyal to the Kuomintang and Christianity at the same time, the young Chiang had said.

*   *   *

'This place is beginning to suffocate me,' I told Ridley.

'I'm glad to hear that,' Ridley said. 'I feared I was being influenced only by homesickness.'

'Homesickness? But you haven't tried to get back to your home in England for years, have you?'

'I don't mean I'm homesick for Northumberland,' he said. 'I'm homesick for Seoul. I miss Yao.'

30

In Korea, it was generally agreed that the social highlight of the 1953 season was Patrick O'Donovan's St Patrick's Day party, which was held at the headquarters encampment of the Commonwealth Division. As a special privilege, I was allowed – the *Sun* was allowed – to help defray the not inconsiderable cost.

Tables were arranged lengthwise along two sides of the large mess tent as a bar and buffet. There were Gargantuan quantities of NAAFI food and drink, augmented by delicacies such as smoked salmon, smoked oysters and caviar, flown over for the occasion from Tokyo by the Royal Australian Air Force. O'Donovan had sent out formal invitations ('Carriages at Three O'clock'), which filled the tent with all sorts of officers, including a group of bewildered Canadians who had just arrived from Ottawa to inspect the battle zone and had expected rigours.

Black Watch pipers in full dress uniforms swaggered around the central stove and inflated the tent with the heroic, vibrant, nasal scream of Scottish martial music, which reminded me of Alaskan Eskimos. The pipers concluded the first part of their open-ended concert with the newest addition to their traditional regimental repertoire, '*Arirang*', an old Korean air melodically similar to, and as plaintive as, 'Over the Sea to Skye'.

John Ridley demonstrated his fortitude as a matador, substantiating accounts of his activities during the Spanish Civil War. The captain who had spent the night with O'Donovan and me in the Tokyo hotel fervently played the part of the bull, using two quart bottles of Asahi beer as horns. In one charge that was confused in the daringly late swirl of Ridley's tablecloth cape, the bull collided heavily with the stove and disastrous incineration seemed imminent. But the stovepipe was successfully straightened, and the party continued unabated, even when the Commonwealth Division's commanding general, Mike West, in the throes of jitterbugging, painfully wrenched a shoulder of a young lady in the uniform of one of the United Nations' relief agencies. The mishap caused widespread consternation, partly because she was one of the very few women available. A medical officer, not noted for abstemiousness, examined her there and then and declared her A-1, and she went on dancing almost as uninhibitedly as before.

The festivities took place within range of Chinese artillery. If the enemy had known of the extraordinary concentration of high-ranking officers and journalists in that tent that night, a single accurate shell might have wrought havoc in Whitehall, if not in Fleet Street.

'We don't want to believe it,' Stephen Barber, of the London *News Chronicle*, pointed out, 'it's hard to accept, but the fact is that we are expendable, all of us. None of our papers, in England or America, would have the slightest difficulty in replacing any of us within a week.' The thought was a sobering one, but not very. It was a good party.

Close to the front shortly after a minor Chinese attack, I encountered a US Army graves registrar. He had been given the job of burying some Chinese soldiers. Koreans were dong the actual digging, so he had time to talk, and seemed to enjoy doing so. He was a very young man, a Tennessee hill-billy with a blank, tan face and unclouded blue eyes. He had been drafted from an apprenticeship in his home-town mortuary. He wasn't complaining, he said; it had happened to lots of fellas, being taken away from civilian professions, just when they were getting ahead good. He always looked on the bright side though. He guessed he had been kinda lucky.

'We're too busy, of course, to handle the cadavers the way we would at home. We're not supposed to fix them up fancy. But it's better than nothing.'

An Army truck groaned up the hill and dumped a load of fresh corpses.

'We get all kinds, in all kinds of conditions,' he said. 'What I do is I look 'em over good and figure out what they need, what I'd do back home if they belonged to clients. I've learned a lot, just imagining what I'd do. It's been right interesting.'

I left him happily whistling between his teeth as he totted up the day's score.

Languishing idly one day, I got in touch with the US Navy for authority to go aboard a carrier in the Sea of Japan. Because news editors were of the opinion that correspondents who went to sea were wasting their time, the Navy justifiably felt neglected and they were eager to receive visitors representing the American media.

I had never before flown to a carrier, so landing on the USS *Oriskany* was exciting. Being suddenly stopped by arrester gear was unlike any of my previous aeronautical experience. It was like driving at high speed into a steel net. After an exchange of courtesies with the admiral of this splendid flagship, which gave me a penetrating, but unusable, insight into the weather, I was offered a helicopter for aerial photography.

The helicopter was securely fastened to the flight deck by three tie-down wires, light but strong cables. The deck crew were supposed to release all three simultaneously, as the pilot gave the engine maximum power for take-off. At this critical moment, however, the crew released only two of the cables. Held by the third, the helicopter was tipped onto its side, the main rotor thrashed the deck, and the damaged fuselage broke free and slid juddering horizontally across the deck to the edge, some fifty feet or so above the waves. And stopped. X-rays showed I had no broken bones. US Navy ships were dry and the coffee was weak, but a medical officer mercifully provided brandy. For me, the episode was interesting, but, of course, entirely devoid of news value.

The day it was announced that the first contingent of sick and wounded United Nations prisoners of war were on their way from North Korean prison camps to be exchanged at Panmunjom with Communist prisoners from the south, I asked Lieutenant General Glen O. Barcus, commanding general of the United States Fifth Air Force, whether it would be possible to fly north for an aerial preview of the first convoy of ambulances.

'When do you want to leave?' was the general's only question. In Korea as elsewhere, the USAF did not mess about with public relations: it did things fast and it did them in a big way. The next morning I was provided with a Shooting Star (a two-place jet trainer) and an escort of *five* Sabrejets for my private sightseeing tour. The size of the escort was so impressive that I was not too upset by the name of the pilot assigned to fly the Shooting Star – Captain Coffin. An Air Force photographer took some shots of me in flying suit and helmet beside the plane. Who was publicising whom?

The Sabres were already orbiting overhead, and their fuel consumption at low altitudes was prodigious, so Captain Coffin apologetically curtailed the photo session. The photographer took only two shots of me sitting in the plane, with my molars clamped together in an expression of determination I hoped would suggest *Hell's Angels*. Life continued to imitate art.

The wing of the Shooting Star dipped like a diviner's wand and pointed to the convoy. It looked like a caravan of matchboxes, moving slowly along the the tortuous, bomb-pitted North Korean road. We flew over the rubble of Pyongyang, the Communist capital. A man in a field waved. Then we were near the forbidden Yalu River, the Chinese border. I saw two condensation trails, like two chalk lines on a blue ceiling, high above us, moving southward from the direction of the MIG bases. We turned about and headed for home in a shallow dive. The Shooting Star flew slower than sound, and the plane started buffeting as we approached the sound barrier. Captain Coffin pulled the nose up and I felt the bladders of my G-suit dilate unpleasantly against arterial pressure points and my helmet press leadenly down on my forehead. Once we were south of the Thirty-Eighth Parallel, the line that divided Them from Us, Captain Coffin sounded relaxed.

'Would you like some aerobatics?' he enquired. I felt I had to say I would. He performed some sickeningly smooth barrel rolls, Cuban eights, Immelmann turns and other convolutions that made me feel alternately like a balloon and meat pâté, while the sky appeared to change from blue to grey and back to blue again.

While my fears were teased on this expensive military roller coaster, a hundred and twenty American soldiers, many of them on litters, were bumping slowly toward liberation with some of the most harrowing stories of the Korean War. There were grim accounts of the first days of captivity after China's sudden intervention during the first winter. North Koreans marched American prisoners in severe cold to camps near the Yalu. One man told of having a gangrenous foot slowly cut off with a hacksaw, without anaesthetic. Prison lectures on Mao's brand of Marxism were excruciatingly boring. There were compulsory sessions of confessional self-criticism. One British POW admitted in class that he had once travelled by Underground from Hendon to Leicester Square without a ticket.

After the exchanges of sick and wounded prisoners, the war anticlimactically dragged on. During the protracted negotiations at Panmunjom, there were arguments, for example, about which side should generate the electricity to light the 'Pagoda of Peace' for the final signing. President Rhee did his best to incite small-scale battles along the front, as though keeping his job depended on them. It did. Four Republic of Korea divisions were badly battered by Chinese artillery and Chinese infantry, who swarmed southward, wave after wave, with the suicidal, inexorable determination of ants. It was raining. I waded about in the mud with harassed UN liaison officers while South Korean soldiers fought hard but fell back. At dusk, as the fighting continued, and 'the situation', as briefing officers used to say during retreats, remained 'fluid', I organised my own strategic withdrawal to a previously prepared position. Our boys called this manoeuvre 'bugging out'. An Army liaison plane managed to take off in a torrential downpour and we landed in the dark on Seoul Racetrack.

I had a shower and shave and changed into a fresh uniform. I ate a hot dinner. Michael Rougier, of *Life*, who had spent the day photographing the ROK's prize unit, the Capitol Division, taking a frightful beating, came into my room and asked: 'Going to the fashion show?'

What was a news story? Obliqueness was needed to stimulate editors wearied by military communiqués reporting inconclusive skirmishes that meant nothing to readers at their Baltimore breakfast tables.

In 'Carnegie Hall', a new, American-style Seoul night-club, Miss Norah Noh, a South Korean hooker who had somehow spent a year in Los Angeles, had picked that night to present South Korea's first 'Western' fashion show. Tommy's Combo, a Korean jazz band, played their version of the Goodman classic, 'Sing, Sing, Sing', while Korean girls modelled black-market impressions of high fashion, and Miss Noh tirelessly raised her thinly pencilled left eyebrow in the *femme fatale* mode of silent movie vamps and pointed out the attractions of her latest designs. 'This has been a hell of a day,' Rougier commented. 'I can hardly wait to tell my grandchildren about the things I've seen – a battle going nowhere and a surrealist nightmare. The most fashionable colours in Korea are recognition-panel yellow, foxhole brown, bazooka grey and Nam Il red.'

The last hour of the war was the longest. I spent it with some US Marines in a bunker on the forward slope of the Main Line of Resistance. We counted the minutes. The cease-fire was due at 22.00 hours. American and Chinese artillery had been particularly active all day. It was assumed that both sides wanted to reduce the weight of ammunition they would have to carry when they pulled back from the Demarcation Zone. While the aimless explosions went on, everyone was extra careful not to get killed. 'I'd never forgive myself if I got killed the last day,' Rougier said. He took a series of pictures of field-hospital surgeons operating for hours on the war's last Marine casualty, in vain. His magazine devoted several full pages to 'The Death of A Marine', a layout that was praised as 'a very nice play'.

On the first morning of the armistice, we shared a helicopter he had been able to get from the Marine Corps, and alertness we got from a bottle of benzedrine. The chopper deposited us in no man's land, beside a steep hill temporarily known as Boulder City. We climbed the hill on foot. The rocky ground was thickly strewn with American and Chinese grenades, mortar shells, mines, artillery shells and shell fragments, burp-gun clips and belts of machinegun ammunition, some supposedly dud, and some believed to be live.

This was the point at which Americans and Chinese had most closely confronted each other at the end of the fighting. The opposing positions were almost connected by deep communication trenches. Americans and Chinese were often no more than twenty-five yards, a grenade's throw, apart. Sometimes they intruded into each other's positions and fought with absurd bravery hand to hand. The day before the cease-fire they had been trying to kill each other. Now they were in each other's trenches retrieving their dead.

The weather was hot. There was a heavy, sweet smell like the smell of funeral lilies. There was a buzz of flies. Bodies that had been unrecoverable during the past few days had swollen and blackened and putrified in the sunshine. Some, like inflated rubber dummies, had split the rotting cloth of their battle dress. Looking from the Americans to the Chinese and back again, I noticed that in death they were beginning to look alike.

Brigadier General J. C. Burger, second in command of the First Marines, visited Boulder City that morning, while Rougier and I were still there. 'The aftermath of war,' the general said. 'There's never been anything quite like this before. And I don't think we'll ever see anything like it again.' He was gazing into what the *New Yorker* derisively used to caption 'The Clouded Crystal Ball'.

Silently, steadily, the stretcher-bearers, heavy-laden, trudged back and forth.

On the way home, I paused in Japan.

At a souvenir stall at ground zero of the atomic bomb that obliterated Hiroshima in 1945, K. Kikkawa, a member of an association called 'The Atomic Bomb Casualty Sufferers', pulled off his shirt with hands like claws and showed me the shiny pink and brown lumps of keloid scar tissue all over his back. He sold me a smooth glass fragment that he said had been fused by radiation. He asked for the equivalent of 28 cents. It would have been churlish of me to refuse the offer, would it not? Afterward, I noticed that the glass had been part of a Coca-Cola bottle, an apt international souvenir.

At Tokyo University, Dr Horotake Kakehi, a physicist, told me enthusiastically of the progress Japan was making in nuclear research. 'We are still far behind you,' he said. 'But — who knows? — perhaps, one day . . .'

*　*　*

On my return to the United States, like many other people in 1953, I became preoccupied with speculation on the probable nature of World War III. My apprehensiveness was sharpened by an assignment to write a series of articles on Strategic Air Command, USAF, which was caricatured with such candour in the movie *Dr Strangelove, or How I Learned to Stop Worrying and Love the Bomb*. I flew to Omaha, Nebraska, a city renowned for its beefsteak.

'Good meat begins with good grazing,' a local restaurateur pointed out. 'But one of the most important factors is hanging it. None of that premature freezing. You've got to hang meat until the tissues begin to break down – this is for tenderness – and the whole carcass ripens – this is for flavour.' At a restaurant named 'The Top of The World' a waitress with an off-duty avocation asked, 'You want to be frenched?' I was ready to visit SAC headquarters at nearby Offutt Air Force Base.

SAC's motto, posted on a large billboard at the main gates, was 'Peace is Our Profession', though it was then well known that the commander, General Curtis E. LeMay, advocated a pre-emptive atomic strike to incapacitate the Soviet Union before it could build a threatening nuclear capability of its own.

One of General LeMay's senior aides assured me that the bomb that was dropped on Hiroshima was now regarded as kids' stuff. 'If the explosive force of one ton of TNT were represented by a one-inch cube,' he said, 'the average load of a World War II bomber would be represented by a column four inches high. The Hiroshima bomb would be represented by a column 1,666 *feet* high, and the thermonuclear superbomb would be represented by a column sixty-three *miles* high! With bombs of such cataclysmic potential and the means to deliver them, the furies of war could be compressed into a very short period. Think what it would be like: your whole city would be in flames. Casualties would be in the hundreds of thousands. The immediate need for plasma in one city would exceed the total amount used in the whole of the Korean War. You might be able to pull a few people out of the rubble. But don't forget that the fire department would have been destroyed, and the police department, and the ambulances and hospitals. And, of course, you couldn't expect any help from the next metropolis; they would have been hit too.'

I flew despondently down to Carswell Air Force Base, at Fort Worth, Texas. Major F. E. Bachmann, Jr, and fourteen other men took me up for a training flight in a B-36, whose wing-span, they said, was longer than the Wright Brothers' first flight. Progress! From our cruising height, the target, a football stadium, looked like a bone curtain ring.

'Is that Dallas?' I asked Major Bachmann.

'That *was* Dallas,' he replied with a mischievous, boyish smile, as the vast plane banked and headed away at 400 miles per hour for the Gulf of Mexico.

I spent a lot of time morbidly brooding about Mr Kikkawa, Dr Kakehi, General LeMay and the politicians all over the world, East and West, and the future they were preparing. Buck Dorsey picked a suitable quote from one of my articles as a title for the series: 'Every Day is D-Day'.

It was a relief to turn my attention to a more immediate, comparatively cosy crisis, the struggle for domination of the Republic of Guatemala. A journalist must have an occasional holiday from the big time.

31

B ack from the Far East, in Baltimore I wrote to all the Latin-American embassies in Washington to get on their information mailing lists. Most of them sent me brochures intended to attract tourists, but one country inundated me with newsletters and political pamphlets. Guatemala's quasi-Communist régime complained that the United States was encouraging and supporting a revolutionary plot. The 1954 revolt against President Jacobo Arbenz Guzman was well advertised before the event.

In May that year the *Alfhelm*, a Swedish cargo ship, sailed from Poland with a load of Czechoslovakian arms. The shipment, believed to be worth about $10,000,000, considered a lot of money at the time, was originally cleared for Dakar, but was delivered to Puerto Barrios, the Caribbean port of Guatemala. After the US State Department denounced the delivery as 'a grave development', my managing editor agreed that it might be interesting to see what was going on down there. I had not been to Central America before and I spoke no Spanish, but I knew how to spell the name of the country and where it was on the map, and Dorsey sent me. Journalists often have to undergo on-the-job training. Very few other managing editors became sufficiently interested to assign correspondents to Guatemala until the airlines stopped flying there, the frontiers were closed, and it was almost impossible to get in.

This was to be my first revolution. I went to the State Department for a briefing. A man in Brooks Brothers clothing closed the door of his small office, sat down at the Central American desk, opened, presumably, the Guatemalan drawer, and produced a creased Guatemalan Esso map.

'May I see?' I asked, moving the map sideways on his desk.

'Sorry,' he said anxiously, seizing the map by one corner. 'I can't let you have it. It's the only one I have. I'll try to get you one.' When he telephoned, however, the State Department's neighbourhood Esso garage evidently was closed.

'Frankly,' he said with a worn Ivy League smile that was half a frown, 'I'm stymied. Still, I can give you the names of the political parties, if they would help.'

Eventually, I got an Esso map from the United Fruit Company of Boston in Guatemala City, who were co-sponsoring the revolution. After the conflict, I learned that leaders of both sides had used Esso maps in their conduct of the brief military campaign.

In Baltimore, I went to Eddie Jacobs's shop and asked him for a couple of suits made of miracle-fabric, suitable for a revolution.

'Bulletproof, you mean?' he said.

How we laughed! I got two washable suits and a white dinner jacket on my expense account. Though somewhat parsimonious about salaries, the *Sun* was lavish with expenses for foreign correspondents.

On the way south, I read a guidebook, *Guatemala. From Where the Rainbow Takes its Colors*. Guatemala, the book said, and the book was right, is 'The Land of Eternal Spring ... ancient, historical, colorful, picturesque, modern'. It was heaven on earth, for a while: the sweet, wooden chimes of marimbas in flower-scented patios kept one from hearing the groans of political prisoners in the basement of the headquarters of the Guardia Civil.

Gerry Robichaud, of the Chicago *Sun-Times*, had arrived in

Guatemala City a couple of days ahead of me and was a model assimilator of local folk ways. A dark, swarthy man, he was growing a wild, black moustache, which, he hoped, would look authentically Latin in time for the revolution. He was properly dressed for it, in an unpressed brown suit, a white shirt and a black tie.

'Don't drink in the hotel bar,' he said. 'The *cantinero* – the bartender – speaks English. Come across the street. I'm learning Spanish. This is better than Berlitz.

'Hey, José,' he said, 'una cerveza Bohémia, por favor, and para this señor here uno martini, muy seco.' Robichaud smiled triumphantly. 'All in two days,' he said. 'Don't feel bad. You'll catch on.

'Hey, José,' he said, displaying more of his erudition, 'bocitas.' Bocitas proved to be strips of fatty ham and bean paste on crackers. 'And I've discovered a new drink, made of pineapple juice, lime, coffee essence and white rum. It's great.'

'How about sources?' I asked. 'Have you found anyone helpful?'

'This bartender knows everything about everything,' Robichaud assured me. 'The revolution's due the third week of the month. That gives us plenty of time to look around. I've lined up most of the cabinet for interviews. Tomorrow I'm doing Toriello, the foreign minister. You can come along, if you want to. The *Sun* isn't in my circulation area. And I've found a good restaurant – chicken and shrimp and rice, and not too greasy. I've just about got this town figured out.'

Antigua Guatemala, the sixteenth-century Spanish colonial capital, was badly damaged by earthquake and flood in the eighteenth century. The eruption was interpreted as a Providential hint to the survivors to move away. Guatemala City was established soon afterward, about a mile above sea level. It, too, was laid waste by earthquakes, in 1917 and 1918, but omens of this sort were disregarded in the twentieth century, and the city was largely rebuilt. It was not

(*Above*) The Age of Innocence.
At four, with my mother, Sheila,
before I learned to type.

(*Left*) Machismo with lion cubs
in the Berlin Zoo in the summer
of the Olympic Games.

Right) Family reunion in 1946,
on my return from the RCAF.
My brothers, Timothy (*left*) and
Duncan, with our mother and
father and Nina, a substitute
or the daughter they never had.

(*Above*) A Macao rickshaw man in 1953, understandably pained, looks at a foreign correspondent imitating a Portuguese imperialist. (*Below left*) Visiting Marcia Lucas in New York on the scenic route from Cairo to Nassau, 1944. Note whimsical uniform, bespoke in Puerto Rico. (*Below right*) As the Governor of the Bahamas in 1944, the Duke of Windsor showed me his own bizarre contribution to the prosecution of World War II.

(*Above*) At RAF Odiham, in Hampshire, 1945. We took our own motorcycles in Dakotas on trips to European ruins where taxis were difficult to find.

Above) In US Air Force gear for sightseeing flight over North Korea, early in 1953.

(*Right*) With Captain Coffin, USAF, who flew me in his Shooting Star to the Chinese border and back, fast.

(*Left*) Billie Holiday sang 'Strange Fruit' about a lynching in 'the gallant South', and saved me with a kiss.

(*Below*) Duke Ellington's recording of 'Jubilee Stomp' introduced me to jazz and improved King Alfred School in the 1930s.

Right) Peggy Lee at her best, in London and Monaco in 1961.

(*Left*) Robert Mitchum, an intelligent actor and a tireless anti-authoritarian, was Jane Russell's best friend. Largely thanks to him, they survived contracts with Howard Hughes that were like penal servitude.

(*Left*) Graham Greene urged me to make the leap of faith and to write more honestly than I dared. He was also a good man with a pink gin.

(*Right*) Sir Pelham Grenville Wodehouse, surely the world's happiest writer, advised me to write 600 words a day – every day. I rarely succeeded.

(*Above left*) Daughter Charlotte,
once a good chaser of rabbits,
now a good architect.

(*Above right*) With daughters Sheila
(*left*) and Ellen, on the Chesapeake
Bay in 1958.

(*Right*) Celebrating Mickey Mouse's
fiftieth birthday at Disney World,
Florida, in 1979, with Diana Laing,
one of the Mouse's most ardent admirers.

Elegiac champagne in Reenacoppul, West Cork, after the freakish Great Snow of St Valentine Day, 1994. There were drifts of depths up to half an inch, so the schools were closed.

a great architectural achievement, but an almost perfect climate makes one feel so well that the minor beauties of the capital are greatly enhanced. The Penitentiary and Police Headquarters are forts with crenellated battlements, but they don't look severe or even serious: the Penitentiary is pale green, and Police Headquarters is pale pink. There are orange-tiled villas in tropical gardens.

The capital is by far the most important city of the Republic, and the Parque Central, a large plaza, is the heart of the nation. The buildings on the four sides of the plaza, the National Palace, the barracks, the Cathedral and offices and shops, represent the four competing powers: the Government, the Army, the Church and Commerce. I found a few chips in the stucco, caused by bullets. In this plaza the revolutions begin and end; whatever happens in the provinces is incidental. The Pan-American Hotel, only a block from the commercial side of the plaza and only a few minutes' walk from a cable office, is the hotel in which most correspondents stayed while covering Guatemalan revolutions. Not knowing the layout of the city when I arrived, I stayed first at the Palace Hotel, which was slightly nearer the Government Tourist Bureau. I wanted to see some of the rest of the country before it was too late.

When I was ushered into the private office of Guillermo Palmieri, the director of the Tourist Bureau, he was sitting at his desk loading a pearl-handled, silver-plated .38 revolver. He looked up and smiled. He had the high sheen of a Latin lover: his black hair, his dark eyes, his white teeth and his black silk sport shirt gleamed. He snapped into place the loaded cylinder of the revolver. He shut first one eye and then the other, as he looked thoughtfully across the sights at various objects in the room.

'You know, it is very interesting,' smoothly said Palmieri, as he pointed his revolver at a bird on a pictorial wall map of Guatemala. 'I look with one eye and see that the bird is in the sights; I look with the other eye and the bird is no longer in the sights: the aim changes according to the point of view. Do you agree?'

'That sounds plausible,' I acknowledged. 'I came here this morning because –'

'Ah!' Palmieri shouted, abruptly leaning forward in his swivel chair and slapping his desk with his free hand. 'Then what is true for one eye may not be true for another! There is no absolute truth. I was taught by Jesuits. They are very clever men. I am a Catholic' – he tugged a fine gold chain dangling from his neck – 'but I tell you that sometimes their religion is not the same as my religion.'

He gestured toward the map on the wall.

'You know what kind of bird that is?' he demanded.

'Some sort of parrot?'

'It is a quetzal,' Palmieri said with sombre pride. 'It is a very independent bird. If you put it in a cage it will not eat. It will die. This is the national emblem of Guatemala. But does your United Fruit Company know that?'

'Really,' I began again, 'all I want –'

'Can you use a gun? Could you shoot the head off that little quetzal with the first shot?'

'I'd rather not try,' I said with what I meant to be an ingratiating smile.

'Ah! I am glad. Because if you kill the quetzal I will kill you. Please write *that* to your Baltimore *Sun* and to all the North American people. Why does Mr Dulles attack Guatemala? How can we threaten the Panama Canal? Do you like Mr Dulles?'

'I do not like him or dislike him,' I replied untruthfully. 'He is the United States Secretary of State. I am a reporter.'

'I have been to the United States,' Palmieri said. 'And also I have stood beside Jacobo Arbenz Guzman while guns were firing. He is the President of Guatemala, and I am a Guatemaltecan.'

'And the director of the National Tourist Bureau,' I reminded him. He accepted the gentle rebuke with a nod and a smile.

'You want to see Antigua and Lake Atitlán and Chichicastenango?' he said. 'Yes, of course – they are the most beautiful places in the world. I will take you myself, tomorrow morning. I will show you the wicked Communistas cultivating their fields and plotting to blow up Miami Beach.'

'I don't want you to take me anywhere,' I said. 'I only want some information.'

'Information! I'll give you information! I insist on taking you. To tell you the truth, I am conducting this tour anyway. You are not the only journalist who has thought of it. We will leave at about 11.30 – in time to get to Antigua for cocktails before lunch. There will be much conversation. I'll pick you up at your hotel.'

'I'm at the Palace.'

'I know.'

'About how much money will I need?'

Palmieri laughed. 'You are joking. As you, yourself, have pointed out, I am the director of the National Tourist Bureau.'

'We are taking with us a young woman from Berkeley, California,' Palmieri said the next morning. 'She is not a journalist and she is not pretty, but she has very splendid breasts. She told me she is interested in agrarian reform and public hygiene. I have met other idealistic, cultured North American ladies. With their mouths they ask questions about the Mayan pyramids at Zaculeu, but with their eyes – even the dried-up old schoolteachers with the faces of horses – they all ask for only one thing. I will explain agrarian reform and public hygiene to the young woman from Berkeley, California. Then I will show her Lake Atitlán in the moonlight.'

I asked him why he was telling me his plans for her.

'As long as I know that you know what I am thinking,' he explained, 'there will be added a certain spice to the political discussions during the drive. The two other journalists will be taken in a second car by my assistant.'

Palmieri drove like a demon. The Californian sat beside him and I sat alone in the back. She had yellow hair, brushed up, surmounted by a circular, rope-like plait. She wore hornrimmed spectacles and no make-up. She was dressed in folksy Guatemalan clothes, a white blouse and a multicoloured woollen skirt. She looked as earnestly, wholesomely romantic as a Scandinavian cellist.

She asked him scores of questions about crop rotation and DDT. He answered them with smouldering glances, gazing at her as languidly as was possible at high speeds on a road winding about between a sheer cliff and a sheer precipice.

At an open space, the car slithered to a halt and Palmieri turned to me and grinned and said: 'Let me show you some of my weapons.' We got out of the car and he opened the trunk. It contained an arsenal. There were automatic pistols and rifles and a submachinegun and several grenades.

'We shall have a contest, you and I,' he told me. I could see why I hadn't been riding in the other car. I was to be his tame rival for an exhibition of his prowess. He placed a Kodak film package on a boulder and led me about a hundred feet from it.

'Go on and shoot it,' he said. 'Like this.' He raised his revolver like an accusative finger and shot. There was a tiny eruption of dust close to the improvised target. It was my turn. Suddenly I wanted very much to succeed. I lifted the revolver in the prescribed training-range manner, until my arm was fully outstretched. My hand trembled. I aimed carefully and gradually squeezed the trigger. When my eyes blinked open, the film package was no longer on the boulder. Palmieri and I looked at the woman. She was looking at her watch.

'Of course anybody can shoot exactly straight if he takes enough time,' he commented. 'When fighting in the streets the important factor is speed. Look. Imagine that the boulder is a man.' He snatched the revolver from me and walked rapidly away from the boulder. 'I hear a suspicious noise!' he shouted. 'Immediately I turn and fire!' There were four quick bangs, four hits. 'That's the way to do it,' he said. 'The man is dead. I am alive.'

'Good grouping,' I said.

The woman said nothing.

'All right,' Palmieri said grimly. 'Enough fooling around. Let's go.'

That night we stayed at a hotel overlooking Lake Atitlán and the volcanic peaks beyond. Palmieri and the woman from Berkeley, California, dined together and left the building soon after dinner.

The next morning his car was gone.

I was finishing breakfast when the young woman came into the dining room.

'May I join you for coffee?' she asked. 'I'd like to tell you what happened last night. I know what you must think. Mr Palmieri took me for a walk. We went to the beach. It was beautiful.'

I sipped coffee and applied what Max Beerbohm, I believe, called 'the spur of silence'.

'Well, yes, he made a pass at me,' she continued in a remarkably matter-of-fact tone of voice. 'I spoke rather sharply to him. And – guess what! It was worse than when you hit that Kodak box at point-blank range after he'd missed the damn thing.'

'What did he do?'

'He burst out crying and ran away.'

32

Colonel Carlos Castillo Armas, who had tunnelled (or bribed his way) out of the Guatemala City Penitentiary a couple of years before, was in the neighbouring republic of Honduras, waging a war of nerves against President Arbenz. The Honduran government, with CIA encouragement, was allowing Castillo Armas to operate a C-47 from a base in their country. He sent it over Guatemala to drop leaflets and, some said, armaments.

'Fight for God, country, liberty, work, truth, justice!' one of the leaflets exhorted the people of Guatemala. 'Fight against Communist atheism, Communist oppression, Communist poverty, Communist lies, Communist police! Fight with your brother patriots – fight with Castillo Armas!'

A rebel radio station, a mobile transmitter, could be heard in the Guatemalan capital. 'Arbenz,' it warned, 'your days are numbered. Your tomb is prepared and the buzzards are flying, awaiting you and your band of assassins.'

The Minister of the Interior announced that police had arrested revolutionary plotters and seized weapons and explosives. Some anti-Communists gained asylum in foreign embassies. One of the fugitives was the editor of the most daringly anti-government newspaper, *El Espectador*. His name was J. A. P. Palmieri. He was the older brother of the director of the Tourist Bureau.

There were rumours of police brutalities.

There were rumours that the government was distributing Czechoslovakian machineguns to the Indians. 'I'd rather be machine-gunned than sliced up with a machete,' said a former mayor of Guatemala City at the bar of the Palace Hotel. 'But after the next drink – let us drink in industrial quantities – I shall return to my plantation. I will make it a fort. Mine will be the Dien Bien Phu of the coffee fincas.' The Indo-Chinese analogy was an unfortunate one, I thought, remembering what had happened to the French.

The government announced the suspension of civil liberties. *Habeas corpus* writs were no longer valid. Public meetings were forbidden. Worst of all, local and outgoing news articles had to be submitted to censorship. The rebel radio said that Castillo would strike soon. A taxi driver was more precise: 'The revolution will begin in ten days.' He proved to be correct. No wonder that foreign correspondents get much of their information from taxi drivers! Metal shutters were locked over shop windows. The Austrian proprietor of La Casita, which the Tourist Bureau guidebook described as 'the most aristocratic of all tearooms', wrung his hands. 'Aie!' he wailed. 'Comes now more heartache. My dears, I can tell you: here no pleasure is.'

The last American journalist to arrive in the capital was Fred Sparks. He had not changed since Seoul. His soft hat was on the back of his head, the last few millimetres of a cigarette hung attached to his lower lip, his trench coat was open, and he was almost entirely unencumbered, except for a brief-case, a few cameras and an umbrella. One of his axioms was: 'Nobody ever hits a man carrying an umbrella.'

I met him on his arrival, hesitating fastidiously in the main doorway of the Pan-American Hotel, into which, by then, all of us had moved. He peered over his spectacles, and, with something of W. C. Fields's querulousness, intoned: 'These are parlous times. Where, may I ask, are the barricades? Where are the babies skewered on bayonets? Where's the cable office? And where's the bar? I have a deadline, you know.'

Sparks had an encyclopaedic knowledge of journalistic tricks and clichés. Late one morning over coffee and pastries, after two of our colleagues had exchanged their collection of unconfirmed and unconfirmable reports from the Honduran border, he peered furtively over one shoulder and then the other, put the back of his hand beside his mouth, and confided: 'I'm putting machineguns in the church steeple at Puerto Barrios in my dispatch tonight, men. In these revolutions they always put machineguns in the church steeples. You guys are going to look pretty silly if you don't get those machineguns up there.'

Telephone calls to the United States now had to be made from the Tropical Radio office, where an English-speaking renegade from what was then British Honduras stood by the switchboard wearing earphones, ready to pull the plug whenever he heard anything that he thought seemed censorable. I found that this newly appointed censor, bearing the exotic monicker Gerald Cattousse Fairweather, was a man of modest means and immodest cravings. He was inordinately fond of natty haberdashery, two-toned shoes and musky after-shave lotion. I took him to lunch. As he munched fillet steak and strawberry shortcake, sealed with a double Cointreau, he said: 'You know, man, in these countries it doesn't pay to be fanatic. Middle of the road all the way, that's me.'

'You and Eisenhower,' I said.

'That's the ticket!' he jubilantly agreed. 'I get along with the government; I get along with you. Everybody happy.'

It was not difficult to persuade him to turn a deaf ear to my telephone calls to Baltimore. There was absolutely no embarrassment in talking about money. Sparks, too, was glad to subscribe to the Fairweather service, and I imagine that he extended it to other correspondents. The fees were not exorbitant. My office did not question one of my favourite expense-account items: 'Bribes to Censor — $160.'

*   *   *

One afternoon I had a private appointment with John Peurifoy, the US ambassador, at the embassy. His secretary said the ambassador was on the roof and I was to go up. He was wearing a one-piece, dove-grey garment like that wartime 'siren suit' of Winston Churchill's and looking through field glasses into the eastern sky. Soon I heard the drone of a single-engined plane, and then saw it, flying at about 2,000 feet, heading our way.

'Wouldn't it be a good idea to take cover?' I suggested.

'It's all right,' Peurifoy assured me, as he checked his watch. 'We'll be OK here. They're going for the Aurora gasoline storage tanks.'

And so they were. This was a well-managed revolution.

The revolution lasted quite a long time by Central American standards – nine days, long enough for a local manufacturer to make Army of Liberation tee-shirts. The populace wanted to demonstrate their new loyalty when Castillo Armas's mob hit town.

The new president honoured the Latin-American tradition of granting safe-conduct passes out of the country to high-ranking enemies who had gained asylum in foreign embassies. New governments are magnanimous in this way, because today's ins may be tomorrow's outs; escape routes are kept available.

Shortly before Castillo took over, police arrested Fairweather, and his surname suddenly acquired further irony. They beat him up quite severely. When things settled down and he was at liberty, he applied to the US embassy for help. He argued that he deserved compensation as a martyr in the cause of freedom of the press. After the embassy turned him down, he came to me. 'I've got a terrific idea,' he said. 'I'm going to organise a Negro tourist agency. I'll allow my friends to invest in it.'

Ex-President Arbenz was said to have reached his ancestral country, Switzerland, with several million dollars.

During the immediate postrevolutionary clean-up, a search party exhumed some horribly mutilated bodies.

I don't know who the President of Guatemala is now. Castillo Armas was assassinated long ago. He successfully performed his Cold War function. It doesn't really matter much who the present incumbent is. Guatemala is still a beautiful country, with humming-birds and butterflies and many friendly people, and the weather is wonderful.

33

Continuing my tour of Central America, I interviewed President Anastasio Somoza of Nicaragua. It was when speaking of this long-ruling, right-wing dictator that President Roosevelt said: 'He may be a son of a bitch, but he's our son of a bitch.' Even before McCarthyism, the United States supported any foreign dictator, no matter how corrupt, as long as he was opposed to politicians of the left.

'The situation in Central America is much better now,' Somoza said. 'The only remaining danger is Figueres. When you talk to Figueres, he walks up and down with his finger to his forehead and a faraway look in his eyes. He thinks he's a visionary and he's looking for visions. He has a Napoleon complex. But you know what Figueres is? He's a lousy Commie. But he's only a small one.' Somoza grinned and sat forward and gently tapped my knee with the blade of the knife he happened to be fondling. 'Figueres is so small and he wants to be so big he wears built-up shoes. You're going to Costa Rica? Good. When you get there, you look at Figueres's shoes. You'll see I'm telling the truth.'

President José María Figueres was not in his capital, named after his patron saint, when I sought an audience. I found him in Puerto Limón, a soporific small town on the Caribbean coast. When he received me he was reclining on a sofa in his bed-sitting room in the provincial Government House, reading the *Atlantic Monthly*. Figueres was a neat little man of early middle age, with receding black hair, a long nose, a short upper lip and a cordial smile. It was true that his shoes looked extraordinarily thick-soled.

'I would be willing to attend any meeting that could resolve the differences between Nicaragua and my country,' he said. 'But there are no real political issues. Somoza doesn't want to end the friction, for the simple reason that he's using it as a distraction from domestic dissatisfaction at a time when he's getting the Nicaraguan Constitution amended so that he can succeed himself yet again as president.

'Let's go for a walk,' Figueres suggested. 'This will be a peripatetic interview,' he said, leading the way downstairs and out through the garden. 'Like Truman's. Peripatetic,' he repeated, relishing the word. We strolled across the street. There was a view of blue sea and blue sky. It was a charming place to be the president of. In a leisurely fashion, Figueres expounded his political philosophy and economic theories, in the fluent American-English he had refined at the Massachusetts Institute of Technology and Columbia University. He politely deplored American foreign policies based on military expedience. He pointed out that there was little to choose between dictators of the extreme right and the extreme left. 'Think of Somoza and Chiang Kai-shek and Franco,' he said. 'Nicaragua and the Dominican Republic and Venezuela are just as bad as Guatemala under Arbenz.'

I was surprised to discover that conversations with presidents were easy, once I had got over initial stage-fright. They were only people. Somoza was a sort of gangster; Figueres was like a professor. I liked Figueres.

'We must have another talk,' he said on our way back to Government House. 'The next time we're both in San José, drop around to the palace and meet my wife.'

*   *   *

I did that, about six months later. Fighting had broken out on the Costa Rican side of the border with Nicaragua. Direct flights from the United States to Costa Rica were temporarily suspended, but I was able to fly to Panama City and from there to San José. I went to a restaurant where any American correspondents in the capital would be likely to have dinner. Sure enough, there was a small group of them, drinking martinis and trying to decide the best way to cover whatever was happening in Guanacaste Province.

'What are *you* going to do?' one of them asked me with the sardonic smile of condescension sometimes shown by a reporter who has been on the scene of a story twenty-four hours longer than a colleague.

'First,' I said, 'I'd like to see the menu. Then I think I'll ask President Figueres for advice.'

'He hasn't been giving press conferences,' a more sympathetic veteran said.

Having placed my order, I excused myself to telephone a number I had obtained in Washington. The restaurant telephone was attached to a wall within sight of our table. I was finishing my soup when the waitress came over and asked for me by name.

'The President wants to speak to you,' she said.

It was a great moment, the first of a series of great moments. Thanks to the President's goodwill, Costa Rica was one great moment after another, a reporter's dream come true.

'Well, what is it? What's going on?' I was asked when I sat down again. Nothing, I said; just a personal conversation. I told the waitress to cancel my order for dessert.

'You're on to something,' someone bitterly complained. 'Is it a Cabinet meeting?'

'The United Nations? Are they getting into this?'

'Has Nicaragua declared war?' It seemed unlikely that Costa Rica had, as Costa Rica had no armed forces, only civilian policemen.

It was none of those things. 'Madame Figueres has baked a

cake,' I disclosed. 'She wondered whether I'd like to try it. Banana cream, she said.'

Nobody was convinced.

The cake was delicious.

Early the next morning, as invited, I reported to the Presidential Palace as a small convoy was preparing to leave for the front. Madame Figueres, an attractive blonde Danish-American whom the President had met at Columbia, was standing in the palace doorway, holding in her arms their month-old son, José María, Jr.

'This is one time I wish I were not a woman,' she said. 'I told Pepe I would have my hair cropped, wash off my make-up, and put on a uniform, but he said no. He said there are ten thousand other volunteers.'

President Figueres drove his own car. One of his ministers, with a machine-pistol on his lap, sat on the President's right. I sat in the back. The rest of the convoy consisted of Jeeps loaded with armed men that were to precede and follow the President's car. President and Madame Figueres fondly waved to each other, as a departing commuter might exchange farewells with a suburban housewife, and we headed north-west, up the Pan-American Highway.

Figueres said he was encouraged by the Organization of American States' commission whose investigations in the field had resulted in a report implicating President Somoza as the instigator of the fighting. The US Navy had sent Marlin patrol planes from Panama to observe the Nicaragua-Costa Rica border region for the OAS, but, Figueres pointed out, they were unable to deter the Nicaraguans. While the Marlins were overhead there were no attacks, but the patrol was not continuous; as soon as the Marlins left the scene, there were further violations.

'The United States should provide a continuous air patrol by aircraft authorised to shoot, if necessary,' Figueres said.

'Why don't you ask for that?' I said, with pencil poised, like a grocer ready to take an order.

'Yes.'

'Perhaps an aircraft carrier could do the job.'

'That's a good idea.'

'But, of course,' I said, 'you really need some planes of your own.'

Figueres frequently stopped the convoy to shake hands and talk with volunteers wearing bandoliers of ammunition over their farm work-clothes and carrying antique rifles. At every defensible bend in the road, men of the civilian home guard arose from camouflaged strong points in the deep ditches. Figueres greeted the volunteers as gratefully as a political candidate greets voters the day before an election. In villages, crowds gathered around the President's car and cheered him. They evidently assumed I was a government supporter, and I shared some of the glory. As a matter of fact, government supporter was rapidly becoming my true role. There went objectivity.

We stopped for lunch at San Ramón, the President's birthplace, where the demonstrations of loyalty were especially fervent. While the others ate, I wrote a gaudy account of the President's triumphal journey, and a report of his plea for fighter aircraft. Then, while I ate some chicken and ham salad, Figueres himself walked to the local telegraph office to file my cables. He told the manager that they were to be dispatched as top-priority government messages and relayed without delay from San José to Baltimore. The President also left instructions that any future messages I might file were to be handled in the same way.

I realised that the President might not be pampering me for entirely altruistic reasons, but the experience was nonetheless delightful. To have exclusive access to the highest news source in the country would have been gratifying enough, but to be served by the President as chauffeur, interpreter and messenger — this, surely, was the ultimate in journalistic luxury. And the Costa

Rican cause, I felt comfortably confident, was a just one.

We arrived at advanced military headquarters, a pink-stuccoed fort in Liberia, late in the afternoon. The President introduced me to Colonel Marcel Aguiluz, an old professional warrior of the Caribbean Legion and now designated Costa Rica's military commander, although there was still no national army. His three-day black beard, dusty fatigues, bulging cartridge belt and low-slung holster gave him the appearance of a villain in a Western. But when he gripped my hand with a big, hairy, thickly padded paw and grinned he seemed more like a jolly pirate. I was glad he was on our side.

Figueres was in the fort's communications room, where bulletins were crackling through the command radio from Costa Rica's forward outpost, a farmhouse north of Santa Rosa, when we heard the drone of an approaching aircraft and the rattle of machinegun fire. The fort was being attacked again by a Thunderbolt. I suspected that it came from the same base, Managua, as the unidentified Thunderbolts that had flown, under CIA auspices, against Arbenz.

Costa Rican small arms banged and chattered ineffectually from the roof of the fort. The Thunderbolt climbed and turned and dived at us again. This time we heard bullets thud into the stucco across the inner courtyard, where swearing cooks were manning a field kitchen that had been established to feed the garrison's rein-forcements. Figueres was indignant: 'We must get some fast planes to put an end to this!' An aide urged the President to take shelter below the stairs.

'How will I know what's going on, if I leave this room?' Figueres demanded.

'But, sir, it is possible that the plane may shoot through the windows.'

'We will compromise,' the President said. 'Look: we will sit on the floor beneath this excellent table.'

There was another snarl of the diving plane and a chaos of ground fire, and the President's voice for a moment was inaudible.

'. . . procure a tiny air force,' he said.

'You should keep saying that publicly,' I urged him with some emotion.

'Yes,' he agreed. 'Certainly. You may quote me in any words you like. Just make this meaning clear: we urgently need some planes. But don't report that I'm in Liberia or Somoza will attack it all the more. He's not a strategist; he's just mad.'

Perhaps because it was running out of fuel – it did not seem to have been disturbed by our defences – the Thunderbolt turned north. The cooks returned to their cauldrons, and the President and I were able to emerge, rather stiff-legged, from under the table. The President occupied himself with maps and I did some more typing.

On the way back to San José, the President wrote an order entitling me to the use of a government Land Rover.

When I telephoned the President the next day he was jubilant.

'It's wonderful!' he exclaimed. 'We're going to El Coco Airport. You should be there. In about one hour, we shall receive four American fighter planes – F-51 Mustangs! Mustangs are very fast, aren't they?'

'A lot faster than Thunderbolts,' I assured him. 'Mustangs have Rolls Royce Merlin engines.'

'Rolls Royce!' the President marvelled. 'Wonderful! You must come to meet them. Ambassador Woodward will be there too.'

President Figueres, Madame Figueres and the whole Costa Rican cabinet were at El Coco to greet the incoming Texas Air National Guard Mustangs.

'They're beautiful, beautiful, beautiful!' the President's wife cried out, so excited that she forgot to take pictures with her new movie camera.

The Minister of Finance gave the President an envelope. 'Here's the four bucks for our air force,' the minister said. In deference to some sort of international protocol, the United States were not *giving* the warplanes to Costa Rica.

'I don't think we're going to have to raise the price of coffee to pay for them,' Figueres said.

My story was so many hours ahead of the Associated Press that one of my editors contacted me to make sure I had a secure grasp of reality.

Hostile military aircraft were not seen again over Costa Rica. With the help of the Mustangs, flown by Costa Rican pilots (airline pilots? crop-dusting pilots?), land fighting was concluded almost immediately. I felt that the *Sun* had legitimately made history.

The crucial moment, as I envisioned it, occurred when Secretary of State John Foster Dulles, over breakfast the day before the planes were delivered, had read President Figueres's anguished plea. Even though his mouth might have been full of toast, Dulles must have grabbed a telephone and called the White House.

'Ike,' Dulles must have said, 'have you read Catling's article — President Figueres's request for planes?'

'Of course I have, Foster. I was going to call you. What d'you think?'

'A persuasive case. I think we ought to send help,' Dulles must have advised.

'I think so too,' President Eisenhower must have said. 'I'll get on to Defense about it right away. Whew! I don't know what we'd do without that Catling.'

'Me neither,' Dulles must have confessed.

34

My next domestic interlude on the *Sun* included a few months of writing editorials, in which, of course, I was required to write as 'we', expressing the Olympian collective will of the paper. The *Sun* in the mid-1950s classified itself as an Independent Democratic newspaper, though it had not endorsed a Democrat for the Presidency since Roosevelt's second term. The paper's policy – the publisher's policy, based, no doubt, on his feelings about taxation – was cautiously conservative, except in its occasional liberal concessions to other nations' colonies. Like most other reporters on major American newspapers, I found myself out of harmony with many editorial opinions. However, as the most junior of editorial writers, I never had to write on political subjects of any importance. I was able to maintain an illusion of integrity by regarding the experience as only a literary exercise.

For a short time, I was amused by my counterfeit pomposity. I assumed in my prose the slow, deliberate, heavy-breathing manner of Colonel Blimp, appraising with controlled outrage or benign whimsy such subjects as the trend in gubernatorial proclamations, the production of synthetic gasoline from peanuts, the decline of the stork in popular mythology, an electrical device for repelling barnacles from ships' bottoms, and the principle that finders are keepers.

The hours were pleasant. We, the editorial we, arrived at our air-conditioned cubicle, a cell in a row of cells, at about 10.30 in the morning and read the newspapers in time for a conference in the editor's office before a leisurely luncheon. The editor-in-chief at the time was a decent gentleman dressed like a senior banker. He was no longer young. The conference was a one-sided affair. He gently but firmly imposed his long-cherished prejudices on a variety of topics, and we carried them to our typewriter for processing by the end of the afternoon. It was possible to leave the office by 5 o'clock. The routine was a restful one, and I detected in the non-editorial me a metaphorical broadening of the rump, a deepening of the jowls. I might have come to regard myself as a leader of the community if my salary had been substantially more than $120 a week. Middle-class penury saved me from the sin of pride.

Late in the summer of 1955 I was allowed to return to the cynical frivolity of the local reporting staff. After the discipline of the editorial chambers, I enjoyed the anarchic freedom of choosing subjects for feature articles. The local editor had apparently given up trying to restrict me to covering news. There were days of fanciful eccentricity. Bishop Charles Manuel Sweet Daddy Grace, a millionaire itinerant evangelist, introduced me to his devoted entourage of nubile 'angels', and baptised me (and some others) with a fire-hose. Miss Gloria Vanderbilt, recently liberated from a senile symphony conductor, told me about her love poems. 'Happiness', she wrote, 'a wing ding is.' James Margaritis, the proprietor of the bar closest to the *Sun*, consented to donate to Mayor D'Alesandro the deeds I had procured to five acres on the scenic south-west corner of the great lunar crater Copernicus. I got the deeds by mail-order, having noticed a classified advertisement in a paper sold at a supermarket check-out counter. Baltimore thus became the first city in the United States to possess a municipal park on the Moon. The Mayor, in grateful appreciation, conferred upon me a Certificate of Merit bearing the golden paper seal of the City of Baltimore, designating me 'an honored and outstanding citizen of Baltimore, worthy of high recognition for contributions to the civic welfare of our community'. Politics was easy, once you knew how.

Then one evening, not for my paper, I was able to see and hear Billie Holiday.

I had fallen in love with her a long time before, in the Downbeat, on 52nd Street, when she was twenty-seven and I was seventeen. She was then a many-splendoured figure of a woman, strong and beautiful, upright and proud and joyful. In those days, she sang a lot of up-beat, happy songs, such as 'What a Little Moonlight Can Do' and 'Them There Eyes', and smiled. When she sang the occasional sad song about betrayal she was defiant. Her emotional power, investing even the most banal popular lyrics with her ironic sensitivity, raised the performance of every jazz musician who accompanied her, as they, especially Teddy Wilson and Lester Young, raised hers.

In his expert and affectionate analysis of 'why Billie Holiday is unique in all the annals of jazz' the late Benny Green wrote: 'In "One, Two, Button Your Shoe", made in the vintage days with Bunny Berigan and Irving Fazola, she virtually abandons the written line completely, using harmonies whose names she did not know, to build a new, sleeker melodic line which reduced the number of pitches by more than half, until a phrase like "tell me you get a thrill", originally linked syllable by syllable to the arpeggio of the major seventh with the major sixth thrown in to make up the number, emerges through the voice simply as the actual note of the major seventh and not its arpeggio, repeated four times, exactly as Lester Young might have played it, or any competent jazzman of experience.'

In 1942 I did not understand those technical reasons that she sounded wonderful, and I still don't. Like Lester Young, whom she called Pres, who named her Lady Day, I loved her beyond reason on that rarefied, top level that men describe as Platonic, when they can't have what they want. As I was about to enlist, at a time when it was difficult to imagine that the war would ever end, she seemed to represent a feminine warmth I thought I would soon leave, perhaps for ever. I did not anticipate the bar-girls of Brazil and Marcia Lucas.

Billie Holiday died in New York in 1959. The police made her last moments cruelly painful by arresting her on her death-bed, for possession of narcotics. In the late 1950s, however, even when she was obviously mortally ill, she continued to make brief, annual, unpublicised visits to her original home-town, Baltimore. When, by chance, I learned very late that she was there, I hurried to hear her sing. This was my first chance, and the last, since those magical times twelve or thirteen years earlier. In those few years, we both changed in many ways.

The venue now was a small club in the black ghetto of north-west Baltimore. As the taxi drove up Pennsylvania Avenue in the rain, I did not expect much of a welcome, and I did not get one. I didn't flash my press card when the doorman halted me. He was not at all like the man outside Ronnie Scott's in Soho, who, Ronnie used to say in his invariable introductory routine, was 'the only bouncer who throws people *in*'. But after a short, silent scrutiny, I was permitted to enter the dim, smoky room where the music was. I was unceremoniously seated at a table by myself, several rows back from the elevated stand within the hollow rectangle of the bar.

Looking around rather furtively, I saw that in all that crowded room I was the only white. Men and women at nearby tables scrupulously avoided eye-contact with me. I tried to concentrate on Lady Day and her trio.

In her customary simple long white dress, she was statuesque, but the statue had diminished. She had been buxom; she had become scrawny. The dress was cut low enough to reveal the emaciation of her shoulders and the stark prominence of her collar-bones. Her upswept hair was decorated, as usual, with a gardenia above her left ear, but her face was shockingly different. She was haggard. Her eyes looked tired and anguished.

I recognised familiar songs – 'Yesterdays', 'Without Your Love', 'Ain't Nobody's Business' and 'Please Don't Talk About Me When I'm Gone' – but her vivacity had faded. Her voice was hoarse and tremulous and yet, more than ever, profoundly moving. Frailty squeezed extra significance from every melancholy word.

Close to two o'clock, she sang the song with which she usually concluded the night-club performances of her final years. 'Strange Fruit' was not merely a song; it was a passionate protest against lynching:

> Southern trees bear a strange fruit,
> Blood on the leaves and blood at the root.
> Black bodies swinging in the Southern breeze,
> Strange fruit hanging from the poplar trees.

It got worse:

> Pastoral scene of the gallant South,
> The bulging eyes and the twisted mouth,
> Scent of magnolia, sweet and fresh,
> Then the sudden smell of burning flesh.

She almost choked on the last line:

> Here is a strange and bitter crop.

When she finished, she first stood motionless and silent. Everybody was silent. I suffered an agony of paranoia, hardly able to breathe, sure that they all hated and despised me.

And then there was a miracle.

Billie Holiday, who had often been subjected to white bigotry and discrimination, particularly when touring America with the Artie Shaw band, somehow extra-sensorially perceived my predicament, as if she could read my mind, although we had never met. She quickly descended from the stand, the goddess from the machine, crossed to my table, and gave me a great, big kiss on the lips.

The whole room seemed to sigh with relief. Normal conversation resumed. She sat beside me. A waiter brought a bottle of gin.

We drank.

Billie Holiday and I sat drinking together until after closing time. Billie Holiday and I . . .

35

Opportunism is a word with shoddy connotations, yet for journalists it is the paramount way of life. My sense of national identity was already chameleonic, so, when I learned that the *Sun*, though Anglophilic, conferred the title Chief of the London Bureau only upon citizens of the United States, it was not temperamentally difficult for me to assume citizenship. I had retained the status of resident alien even in long absences during wars. Complete, formal Americanisation was accomplished in the briefest of legal ceremonies, in Baltimore in February 1956.

In the same month, with a new passport, I sailed first-class aboard the *Queen Elizabeth* from New York to Southampton. Suddenly I was one of the most affluent people I knew. I travelled on my own, dining gluttonously in black tie in the Veranda Grill. English cuisine, or French cuisine under English auspices, had made spectacular progress since the lean days of rabbit pie and dehydrated eggs. By the end of five days of truffles, béarnaise sauce and brandy butter, I was reminded of the Pont cartoon of a sulky débutante despondently looking down at her plate and saying: 'Gosh! Quails in aspic again.' Susan and our daughters, Sheila and Ellen, were to follow a few weeks later, when I was supposed to be settled.

London Correspondent, the very apotheosis of an American

newspaper career! London is the greatest newspaper city on earth, in the sense that more newspapers of national circulation and international significance are published there than anywhere else. London performs for England the functions that Washington, New York and Los Angeles together perform for the United States. In England, government, commerce and the arts are all concentrated in one place. The principal language spoken and written in London is English. Greenwich Mean Time is five hours ahead of Eastern Standard Time. Reports from London easily beat American deadlines. In London, it is almost impossible to miss major news stories, unless everyone else also misses them, and then they are not news. News is what is reported.

Nearly ten years had passed since the last time I had left London. I returned with the nostalgia of a native and the wide-eyed enthusiasm of a friendly alien. I had lived there before as a schoolboy and had stayed there as a serviceman on leave. Now I was able to penetrate the life of the place more generally and more intimately, partly because I was an adult and a civilian, mainly because I was a journalist. Although all classes of people in London were voracious readers of newspapers, reporters as a group were not universally respected there. They had not the high standing that reporters could attain in Washington. Britons on the whole were less sophisticated and calculating than Americans about how to achieve favourable relations with the public. Die-hards in London still resisted invasions of privacy. Vulgarity in the press was still deplored as often as it occurred – every day. Libel actions were taken against newspapers for offensive allegations that would have passed almost unnoticed in Broadway columns. British judges and juries tended to favour the plaintiffs in that sort of case. But in spite of certain reservations, London opened most of its doors to newspapermen; and the more important doors opened more readily than some of the lesser ones.

An increased salary, a cost-of-living allowance, a company car and an apparently unlimited expense account enabled me to rent a pleasantly furnished flat in Knightsbridge conveniently close to Harrods. London at that time was a grey city of Portland stone and red brick, darkened by soot and weathered pale at the edges. This was before the time of towers with glass façades. The streets were not yet almost paralysed by too much traffic. To me, the red buses and black taxis looked as handsome as ceremonial military parades. Everything gloriously glittered in my eyes. I wondered why I had stayed away so long.

While gaslights were popping into flame in the blue dusk of late afternoon, I called on Dr W. R. Matthews, the dean of St Paul's, and Mrs Matthews, at the Wren deanery. 'I remember the time', Mrs Matthews said, as she carefully sliced through lemon icing, 'when an architect warned me that the house might at any moment collapse – and the Queen Mother was expected for tea. "How awful it would be", I thought, "if the Queen Mother were to fall through the floor into the kitchen sink." I'm sure she would have been most gracious about it, but she might not have come to tea again.'

I heard about economic decline from bankers at their port and Stilton in the cheerful fug of the George & Vulture, a small seventeenth-century chophouse in the City. There were conversations with Foreign Office spokesmen over Aylesbury duck and claret at Simpson's in the Strand, with R. H. S. Crossman, MP, over pink gins in the House of Commons, with Frank Allaun, MP, in Kettner's restaurant in Soho. 'Do you realise that this dinner is costing more than most of my constituents earn in a whole week?' Allaun balefully asked, as his glass was refilled. Julian Amery, MP, showed me in his library 'a reminder of a danger we mustn't forget', a photograph of an Egyptian chess player, President Gamal Abdel Nasser.

I drove the pea-green Ford Anglia along Downing Street and through a dark archway into the Foreign Office courtyard and parked beside official black limousines. Two policemen watched disinterestedly as I lifted and dropped the heavy knocker against the black door of Number 10.

William Clarke, Prime Minister Sir Anthony Eden's press secretary, received me in his plainly elegant office. How was Patrick O'Donovan getting on in Washington? Clarke wanted to know. Had I had a smooth crossing? Would I prefer tea or coffee? The room was silent for a few moments, except for the delicate chink of silver against china. Clarke fingered the knot of his grey silk tie. 'Incidentally,' he said, 'you've come at an interesting time. Actually, there's a sort of crisis.' He spoke as gravely as Bertie Wooster might have announced the misplacement of a collar stud. 'The Jordanians have just sacked Glubb.'

It was ominous that my first article from London was an account of the ousting of Lieutenant General John Bagot Glubb, Glubb Pasha, from command of the Arab Legion. Although I was now a London correspondent and wanted nothing more than to preoccupy myself with the charming minutiae of the immediate environment, I was no better able than Britain itself to avoid spending much, and then more, and then almost all the time considering the growing threats of Arab nationalists in the Middle East.

One of Eden's ancestors was a Governor Eden of Maryland. The Prime Minister seemed kindly disposed to a newspaperman from Baltimore, and I was invited to be one of the small group of American correspondents who visited Number 10 once a week for suave brain-washing. On one such occasion, he himself stirred shakerful after shakerful of excellent dry martinis (he prided himself on their New World authenticity), and told us, as he had told Nikolai Bulganin and Nikita Khrushchev, that if anyone interfered with Britain's access to their main sources of oil, Britain would fight. Lady Eden said she felt as if the Nile were flowing through her drawing room.

There was still a little time for minor pleasures. I wrote about Lord Windlesham's lament for the decline of practical joking, the Icelandic general election, the Henley Royal Regatta, the Anglo-New Zealand croquet test matches, and Nina Ponomareva's theft of five hats from a West End shop. But soon after President Nasser expropriated the Suez Canal, I flew to Cairo. The diplomats were still talking, but preparations were being made for another war.

36

War is an unpopular way of settling economic conflicts of interest. I have never met anybody who advocated it, except as a defensive response to unreasonable leaders on the other side. Nations devote a large part of their wealth to building vast arsenals to maintain a balance of terror. But sometimes 'the situation', as it is called, deteriorates to the point at which peace-loving statesmen are honour-bound to let war happen.

'Speak to me not as an American to an Egyptian,' begged Sayed El Gabry, the proprietor of Azhar Bazaar, a small Cairene gift shop specialising in brass trays and embroidered cushions. 'We are both human,' he said. 'Speak to me the truth, as brother to brother. Will there be war?'

His shop looked so desolate – I was the only potential customer that morning – that I hadn't the heart to talk about the growing concentration at Aldershot of tanks painted the colour of the desert, the paratroops clambering aboard air transports at Blackbushe aerodrome, the naval reinforcements at Malta, the troops alerted on Cyprus.

'No war,' I said. 'Everything will be fixed by talking.'

'No war!' he echoed. He seized upon the assurance, although neither of us was truly convinced. 'That is what the Congressman from the Philippines said yesterday,' another authoritative prophet. 'War is bad for all peoples.'

The bearded merchant contrived a smile and clapped his hands, as though ordering a celebration. A few moments later a barefoot young man in a white gown and a brown skullcap slapped into the dim back room with a salver bearing glasses of bright yellow lemonade for me and my guide.

'It is hospitality,' said our host. 'There is no charge. You have made me glad. Things will improve this week? Business is very bad for us now. But soon Gamal Abdel Nasser will make everything all right.'

'Hmmm,' I said. 'How much are the dressing gowns?' Correspondents traditionally return home with gifts. Sayed El Gabry politely began the probe and withdrawal of Oriental bargaining.

Moses, who wore an armband identifying him as an 'Official Dragoman', a splendid figure with distinguished grey hair, a grand, aquiline nose and the sticky persistence of a horsefly or camelfly, guided me away from the bazaar to visit pyramids and mosques.

We drove out to Mena House for lunch. The last time I had been there senior British army officers and their pneumatic mistresses had been dancing on the terrace. Now the hotel was empty but for waiters in white gowns, red cummerbunds and red fezzes, standing about waiting for people to wait on.

I relayed the bazaar proprietor's anxious question to the Sphinx, and the Sphinx told me as much as I had learned from the Ministry of National Guidance.

Moses took me to the Mohammed Ali Mosque and preached against the decadence of ex-King Farouk. From a parapet we gazed down at a low-lying panorama of greyish-ochre buildings and the brownish Nile glimmering mercurially through heat haze and pollution.

'One day,' Moses said proudly, 'we have new dam, all you see covered with water, grow plenty food, everybody live in nice new house in the mountains with air condition.'

Moses spoke sharply to an old man holding out a supplicatory hand. We got back into the car.

After my last infra-red treatment in a Catholic hospital for a poisonous bite that I had suffered when sitting on a spider, I arranged to go on to Suez. I was supposed to be filing features while staying close to the probable centre of imminent events. A taxi took me across the desert to Port Tewfik, the southern terminus of the Suez Canal. Fortunately, the British consul there was an old acquaintance, Joseph Mulvenny, who had served as the consul in Baltimore for several years. British women and children had been sent home from Port Tewfik, always a sure sign that trouble was scheduled, and there were many vacant rooms in his dazzling white new consulate on the west bank of the canal.

'Sitting on my balcony, I can see both Africa and Asia,' he pointed out in the flat voice of a man who had long since tired of the view. Egyptian police in crumpled white uniforms leaned on their rifles in the shade of palm trees.

'I give them cigarettes,' Mulvenny said. 'They're not bad fellows. But we're all beginning to get a bit irritable. It hasn't rained for ten months. The midday temperature recently reached 114.' He mopped his brow at the thought. 'The mango tree that the Bishop planted when he dedicated the consulate last spring is still all right, but if we leave I doubt that the Gyppos will water it. Shall we have a whisky?'

British shipping agents and oil company engineers came over for dinner. One of the agents made some telephone calls and arranged to get me aboard a ship that would be heading for Port Said the following day. We all went to the French Club, abandoned but for the bartender and waiters, and we had a pessimistic party on the patio.

'This used to be very gay,' Mulvenny said.

I drank arak, defined by Chambers as 'an ardent spirit used in the East, procured from toddy, or the fermented juice of the coco and other palms, as well as from rice and jaggery sugar.' It was like drinking a mixture of Pernod and napalm.

'If only they'd play some music,' someone said.

'The orchestra's broken up,' Mulvenny dolefully informed him.

'They've got a loudspeaker system. How about requesting "Nearer My God to Thee"?'

But the first record, played very loud, was 'Rock Around the Clock'. We became slightly manic as time ran out.

John Walters, of the London *Daily Mirror*, met by chance, and I visited Bethlehem together.

'Business is very bad here,' said Bishara Canavati, the mayor, director of the Bethlehem Chamber of Commerce and president of the Bethlehem Lions Club. 'Last year we had a quarter million visitors — twenty-eight thousand Americans. Wonderful year. They spent plenty money, bought plenty things.' Now, if it had not been for the export business (he supplied US Army post exchanges from Frankfurt to Tokyo), he said, his souvenir factory might have had to close down. As things were, he had already been obliged to get rid of some of the assembly-line girls who made the mother-of-pearl crucifixes.

'We hoped Point Four Programme would build a nice, big hotel beside the Church of the Nativity,' he said, indicating the church courtyard. 'A hotel would be a big attraction. All the modern churches are in Jerusalem. We need one. Think how sensational! Visitors could stay close to the exact, genuine spot where Jesus Christ was born.'

An Arab accosted Walters and me in a dingy café, where we were sharing a quart bottle of Stella beer, brewed in Egypt. The Arab said he had heard we were journalists. Would we be interested to know that there was much discontent, talk of a strike, in Mayor Canavati's factory? Walters wearily passed over a small sum

of money and we got a small story. It had been suggested that the
workers should steal the bells from the Church of the Nativity at
the time of the annual Christmas broadcast, thus calling the attention of the West to the plight of refugee artisans from Palestine.

'What other countries are there?' I asked Walters.

'There's always Lebanon. The Switzerland of the Middle East.'

We flew to Beirut.

Beirut's a good place to get laundry done.

I went by taxi to Aley, a gambling resort in the hills near the
capital. I had an appointment with ex-Queen Narriman of Egypt,
who was living in exile in a villa there.

She looked like a superannuated movie starlet who had been
eating too many marshmallows. Her face was like a beige silk
cushion. She had beautiful, pouting, fat lips, like the lips of an
unhappy African angel. She was wearing a skin-tight yellow sweater,
a charcoal-grey ballerina skirt, yellow shoes and a gold ring bearing
a topaz the size of a lump of sugar. She sat in a gold-brocaded
Empire chair, in front of Flemish tapestry nudes, beneath a glittering chandelier and beside a recent pastel portrait of herself, done
before she had changed her hair from ash-blonde to dark henna.

She whispered huskily that she had arrived at a momentous deci-
sion: she had renounced romantic love for all time. Wasn't twenty-
two a bit young to be giving up love? No, she said; she was going
to consecrate herself to maternal devotion to her son. Where was
he? At the moment he was with his governess, in the Lebanon of
Europe.

How did she feel about ex-King Farouk? She said she did not
wish to throw mud at him, though she was still a little sore about
having been forced to leave most of her jewellery and most of her
clothes, including an unrivalled collection of lingerie, with his
library of erotica, in Cairo. She sighed, and her bust measurement
shrank to about 40 inches.

'But I have hopes that President Nasser one day will restore the
monarchy – he is very anti-Communist,' the ex-queen said. 'And

then, of course, my son will be recognised as the King of Egypt.'
Exiled royalty always cherish a belief that they will be restored to
their thrones, one day.

I flew to Israel, by way of Cyprus.

Menachem Begin, the leader of Herut, Israel's most militant
opposition party, received me in his office in Tel Aviv. He said he
and his colleagues were agitating for an all-out attack against Egypt.
Like General LeMay and President George W. Bush, Jr., Begin was
an advocate of the pre-emptive strike. 'The best defence is attack,'
he pointed out.

Back in London, I sought the comments of the leader of the
Labour Party. Hugh Gaitskell let me join him at a dinner meeting
in Hendon. His primary concern was Soviet savagery in Hungary.
He did not seem to share Eden's anxiety about the Suez Canal.

I had been in London almost two days when it was reported
that the Israeli Army was moving into the Sinai Desert. On the
telephone my managing editor sounded surprisingly patient. He
said that everyone else had been caught flat-footed too. At dawn
the next day I was in yet another plane, on the way to Tel Aviv.

Donald Wise, of the London *Daily Express*, said he was glad to
see me back, because he needed somebody non-competitive to share
the cost of retaining a taxi on call twenty-four hours a day.

'This is a very expensive little war,' he said. 'You've got to keep
your room at the Dan Hotel; you've got to come back to Tel Aviv
every night to file. There's no censorship or communications in the
field – wherever the field is right now. The Israelis are moving so
fast they aren't letting correspondents go all the way forward with
them. They are issuing quite good communiqués at headquarters,
though, and you can pick up some colour in a few hours on the
road to Sinai.'

Once again I experienced the guilty pleasures of being a witness
without being a partisan at a time of crucial action. Orange juice,

scrambled eggs, hot-buttered toast and black coffee on the balcony of an air-conditioned bedroom overlooking the Mediterranean; a quick swim; then, in sports shirt and Bermuda shorts, with paper and pencil and picnic hamper, off to war in a taxi . . . It was an American taxi, two-toned, chrome-laden, with a radio. An enthusiastic Israeli disc jockey was playing everything martial he could lay his hands on. Wise and I lolled on soft cushions and the radio blared 'Praise the Lord and Pass the Ammunition', a Tin Pan Alley top-ten hit from World War II, as we were driven past women in uniform carrying weapons.

We visited a kibbutz about half a mile from the Gaza Strip. The Israeli Army was about to take Gaza. Israeli jets flew low over the irrigated green Israeli fields and over the sand dunes and palm groves of Egyptian territory. 'For eight years I have waited to march along the road to Gaza,' said an Israeli with fierce blue eyes and a sun-bleached yellow beard. 'Today we are going to do so.' Wise and I walked with them.

We walked through an Arab village that had been abandoned so hastily that there was burnt food on a cooking stove. There was some machinegunning, some mortar fire, almost all outgoing. We saw one dead Palestinian soldier.

Another day we drove as far as we were allowed into the Sinai, to within a few miles of the Suez Canal. The roads were littered with destroyed and damaged Soviet equipment.

The story shifted to the United Nations. In the Israeli sector of Jerusalem, Major General E. L. M. Burns of Canada, who had been ordered to organise a United Nations Emergency Force to occupy the Suez Canal Zone, advised me to go to Naples to join the first UN troops when they assembled there for the journey into Egypt.

I flew to Rome. I rode in a train to Naples. The United Nations spokesman there said that correspondents would have to make their own way into Egypt and could apply for accreditation to the UNEF in Cairo. The Egyptian consul general, in a decrepit mansion high above the Bay of Naples, suggested a ship from Naples to Benghazi, in Libya, from where I might be able to travel by train and bus to Cairo. He gave me two personal letters and asked me to post them when I got there, and I assured him I would be glad to try. I flew from Naples to Valletta. In Malta, I boarded a British European Airways Elizabethan bound for Benghazi. The plane ordinarily carried forty-eight passengers, but that day I was the only one. The stewardess gave me the customary briefing on how to don a life jacket and offered me barley sugar before take-off. In flight, the captain sent back a position report addressed to me alone. In Benghazi I chartered a taxi to take me to the Egyptian border. The drive was a delirious one, fast, on broken springs, along a winding, switchback road, across a lunar landscape, in mist and moonlight. At the border, a few miles west of Salum, by luck I picked up a Cairo taxi that had brought a French refugee out of Egypt and was about to return to the capital. Apart from being arrested as a spy near Alexandria and held at bayonet-point by a sentry who spoke only Arabic, I reached Cairo uneventfully.

Distance, time and money by then had lost most of their normal significance. The investment seemed worth making, until I reached the Semiramis Hotel on the Nile and saw the vague faces of United Nations officers sitting in the lobby, waiting, as though for an unscheduled train to an unknown destination.

Fred Sparks, of course, eventually turned up. No international muddle reported on front pages was complete without him. He looked strangely younger than in Guatemala. 'The toupée', he pointed out, 'makes a difference.' In New York, he had recently written a column on the advantages of false hair, and America's foremost manufacturer of wigs and toupées had presented him with a realistic Ivy League toupée, a middle-aged one, grizzled and apparently beginning to grow out and bend flat in front.

Sparks sometimes wore the toupée; sometimes he left it off.

When wearing it, he told strangers in an anxious, confidential whisper that if they ever encountered his older brother in the bar they should not be alarmed: he was perfectly harmless, and he, Sparks-with-hair, would pay any debts incurred by the bald Sparks. The toupée engendered more drama than was to be detected in the establishment of the United Nations Emergency Force. A chambermaid saw the toupée crouching menacingly on a chair in Sparks's bedroom and almost screamed the roof off. Sparks himself momentarily panicked when a kite dived at him when he was eating lunch on his balcony. The big bird swooped and grabbed half a chicken off Sparks's plate. 'What a relief,' he said afterwards. 'I thought it was after my hairpiece.'

The *Statue of Liberty*, an oil tanker, was stuck with other ships in the Canal. Sparks and I got permission from the new Egyptian canal authority at Ismailia to go aboard the tanker to interview the captain. He was in the middle of reading *War and Peace*.

Sparks and I spent an evening sailing in a felucca on the Nile. The swarthy master of the small boat grinned wickedly as his crew, a small boy, handed him his hubble-bubble and took over the tiller. 'In the old time,' the ancient mariner said, settled in a nest of dirty cushions, 'everybody all time go to gay house, gamble, smoke hashish, love gorls. Too much gorls, too much money, verra nice. Now Gamal Abdel Nasser say: "Everybody got to work; everybody got to fight for new Egypt."' The only people in the new Egypt easily able to indulge in the old vices, the master concluded, were officers of the armed forces and the police. As he lapsed gradually into a blissful stupor, he reminisced about the tourists he had entertained aboard his felucca. He said his favourite patrons were rich American ladies of a certain age . . .

Captain George Mendes, a Columbian infantry officer seconded to the United Nations, seemed to speak for many of his colleagues and for several correspondents when he spoke of Korea as 'the good old days'. 'There we had authority,' he said wistfully.

There are very few happy memories of the Middle East of that period, and those are overwhelmed by the central fact that justice, unfortunately, prevailed. Anybody believing in the rule of law, yet not sympathising with President Nasser, was sure to come away from Egypt feeling schizophrenic, in addition to suffering from the famous digestive disorders of the region.

37

My journalistic ambition was perceptibly shrinking. Getting my by-line on front-page news stories no longer seemed to matter very much. Not having taken an official holiday during my first year as London correspondent, I was entitled to six weeks off and made the most of them. With an *au pair* girl to take care of our children, we went skiing in Austria and swimming in Spain. There was purple prose in my diary after I hissed downhill through powder-snow between conifers toward a sunlit Tyrolean village; sipped mulled claret on a terrace; floated in the Mediterranean as the sun shone orange through closed eyelids; drove past the dull glare of olive groves and eroded rock in the dazzle of midday, into the cool, dim green tunnel of a sudden avenue of trees; walked between white-washed wineries and cottages and into a dark Catalonian church with a single window of red glass like an inspired shout of revelation. Gosh! I felt I might soon be ready to write a sonnet.

Back on duty, I spent much time with innumerable other reporters in a shepherded flock, processing communiqués and intelligence from 'informed sources' and 'diplomatic observers'. It was necessary, and sometimes interesting, to sit in the press gallery of the House of Commons, especially during preliminary question times. ('Is the Minister aware that since the installation of atomic reactors at Windscale there has been a diminution of migratory flights of wild birds into the surrounding countryside?') But for every five days in Westminster and Whitehall I spent two days elsewhere, often outside London. The *Sun's* correspondent was required to write a Sunday column about odds and ends, not necessarily connected with momentous current happenings.

There was an opportunity to try Evelyn Waugh's ear-trumpet. The *Spectator* threw a party every month in its spacious old office in Gower Street. The guests, most of them invited, were a volatile mix, including all sorts of politicians and writers, as well as the publisher and editors of the magazine. Waugh attended one of these parties, having come up to London from the house in Somerset where he was playing the part of a country gentleman. At the party, wearing the loud, tweed country-gentleman suit with which he teased fellow Londoners still compelled to work in London, he flourished an ear-trumpet of antique design, a symbol of grand-old-boy decrepitude. Patricia Gale, whose husband George later became the editor of the *Spectator*, snatched the ludicrous hearing aid from its owner and passed it around while Waugh's mock irascibility became almost apoplectically genuine. After I had my turn sticking the trumpet in my ear, Waugh complained how disgusted he was by 'all the alien wax'. However, the next day, when he was Christina Foyle's guest of honour at a literary lunch to celebrate the publication of *The Ordeal of Gilbert Pinfold*, his autobiographical novel about paranoiac hallucinations caused by excessive brandy and sleeping draughts, I saw he was still using the ear-trumpet as a prop. Perhaps he had had it sterilised. He listened attentively to a series of eulogies, and ostentatiously removed it only during the principal speech in his praise, which was delivered by Malcolm Muggeridge, of whom he disapproved.

I marched with Vivien Leigh with banners deploring the plan to raze the St James's Theatre. I witnessed her impassioned cries of protest from the public gallery of the House of Commons, watched her perform with her husband, Laurence Olivier, in

Shakespeare's worst play, *Titus Andronicus*, and consoled her with lunch at Caprice, where she spent most of our mealtime visiting admirers at other tables.

Yves Klein, a French monochromatic abstractionist, told me he was experimenting on the relationships between colours, sounds and smells. He was working on 'the blue smell' of lapis lazuli, and had high hopes of setting it to music.

Madame Pandit seated me at her right hand during a splendid luncheon in her mansion in Kensington Palace Gardens, and explained the causes of starvation in Indian villages. As peasant women were reluctant to use mechanical contraceptive devices, the government distributed strings of red and white beads indicating periods when sexual intercourse would not cause pregnancy. The women were instructed to move one bead a day to mark the days of the month, but 'unfortunately', Madame Pandit said, 'they sometimes impatiently moved the beads to satisfy their desires.'

Anthony Crosland, the socialist economist who later became Britain's Foreign Secretary until his death, fed me steak pie and strawberry mousse in the fellows' dining room at Trinity College, Oxford. Gaitskell also was present. After lunch, the three of us walked to Blackwell's bookshop. Gaitskell asked a salesman for a copy of *The Future of Socialism*, Crosland's authoritative right-wing Labour Party forecast that attained complete fulfilment under Tony Blair. I heard the salesman mutter to a colleague, 'If Gaitskell doesn't know its future, who does?' The question seemed funny at the time. Crosland became acquainted with my wife while I was away in the Middle East. When I returned and met him, I used to give him pairs of front-stall tickets to opera and ballet, art forms that did not interest me. He used to take Susan for cultural soirées and they got to know each other better.

38

Crosland gave us a farewell party in his flat in South Kensington. 'I have invited one or two economists,' he said, 'and a young man from Buenos Aires that nobody knows. Their presence will inhibit expressions of sentimentality without cutting down the drinking.' On the night, about twenty men and women turned up, including Hugh and Dora Gaitskell, Kingsley Amis and Lady Jane Heaton, a marquess's daughter who tended to sing Russian folk songs late at night. She had been warmly hospitable to me while Susan and Tony cultivated their affinity. Some time after four in the morning, when only the most dedicated guests lingered, tears were shed and promises of eternal friendship were exchanged. These pledges were endorsed the next evening: Tony and Jane surprisingly flew down to join us in Cannes for a lavish second farewell, before we boarded an Italian liner named after Christopher Columbus. Indulging in expense-account luxury as long as possible, I had arranged to sail first-class via Gibraltar to New York. The valedictory F. Scott Fitzgerald flourish was really rather pathetic, as I was about to revert to local reporting in Baltimore.

In those days, before the grasping Internal Revenue Service tightened its rules, United States citizens had their income tax refunded after staying abroad at least eighteen months. With a two-year refund, I was able to make the down-payment on our apartment.

The Baltimore Museum of Art, noted for its collection of Post-Impressionists, offered Susan an increased salary to return to the staff. I was informally assured that one day, before very long, I might be sent to Washington, perhaps to cover the State Department. The two lures were incongruous. In the meantime I would write whimsical little features. We would be secure for ever, and quite well off compared with most of my *Sun* contemporaries.

My stepfather, an elderly retired distiller who had done very well during Prohibition, invited my family to spend our summer holiday with him and my mother at his place on the Eastern Shore of the Chesapeake Bay. It was the grand sort of waterfront estate that my father, a journalist until death at the age of fifty-four, had never had the means to aspire to. We swam and water-skied, played croquet, ate terrapin and crabs and drank plenty of fine Chablis. In the mornings, I wrote most of a book about my newspaper days till then. William Manchester, who had a job on the *Evening Sun* while writing *Disturber of the Peace*, a biography of H. L. Mencken, and later made a fortune with *The Death of a President*, about the assassination of John F. Kennedy, introduced me to a New York literary agent and the book was eventually published, in New York and London, with astonishing ease but small monetary gain. In the meantime, on the Eastern Shore, we spent the evenings in a digestive coma, in the flickering glow of television Westerns. My stepfather admired John Wayne.

I wrote to Gerard Fay, the London editor of the *Manchester Guardian*, now the *Guardian*, and asked for a job. He said I should come on over. This time we sailed across the Atlantic in a one-class, 25,000-ton Cunarder from New York to Liverpool. Family travel without a salary and expense account was much less extravagant.

The *Manchester Guardian* was such a distinguished newspaper that it paid its people largely in prestige. For the sake of morale, we took with us a used but immaculate Buick Roadmaster convertible, dark green with a tan top. It did about twelve miles to the gallon.

I was able to keep it in London for several weeks before having to sell it.

In a small house in Fulham, our marriage lasted only a few weeks longer.

39

The London office of the *Manchester Guardian* was a dusty, comfortable suite of small rooms above the Fleet Street Post Office, opposite Fetter Lane. Although I was the ultimate link in a chain of command stretching all the way to Manchester, I was made to feel happily unfettered. The paper's honourable and humane tradition of liberal morality, inherited from C. P. Scott, permeated the whole organisation. Though inconveniently underpaid by Fleet Street standards, we shared an illusion of incorruptible loyalty, to the paper and to each other. There were other papers – not only tabloids – that had to pay much more to enable their employees to stomach unsavoury policies. On the *Guardian*, we were sometimes disgruntled but never ashamed.

In London there was an editorial staff of only about half a dozen men and a secretary, a young woman with the firm but gentle manner of a good nurse. Somehow, this small staff made the paper respected for its coverage and interpretation of national and international events. The style was serious, but idiosyncratic asides were not forbidden. We were a heterogeneous group of individuals whose originality was untrammelled, or very little trammelled; we were as free as possible within the limits of daily journalism.

For many years the *Guardian* and the Baltimore *Sun* had been congenial. During the darkest days early in World War II, it had been agreed that if Britain fell the *Sun* would publish a fugitive *Guardian* in Baltimore. Gerry Fay, an affable Irishman whose face had the lived-in appearance of Trevor Howard's near the end of his life, knew the *Sun* and its successive London correspondents well and was entirely sympathetic. The only instruction my new boss gave me was to write English. He said the paper avoided the use of foreign words. He approved of expertness, for example, not expertise; fellowship was preferred to camaraderie. There were no other stated rules; a certain harmony was achieved naturally.

Most of my colleagues were specialists, covering clearly defined beats, such as Parliament, the Foreign Office, the courts, and industry and commerce, especially as they were affected by the trades unions. The paper was also eminently concerned with the arts. There was a man who wrote mostly about music. The man who set a journalistic fashion in describing the proceedings of the House of Commons as though criticising a daily theatrical performance also reported publishing news and reviewed books. The regular theatre critic wrote authoritatively on the opera.

There was only one man-of-all-beats, assigned to write news features. I was given the same sort of general duties, on the periphery of every department. I enjoyed the vagueness and unlimited potential of my job. It meant that every day was a surprise. The secretary kept a diary listing invitations to a great variety of special events and access to many men and women of note. The time soon came when I was allowed to take my pick. There were opportunities for the quirkiness which the *Guardian* cherished, and more conventional papers overlooked. Some of the paragraphs in our London Letter were like anecdotes told by an eccentric don. I strove to develop this minuscule art form and achieved a gratifyingly high percentage of acceptances. Though I spent more and more time in search of choice morsels for the London Letter, the secretary came around to my desk at the beginning of each week, in her tour of the office to try to discover the staff's plans. As I had recently met

Peter Huen, a North Korean poet in exile in Paris, I repeatedly announced that I was going to continue my research into his work. After a while, the secretary routinely said, 'Korean poet?' thus recognising my wish to keep my options open. Gerry occasionally rewarded me for my contributions with unimportant excursions to the Continent – a tour of Belgium's famously unexciting provincial resorts, a wine-tasting in Beaune . . .

Most days, however, wine-tasting took place more conveniently at El Vino, the celebrated bar situated immediately next door to the office. Gerry was an habitual patron. I had already become equally devoted to the place when I was on the *Sun*. In those days of affluence, I had established apparently unlimited credit there, an unusual privilege, and still enjoyed it. Regular attendance from soon after midday until three o'clock, when Frank Bower, the proprietor, stentorianly demanded 'the company's glasses', was a delightful but insidious and expensive habit. It was useful as well, we told ourselves, because when Fleet Street was Fleet Street, before the dispersal of newspaper offices to Kensington, Wapping and the Isle of Dogs, El Vino was headquarters, where the gossip of the day inspired the next day's headlines. Journalists just back from foreign assignments made El Vino their first port of call, to find out what was going on in London. Henry Fairlie, Derek Marks, Donald Edgar, John Raymond and others were always ready to tell them.

There was a time, not very long ago, before the feminist revolution, when ladies, as they used to be called, were not permitted to drink at the bar; they had to sit at tables in the back. I often sat at the foremost of these with Philip Hope-Wallace, the *Guardian*'s drama critic, who was himself charmingly dramatic, a Balliol man of exquisitely cultivated literacy, who told wonderful stories, never repetitiously, in carefully wrought sentences, in a splendidly camp voice. A golden plaque, identifying the chair where he sat for his bottles of champagne, must baffle the present clientele, the stockbrokers, accountants, solicitors' clerks and Japanese tourists, who may now fortuitously glance at it.

Bower attempted to personify old-fashioned grandeur with a high collar, silk cravat, ornately embroidered waistcoat, black jacket and pin-striped trousers, but succeeded only in making himself a Dickensian figure of fun. Regular patrons teased him for his pomposity and parsimoniousness. He played up to this reputation, because he enjoyed attention. The more men laughed at him, the thinner he sliced the lemons for gin and tonic. When anyone requested extra bitters in a pink gin, he himself doled out the Angostura at a penny a drop. He was so pleased to see his name in print that when I wrote something about him that was not unflattering he astonished all who knew him by taking me to dine at his Catholic club in Pont Street – providing his own wine (a bottle of Château Margaux) and two Cox's Pippins to eat with our Stilton. Grumbling like W. C. Fields at his most misanthropic, he reluctantly conceded that a token payment for corkage might be added to his bill. And yet, at the same time, he was a lavish host, grandiloquently ordering the best of everything, with grand gestures.

In journalism, it is not difficult to achieve exclusivity if one picks subjects that nobody else thitherto ever bothered to investigate. When I expressed an interest in the man who beat the gong at the beginning of the current films produced by the J. Arthur Rank organisation, a Rank spokesman said he did not know who had conceived the animated trademark. He seemed uncertain that the gong-beater could be traced.

'Once it's done, it's done,' the spokesman said, 'and the personality who did it is finished. It's rather like trying to find what's happened to Leo, the M-G-M lion – probably turned into meat pies by now.'

However, at last I discovered Ken Richmond, a friendly, gigantic Jehovah's Witness, in high spirits in a terrace house in Mimosa Street in West London. At the age of thirty-three, he was still the amateur heavyweight wrestling champion of Britain and expected to wrestle again for his country in the next Olympic

Games. He had recently become a full-time minister of his new-found religion and travelled about to lecture Kingdom Hall meetings and Bible study groups. 'It's no good using your body if you don't use your mind,' he told me, as we drank mugs of tea beside a paraffin stove in his purple and orange kitchen, 'and it's no good using your mind if you don't use your body.' His wife Valentina, a former professional dancer and now a Jehovah's Witness, nodded in agreement. He used to do occasional stunt work, especially fight scenes, in films. He was offered jobs as a model, but modelling was 'much too boring'. By the time he was selected to beat the gong he had decided that he was 'not very keen on the film environment. It's a cut-throat rat-race.' He preferred preaching.

'But being a witness doesn't mean you have to wear sack-cloth and go around with a long face,' Richmond pointed out. 'We go to the cinema quite often. I like musicals and the better English comedies, such as Norman Wisdom's. Of course, it's funny seeing myself beating the gong. I always have a smile when I see it. We usually give each other a nudge, don't we, Val?'

He recalled the making of the gong-beating films as a day of hard work. 'I did it for conventional screens in black and white and in colour, and then in black and white and colour for wide screens. I wore orange panchromatic make-up – ordinary skin would come out wrong – and my back and arms were oiled. Of course, the stance and the slow motion are not really natural. I wouldn't really beat a gong like that, would you? But it's for the effect.' The timing of the strokes was important, he said, 'because they had to coincide exactly with recorded sound. The boom was dubbed in. The gong's a prop gong, made of plaster. I hope it won't spoil it for anyone, knowing that. I moved to the count of six – and at six the head of the hammer had to be there.'

There was no gong in the Richmonds' house. 'When the food's ready, Val just shouts.'

I found that almost anything, no matter how trivial and obscure, became interesting when I learned all about it. I enjoyed my new experience of journalistic minimalism. Then it suddenly proved to be a turning point in my career.

40

Harold Stassen, the United States disarmament negotiator during my last days as the *Sun*'s London correspondent, gave American journalists a vaguely abstract briefing in the Grosvenor Square embassy at the end of every day's proceedings in Lancaster House. He and other members of the United Nations Disarmament Sub-Committee were repetitively discussing the unfeasibility of the non-testing of nuclear weapons. They devoted a lot of time to debating the proposition that a non-member of the Big Five might not be awarded credit for not testing a nuclear device without first having proved possession of one of devastating power. The Sub-Committee were evidently making as much progress as caged mice on a backward-revolving treadmill. The briefings were brain-numbingly dreary, but they always ended by 6 o'clock. One happy hour, drinking bourbon on the rocks in the embassy bar, I imagined how a peaceful South Sea island tribe might use coconuts to develop a nuclear device and bring the East–West disarmament deadlock to an end simply by blowing up the entire northern hemisphere. Then that unconsidered island's Minister of Off-Island Affairs (retired) could loll tranquilly on the beach and enjoy contemplating a reformed map of the world.

Malcolm Muggeridge, then the editor of *Punch*, accepted the story of my wishful thinking, my first contribution to the magazine. When

Punch was founded, in 1841, it gained an early reputation for radicalism. Some of the witticisms daringly subverted Victorian family values. Richard Doyle, who designed *Punch*'s best-known cover, said that '*The Times* is a monarchy, whereas *Punch* is a Republic.'

The Muggeridge régime restored some of *Punch*'s original anarchic boldness. There was a brief period of heterodoxy. There were surprises! One week the principal cartoon, which was meant to be a declaration of the magazine's true beliefs, portrayed Churchill sagging in senility, which the media in general respectfully disregarded. Muggeridge attracted younger readers, but they were not the people the advertisers wanted to influence. When he wrote an article for a mass-circulation American magazine, the *Saturday Evening Post*, in which he ridiculed the Queen, the BBC (temporarily) banned him from radio and television. Sacred institutions, such as the Cavalry Club, cancelled their *Punch* subscriptions, and the proprietors panicked. They got rid of Muggeridge with a farewell handshake less than golden.

41

Joining the editorial staff of *Punch* was like retiring – not a bad feeling, at first. The office was as substantial and dignified as a merchant bank, a men's club, a sanatorium for gentlefolk. It was situated at 10 Bouverie Street. Bernard Hollowood, Muggeridge's successor as editor, was only semi-facetious when he called the premises and all they stood for 'more respectable than that other Number 10', the one in Downing Street. He was always only semi-facetious; humour was his solemn vocation, an onerous labour.

Punch's immediate neighbour, the *News of the World*, was a reminder of journalism at its crudest and most scandalous. The huge rolls of newsprint delivered into its maw each week represented the destruction of great tracts of Canadian and Scandinavian conifers and millions of gullible British minds, causing the dedicated jesters of *Punch* to raise their eyebrows, purse their lips and shake their heads, deploring the vulgar era in which we lived, for they were custodians of all things bright and beautiful, besieged in a society of barbarians who would rather read about sex and violence than savour *Punch*'s little intellectual sallies.

The office felt as secure as a monastic enclosure, and the staff immured in it were reluctant to venture out into the hurly-burly of literary competition. In the very beginning, I attempted to soften some of the printed rejection slips by adding a scribbled 'Sorry, not quite', but that usually insincere consolation did more harm than good, encouraging would-be contributors to try again, prolonging their agony, and mine. Routinely my out-tray was soon full and it was time to walk around the corner and along Fleet Street to the animation of El Vino. I was an almost entirely negative editor.

'What do you actually *do*?' someone asked.

'Well,' I murmured modestly, implying, with a small, circular gesture, all sorts of technicalities too complex to explain over a glass of wine.

What I actually did was return to the office not much after three, to finish reading the newspapers while waiting for tea. *Punch* was written by the staff (half a dozen of us) and a small coterie of favoured outsiders who could be counted on to write pieces of the right length in the house style and to deliver them on time. The principal sources of ideas were the newspapers and our navels.

'Do you mean to say you write only a thousand words a week?' asked Michael Frayn, then a satirical columnist and incipient playwright, when I met him at one of Peter Dickinson's parties.

'Not every week,' I confessed. Some weeks I only *thought* about writing a thousand words.

To relieve my darkening mood of stagnation, I persuaded Hollowood to allow me to get out and about a bit. BOAC, the ancestor of British Airways, said they could give me free tickets to any British destinations. First, I visited Nassau for a long weekend – the Royal Victoria Hotel, of fragrant wartime memory, the Pilot House Club, Blackbeard's, Junkanoo, the Silver Slipper, Chippie's Confidential and other refreshment parlours – and interviewed Hedley Edwards, a fifty-nine-year-old Jamaican with a smile like the beam of a lighthouse, who exhibited a flock of flamingos doing military drill. Before going to Ardastra Gardens, with about a hundred tourists, mostly Americans off an Italian cruise ship, for the morning performance, I did some research, which I passed on to any *Punch* readers who might have been interested in that sort of stuff. What I enjoyed most was the idea of flying to the

Bahamas to gather material that was so unimportant and yet to me so important.

'On behalf of the birds,' Edwards told the audience, 'welcome to Nassau. After fourteen months of secret experiments and altogether over three years of training, they're doing quite well and keep doing better. I hope they will convince you once and for all that people don't really know what they're talking about when they say "bird-brained". These flamingos are intelligent birds, under disciplinary training. The only reward they get for their performance is your applause, so please be generous with it; it means a lot to them. They have been applauded by Lord Beaverbrook and the Prime Minister of Canada and Winthrop Rockefeller.' The male birds were inclined to be vain, he said, and he got better results from the females – 'but then all females respond better than males to loving kindness,' he added, with a wink at an appreciatively giggling matron in Bermuda shorts.

The flamingos were standing at ease in an artificial pool that looked like pea soup. The water was surrounded by mauve hibiscus blossoms, a pleasant colour scheme. Edwards turned to them and asked, 'Are you ready?' and there was an excited flutter of wings and some soft bleating honks, and they obediently marched to and fro.

Shortly after my return from the Bahamas – her timing was not a big surprise – my wife one morning made a formal speech of renunciation. Some of Tony Crosland's Parliamentary style had rubbed off on her. She had been sick and tired of my presence; when I had flown to see a man about his flamingos, my absence had been the last straw. The gist of her monologue, a three- or four-minute recitation of my major faults that seemed longer, was that I should pack my things forthwith and go away for ever. I was able to take my Olivetti and two suitcases but was obliged to leave all my books and two small girls I was very fond of. I later discovered that my woeful experience was not uncommon in my trade.

A couple of friends apparently had not been unaware of the imminent inevitability of this marital dénouement. One of them telephoned only a few anxious moments before I was due for the old heave-ho into the street with no planned destination. Peter Alexander and Tessa, who was then his wife, were expecting me and had prepared accommodation, the basement of their house in Belgravia. The house and its address were elegant; my flat was simply troglodytic. Private access to it from Wilton Place was by steep steps past garbage cans. There was a large bed-sitting room with a single, narrow window that enabled me to detect daylight. There were a telephone, a bed, a wardrobe, a desk and a couple of chairs. A doorless inner doorway led to the only other room, which combined the functions of kitchen, bathroom and loo, an intimate coalition favoured by Francis Bacon in the Kensington mews house where he had his studio. Willy-nilly, I had attained fashionable squalor for a rent that was little more than a peppercorn. As I was reviewing jazz records for a new, occasional column in *Punch*, I installed a state-of-the-art record-player, and record companies sent me free copies of all the records I requested. My lair was soon loud with the music of Ellington, Armstrong, Count Basie, Miles Davis . . .

My banishment aggrieved me sufficiently to confer a sense of freedom to do any damn thing I pleased. Loneliness was easily overcome. I drank a lot and my social life was not at all finicky. Bacchus and Aphrodite, a potent team, awarded my conscience a holiday. Buddy Greco sang my favourite song of that era, 'Like Young'.

42

On *Punch*, when I wrote profiles, Hollowood begrudged me any more than one week to do each job, though he said he quite liked the results. I wrote a superficial impression of Hong Kong after spending only a long weekend in the colony (I still had some notes left over from the Korean War visit). I squandered about ten days on Alan Bennett, Peter Cook, Jonathan Miller and Dudley Moore in their epoch-making satirical revue *Beyond the Fringe*, and even longer on John, then known as Johnny, Dankworth and his powerful swing band. Mrs Dankworth, Cleo Laine, had repeatedly been voted Britain's most popular woman jazz singer, but she had not yet achieved pre-eminence in their musical partnership and was allowed only a mention.

I was unable to probe deeply into the characters and work of the people I interviewed, but I was at least able to meet them and get an idea of what made them tick. Some of them, especially Dudley Moore, remained friends. I admired the way he adapted and transcended the piano style of Erroll Garner. Even the last time I spent in his company, in Venice, California, at the beginning of his tragic physical decline, he made me laugh so hard that I ached.

Louis Armstrong and his All-Stars paused in London on their way, under the auspices of the US State Department and the Pepsi

Cola Company, to give concerts in Africa 'to strengthen international ties by demonstrating the cultural interests, developments and achievements of the people of the United States'. Trummy Young, trombone; Barney Bigard, clarinet; Billy Kyle, piano; Mort Herbert, bass; Danny Barcelona, drums; Velma Middleton, vocals, and Mr and Mrs Armstrong were staying briefly at the May Fair Hotel. I got there at 10.30 on their first morning and found Trummy Young and Velma Middleton in the lobby, toying with a little whisky and ice.

'The way I hear it,' Trummy said, 'that Lumumba wants us to go over there. "Send some more musicians," he said. "The last troupe was delicious."' The State Department had assigned a photographer to record the tour. 'He used to make pictures down at Cape Canaveral — where they shoot the rockets. I'm not at all interested in those war-heads, not at *all*. I'm not built for spares.' Trummy said he and the others felt that the goodwill they hoped to engender in Africa would help to preserve peace. Velma's smile was sympathetic. Sometimes women are able to believe that men really don't like war.

Danny Barcelona, the young Hawaiian drummer, emerged from a lift, rubbing his eyelids. 'Hey — what country's this?' he demanded. 'Where do they keep the coffee?'

In the Monte Carlo Suite there was a photo opportunity and an opportunity to ask the great man some questions. He and his wife, Lucille, looked happy. It was the twentieth anniversary of the night they got married, in, appropriately enough, St Louis. How were they going to celebrate? 'We're celebrating right now,' Louis said. 'Any time we're together we're celebrating.' Lucille was wearing a gold bracelet from which dangled charms representing countries they had visited. There were an Eiffel Tower, a Big Ben, a lump of jade from Hong Kong and many others. How about Africa? His band had played in Ghana before.

'Them cats down there,' he said, 'all the chiefs and all the ordinary people, everybody, they really dig our music, and, daddy, I dig swinging for them. We played an outdoor concert for a big crowd of them, and we played "Royal Garden Blues", and I played some of them high notes – you know? – and some of them pretty notes, and they really dig all that. There was one old fella, about a hundred and ten years old, and he was really wailing. He danced all over. When we left that country, all the cats came to the airport and said "Satchmo, goodbye". There were nine trumpets all playing for me, so beautiful, and I played with them, and they sang "All for you, Louis, all for you". So of course what we want to do now is go on back down there and lay it on them again.'

I managed to exchange a few words with Louis's private physician, Dr Alexander Schiff of New York. 'At the age of fifty-nine Louis Armstrong is healthier than you or I,' he said. 'And I'm going to keep it that way. I've sent ninety-three pounds of medical supplies ahead to Accra. Louis isn't a hypochondriac, but he does like pills, especially a good, strong physic at the end of every day. His lips have tough spots, like corns, but they're in good shape. He's his own dietician – he eats and drinks everything that comes along. He can still play his trumpet hard for two hours a day.' On days when he wasn't performing for the public, Louis played for himself.

'You can't take nothing for granted with no trumpet,' Louis told me. 'I touch that horn *every* day. You got to keep your chops eulogised.' And every night, after he took his pills, he sterilised his trumpet mouthpiece in witch-hazel and put it away wrapped in a handkerchief, safe from germs.

What did he think of 'progressive jazz'? He said he was reminded of a groom in a New Orleans livery stable who attracted a lot of suckers long ago by putting up a sign offering for a dime each to show them 'a horse with its tail where its head ought to be'. 'He'd just turned that old horse back to front,' Louis said. 'You can get away with that just one time.' However, he liked Miles Davis. 'I buy his albums because he sounds good. But it was Joe Oliver who taught me how to *live* music.'

Photographers interrupted. 'Just one more,' said one. 'Turn this way.' 'Give us an expression, Mr Armstrong.' 'This is it,' he replied. 'This *is* my expression, dad.'

Would Louis Armstrong ever retire? He frowned. Real musicians never retire, he suggested. They only die.

'But if it all stopped tomorrow,' he said, grinning cheerfully, '— hallelujah! Everybody's had a good time.'

The brief encounter was wonderful. But in my basement room that night, as I listened to Louis Armstrong and his Hot Five playing 'Alligator Crawl', I wanted more, a whole lot more than the ephemera of press-conference interviews. It was time for what Dulles called 'an agonising reappraisal'.

In *Alfie*, Michael Caine's film about the life of a social parasite in what would be known as 'Swinging London', the theme-song mockingly demanded: 'What's it all about, Alfie?' Writing for *Punch* provided me, if not many readers, with a certain amount of amusement, but what was it all about? Did it mean anything? Why was I writing?

Some successful writers had asked themselves that question, but the answers they made public were sometimes flippant. For example, George Bernard Shaw said: 'My main reason for adopting literature as a profession was that, as the author is never seen by his clients, he need not dress respectably.' Irwin Shaw, discussing John O'Hara's motivation, said, 'he wrote a great deal . . . because he went on the wagon and had nothing else to do.' Evelyn Waugh approached close to honesty by his standards when he declared: 'I wanted to be a man of the world and I took to writing as I might have taken to archaeology or diplomacy or any other profession, as a means of coming to terms with the world. Now I see it as an end in itself.' According to Gore Vidal, 'A writer is someone who writes, that's all. You can't stop it; you can't make yourself do anything else but that.'

George Orwell, characteristically, did his best to tell the truth.

In an essay, 'Why I write', he said the four great motives for writing prose are 'sheer egoism', 'aesthetic enthusiasm', 'historical impulse' and 'political purpose'. I immediately recognised the first two.

By 'sheer egoism' he meant: 'Desire to seem clever, to be talked about, to be remembered after death, to get your own back on grown-ups who snubbed you in childhood, etc., etc.' As a writer, he defined 'aesthetic enthusiasm' as 'perception of beauty in the external world, or, on the other hand, in words and their right arrangement'. Peter Cook was later to say to Dudley Moore in 'The Dagenham Dialogues' that 'No one knows when God in His Almighty Wisdom will choose to vouchsafe His precious gift of Death'. I had already perceived an inkling of mortality. I had used up half of the Biblical allotment of years and had produced only one small children's book for posthumous remembrance. It was obviously time to write more than the sort of things I was writing. I was increasingly reluctant to write under the discipline of an editor, even one as apathetically benign as Bernard Hollowood.

It is difficult to overcome the inertia of secure and not very demanding employment. But then I met Peggy Lee.

43

Norma Deloris Egstrom, a Swedish-Norwegian-American, was born in Jamestown, North Dakota, in 1920. Life was hard and lonely, up there on the Great Plains, with arctic winters and sweltering summers. She endured an austere girlhood. Her family had very little money. When she was four her mother died. A year later, Norma's father remarried and they moved to an even more remote and smaller town, Nortonville (population 125), where he had a boring job at the railroad depot and drank a lot. His new wife was as cruel as a wicked stepmother in a fairy tale. Norma was often beaten. At the age of fourteen she was able to manage the depot when her father was too drunk to cope with it. As soon as she graduated from high school, she left home. Living on her own in cheap rooming houses, she subsisted as a dish-washer and waitress, until, still in her teens, she attracted attention by singing. Then, also as in a fairy tale, she was suddenly transformed. A local, small-time bandleader named her Peggy Lee. A little later, in Chicago, Benny Goodman happened to hear her sing 'These Foolish Things' when Helen Forrest was about to leave his band and he urgently needed a replacement.

I became aware of Peggy Lee, and was instantly infatuated, when she was twenty-two and I was eighteen. During that unexciting in-between time when the RCAF was teaching me mathematics at the

University of Toronto, I heard her sing 'Why Don't You Do Right?'. Early in 1943 that swinging number, one of the outstanding hits of Benny Goodman's heyday, was still getting a big play on Canadian juke-boxes. In a café near the campus, I contributed more than my quota of nickels, and listened over and over again to her marvellous rendition of that hard-boiled lyric, addressed to an improvident drunkard.

It was not a tragic plea; it was a command, an ultimatum. She made the song more than jazz. It was a dramatic performance, tough, erotic and caustically humorous. She knew the subject intimately. Having already travelled with musicians, she had lived it.

By the time we met in 1961 she had come a long way from North Dakota. I was thirty-six, a good age at which to get to know a good-looking blonde of forty whose singing I had enjoyed for half my life. There was champagne at the press reception in the West End of London, and there were many of the usual banal questions and answers. When the formula routine was over, the champagne continued to flow (non-vintage but marginally better than nothing), and I had a chance to speak to her. I said I reviewed jazz for *Punch* and wondered whether there would be time for an interview. She smiled knowingly and nodded. It was a Good Day; I got That Old Feeling, an early symptom of Fever, and the interview was conducted *tête-à-tête*, without a public-relations chaperone, in the Oliver Messel Suite at the summit of the Dorchester Hotel.

The Dorchester was then the epitome of Park Lane high fashion and Peggy Lee's suite was the quintessence of the epitome – theatrical, glitteringly ornate and voluptuously cushioned. It reminded me of the Prince Regent's grandiose Oriental love-nest in Brighton. The Oliver Messel Suite's reception room was vast, yet meticulous consideration had been paid to even the smallest details. There were no books, but a secret cupboard was concealed by a row of leather bindings, with the key in the spine of *The Life of Saint Francis of Assisi*.

Perhaps it would seem ungallant to repeat the little I remember of our conversation that first night, except that Peggy told me the suite had been occupied recently by Richard Burton and Elizabeth Taylor. What a heritage! What an inspiration on Peggy's first journey to the Old World!

We established an invariable programme. I would hurry back from El Vino to my basement flat, bathe and change, and get to her dressing room at Pigalle in time for her evening performances. Her preparation was long and careful, including a couple of hefty jolts of brandy, not that she needed any anaesthetic to numb stage-fright. She was a seasoned professional and supremely confident in the excellence of her make-up and costumes, her lighting and sound men, the quartet she had rehearsed to accompany her, and, of course, in her own carefully disciplined musical talent. She drank brandy before going on because she liked feeling high.

Well before show-time, I wished her luck and settled at my reserved table, which was central and close to the stand, but not embarrassingly close. I didn't want to seem to believe that she sang 'Mr Wonderful' just to me. The menu was always the same and so were the songs she had chosen for her two sets. There was a group of Ray Charles hits, with suitable gender changes – 'Hallelujah I Love *Him* So', for example. But my appreciation never faltered. I felt an irrational sense of pride in her singing, making love to the microphone in smoky, blue whispers, in the applause, and in my special, privileged access to her. Nightly, I went with her to the hotel, and returned to my flat for three or four hours' sleep before having to go to *Punch*. The adrenalin supply was sorely taxed.

The only fly in the fragrant ointment was Nicki, Peggy's daughter, who, applying Californian standards with the dogmatism of early adolescence, said the Dorchester was 'pathetic' when room service failed to deliver pizza with everything on it and pistachio ice-cream with chocolate sprinkles. Fortunately, she needed no coaxing to withdraw to her bedroom and television, though the BBC and ITV were also both 'pathetic'. Thus, eventually, Peggy and I were left undisturbed, for nightcaps and talk of Peggy Lee, a subject we found fascinating. I admired the laser focus of her intelligence, her resolute stance, the allure and defiance of her attitude to the world. She worked hard to achieve part-time hedonism, and exerted her powerful will to the utmost to control it. Yet there were laughs.

The London engagement was a great success. One thing led, as it usually does, to another. She accepted an invitation to Monaco, to star in a charity gala sponsored by Princess Grace for the Red Cross. How would I like to accompany Miss Lee and her entourage as her interpreter? My elementary school French had recently progressed enough to decipher restaurant menus, but my accent seemed to attain authenticity only late in the evening. However, as Peggy patiently explained, I did not really have to be much of an interpreter; I merely needed the title. The point was that as her interpreter I would have my expenses paid by her charitable hostess, who herself would undoubtedly be reimbursed: that was how charity galas worked.

At the Hôtel de Paris in Monte Carlo, I was assigned an interpreter's small, air-unconditioned, single bedroom overlooking the harbour, but I was allowed to sign for gourmet food and drink. Peggy visited my room at night, furtively, as if electrifying our liaison with a frisson of naughtiness, though the hotel has never been noted for puritanism. In her 1989 autobiography, the memoirs of a selective amnesiac, she wrote: 'I spent most of my time in France in bed – alone, of course . . .'

While Peggy prepared for her gala performance, I repeatedly confirmed that the Michelin Guide Rouge was not exaggerating when it stated that one could always eat very well in the hotel's three-star Louis XV restaurant and sometimes 'merveilleusement'. While toying with an elegant sufficiency of poitrine de pigeonneau with foie gras de canard, I wrote her a 100-word speech in what I hoped was acceptable colloquial French, spelled phonetically, in easy-to-read capital letters. Near the end of the meal, I showed the script to the waiter and asked his opinion. He protruded his lower lip in that inimitably Gallic expression of non-commitment and muttered, 'Ça va.' Peggy put a lot of feeling into the simple words – '*Je suis très heureuse ici au Sporting Club . . .*' – and the cosmopolitan audience's laughter and applause seemed sympathetic. Of course, there was nothing naive about her singing, which was rewarded with much hand-clapping, cheers and shouts of '*Bravo!*'. We celebrated her triumph by driving to St Paul the following day for lunch in the garden of the Colombe d'Or, noted for its collection of modern art. We were accompanied by Moe Lewis, the proprietor of Basin Street East, Peggy's favourite venue in New York, who concluded the meal with a sort of courtship display of a massive roll of thousand-franc notes.

A couple of weeks later, in response to a most cordial invitation, I moved into Peggy Lee's bijou residence in Kimridge Road, on a peak of Beverly Hills. In my mood of *carpe diem* opportunism, I had severed my London ties with brisk informality, retaining only a tenuous but gratifyingly friendly connection with *Punch*. Hollowood was probably relieved by my resignation from the staff. My assistance had been nugatory, but sacking editorial colleagues, however ineffectual, was unheard of at *Punch* in those days. Hollowood assured me that he would welcome any future written contributions I would care to submit from a distance. My only regret was that I had to abandon some cherished possessions in the basement in Belgravia, even my *yee woo*, the two-stringed violin with a dragon's-head handle I had picked up in the China Products Company department store in Kowloon.

Peggy's home was palatial on a small scale, a compact, single-storey structure, with an artificial fish-pond, a Japanese-style rock garden and a circular swimming pool in the rear, and a car-port in front, for the obligatory Cadillac. From the back of the house, on a clear day, Peggy said, there was a view of seven mountain ranges. The rooms were small, with low ceilings, but exquisitely ornamental, in pastel blues and pinks, with marble floors, white fur rugs and crystal chandeliers – much fancier than that suite designed by poor old Oliver Messel.

There was a middle-aged Belgian couple whose quarters were concealed behind the kitchen. She did the cooking, which was not an onerous task, as Peggy, though winsomely svelte at the time, was anxious about her ever-threatening 'weight problem'. For dinner we had a narrow strip of New York cut sirloin steak and a green salad with a low-cal dressing – *every* evening, without exception. The cook's husband, a plump, taciturn man, was the chauffeur, waiter and *sommelier*. My first evening there, he brought us a wicker basket cradling a bottle of wine. He took out the bottle and only then extracted the cork.

'What is it?' I asked with an ingratiating smile.

'Red,' he said.

He allowed me to look at the label: Château Latour. The bottle was frosty, because he always kept the wine for at least two hours in the freezer. He had lived in California for many years but had not picked up the state's great viticultural knowledge and appreciation of wines. When I suggested that it would be nice to drink Château Latour less cold, he did not argue. He silently raised his eyebrows, turned with a smile to my hostess and filled her glass to the brim. He and I never really quite got over that first confrontation. Thereafter, he continued to serve the wine numbingly chilled. Peggy, deferring to his Belgian-American know-how, did not intervene.

When I met Michael Caine in Beverly Hills, many years later, he said he was tired of living 'the fortress life' behind an electric gate and looked forward to returning to London. While I was with her, Peggy was reluctant to emerge from protective isolation. The few times we went out together she did so in disguise, exchanging her blonde wig for a brunette one. One night she let me take her to the Crescendo to hear Mort Sahl do his brilliantly improvised satirical monologue on the news of the day. On his recent visit to London, I had introduced him to Gaitskell, a fan of his record-ings, in the office of the Leader of the Opposition in the House of Commons. Now, as Peggy and I entered the Hollywood night-club, Mort gave me a big hello, amplified by microphone in mid-performance, and didn't greet her. She was somewhat miffed. Like many other local celebrities, she said she disliked being recognised in public, but even more disliked not being recognised. We did not stay long.

She was proud that Frank Sinatra always telephoned her and sent her flowers when she was in hospital. Duke Ellington, with whom she wrote 'I'm Gonna Go Fishin'' for the soundtrack of *Anatomy of a Murder*, called her 'the Queen', and Louis Armstrong said she knew how to swing. I have never met a musician who didn't admire her singing. She had a wide circle of show-business acquaintances, and yet she seemed to have hardly any social life. Her best friends were her doctor and his wife. He gave her a daily hypo-dermic shot – 'vitamins,' she said. She depended on the treatment's immediate euphoric uplift, and the doctor's manner was possessive. That was the time in New York when 'Doctor Feelgood' was almost as famous as his patients or clients, including, it was said, JFK, into whom he regularly injected a stimulating cocktail of amphet-amines.

My favourite room in the house was her studio, where we spent happy hours, playing records of her own performances and other music she loved, reproduced bigger and better than life through a sound system of the highest fidelity. I was besottedly enamoured of almost everything she ever did, especially the sort of numbers she sang with the George Shearing quintet at the 1959 national convention of disc jockeys in Miami, on a record titled *Beauty and the Beat!*. In 'I Lost My Sugar in Salt Lake City' she was able to express regret without self-pity; in 'You Came a Long Way from St Louis' ridicule without bitterness; and in her own lovely compo-sition 'There'll Be Another Spring' there was romantic consolation without cloying sentimentality. In the studio we danced, hardly moving, to Count Basie's 'Li'l Darlin''. Was it Catullus or Frankie Howerd who called dancing 'a vertical expression of a horizontal intention'? In the studio at twilight, she sang Billie Holiday songs with uncanny verisimilitude in Billie Holiday's voice. Even Miss Peggy Lee deferred to Lady Day.

The studio was ideal for creativity, but in all the time I was there Peggy wrote no lyrics and I wrote absolutely nothing. She professed an interest in reading but I never saw her read a book. She said she painted but I never saw her paint. I should have exerted myself as her ghost-painter. Tony Bennett paints amateurishly for top professional prices. If I had painted a series of purple, red and orange abstractions bearing the title 'Fever' and her signature they could easily have been marketed for at least five grand apiece. No such scam occurred to me in my innocence at the time. Peggy did not complain about the discrepancy of our incomes, though hers that year was about $300,000 and mine (payments from *Punch* and royalties from my children's book) was . . . less. The thought made me squirm.

The hydrogen bomb, then as now, seemed to be suspended above the world like the sword of Damocles. There was much talk of nuclear shelters. In an effort to do something constructive, I visited the Civil Defence headquarters downtown and was given a booklet *Survive Nuclear Attack*. 'Face these facts,' it began. 'A 20-megaton explosion on the surface of the earth can kill most people and destroy most buildings within a five-mile radius of ground zero.'

The next day, I telephoned some of the nuclear shelter-builders listed in the Los Angeles classified telephone book and asked for their brochures. 'We can send a highly skilled consultant to measure your space for an excavation right away,' said the man at the Nuclear Survival Corporation, 'Los Angeles' Original Designer-Builder of Quality Shelters since 1959', which offered 'a highly blast-resistant fallout shelter'. 'You know our slogan,' he cheerfully told me, '"The Day You Need Us Will Be One Day Too Late."' I declined his offer 'for the time being'.

The following morning was blue and golden, but my mood was sombre as I sat near the pool and contemplated everlasting plastic hydrangeas in the Japanese-style rockery. One of the witticisms in Walter Winchell's column that day was 'Love Thy Neighbor: he may build a fallout shelter before you do'. This item reminded me of a recent report from Philadelphia that the people's favourite evangelist had assured anxious parents that their first duty was to protect their families, so it was perfectly all right to keep guns and use them, if necessary, to keep intruders out of family shelters. One commentator had responded by suggesting that intruders might be beaten to death with heavy family Bibles.

My reverie was ended by a black mailman in a pale blue pith helmet and pale blue uniform who emerged from a miniature grove of palm trees. 'Hi, Pat!' he said with a congratulatory smile. 'You got *plenty* of mail today!' He handed me bulky packages headed Lancer Fiberglass Blast and Fallout Shelter, Protective Enterprises, Inc. (whose writing paper was decorated with a red mushroom cloud and the rather theological question 'Are You Prepared?') and Fox Hole Shelter, Inc. (slogan: 'Everyone Is A Target'). Fox Hole's letter recommended rules of conduct under-ground after the bombs fall: 'Have good thoughts in mind. Good thinking will help pass the time away.' Paranoia is not a new disease. But Peggy was relieved when I assured her that I wasn't proposing to build a shelter, only to write an article for *Punch*. The fee was £50.

As the weeks drifted by, what did we *do*? We lolled about. It would be difficult to imagine a way of life more demoralising than idling in a long showbiz hiatus. Even so, one morning when I was reclining on the queen-size bed in her boudoir, Peggy summoned her daughter Nicki into the room and announced plans for a Mexican wedding. I learned then that Peggy had already told her doctor, her lawyer, her public-relations consultant and her hair-dresser, but nobody had told my wife. Of course, Peggy easily brushed aside that impediment. In Hollywood, marriages over-lapped more often than not, and, besides, after all, wasn't Susan contentedly fixed up with Tony?

'We'll run on down to Juarez,' Peggy said. 'Divorce, wedding – everything can be done in a day.'

Nicki did not look overjoyed.

I flew to New York a few days later. Alone.

44

People traditionally pity single men on their own in New York at Christmastime, but I found the regained status of pseudo-bachelor exhilarating. When I was on the staff of *Punch* it had been virtually mandatory to join the Savage Club, so, on arriving in Manhattan, thanks to a reciprocal arrangement, I was permitted access to the Players Club, in Gramercy Park, a sheltered, quiet, downtown enclave like a London square. The club was situated in a handsome house of old-fashioned dimness, like the setting of a novel by Henry James. It was an asylum of masculine exclusivity, founded by men of the theatre for men. Like other men's clubs, on both sides of the Atlantic, financial exigency had broadened the membership. It included a number of men from the fringes of New York theatrical culture and beyond, even public-relations consultants and critics. However, generation after generation of earnest committees had done their best to maintain an atmosphere of dramaturgic authenticity. There was a theatrical library. There was a downstairs bar lively with witty and scurrilous gossip, where men in shirtsleeves bet on games of pool.

'You can stay as long as you like,' said Howard Lindsay, the playwright and club president. 'While you're in New York, think of this as your home.' I had no clear-cut plan, but I looked forward to a productive winter of reading and writing.

As things turned out, I managed to send *Punch* a thousand words on those Californian nuclear shelters and sell *Esquire* a piece on Jonathan Miller and others who were introducing fashionable English satire into New York. Then fate intervened. One day when I descended unwarily from my attic bedroom for a lunch of oysters, brown bread and ale in the bar, I found myself in conversation with a middle-aged gentleman in a Brooks Brothers grey-flannel suit, blue button-down shirt and Ancient Madder bow tie, an unlikely Cupid. Sherman Baker was a senior editor at St Martin's Press. He felt sure that one of his colleagues would like to meet me. He suggested a drink the following afternoon, in a bar near their office in the Flatiron Building. Yes, of course. I did not have to look in my diary, because all the pages were blank.

Thus I was introduced to Diane Wheeler-Nicholson, a brunette of just the right age and aspirations, who proved to be an editor of galvanic energy and enthusiasm. She had a smile of phenomenal incandescence. We were both on what is known as the rebound, and Christmas was imminent. There was a sort of amorous explosion. She took me to Long Island to spend the holiday with her parents and two brothers. Within a few days, she agreed that it would be nice to live together in Guatemala, while I tried to write my first novel.

First, there were a few practicalities to attend to. Diane had to explain why she was so abruptly leaving her publishing house. Sherman could hardly complain. I had to go to London to raise some money. Cunard public relations gave me a complimentary ticket so that I could write an article for *Punch* on travel aboard the *Sylvania* from New York to Liverpool.

The future seemed adventurous but somewhat precarious. I refrained from mentioning the biggest uncertainty. Would I be able to write a publishable novel? The afternoon of my departure was bleak. Packs of light grey ice drifted in the dark grey East River. The sky was medium grey and the January sun gleamed as palely as a jellyfish. Diane looked small in the crowd on the pier, but she was waving bravely as the machinery of alienation began to move.

A sailor shouted. Chain clattered. An impatient, monstrous blast of the hooter caused some melancholy blowing of noses, ashore and afloat. There were tears. I went below, to the lounge, modelled after the boudoir of Madame de Sérilly, and was consoled by tea and cakes and a trio playing selections from *South Pacific*.

Most of the passengers were British. There were only a few Canadians and Americans. Around the bar in the oak-panelled lounge, conversations began hesitantly with the conventional British diffidently cautious probings and disclosures of identity and character. Most of the first-class passengers were not young, and most of them were experienced travellers: they were expert at tactful interrogation and social recognition; quite soon they got themselves sorted and graded and combined in the small groups that were to cohere throughout the voyage.

Now there were omens of difficult weather ahead. The porthole in my cabin was secured and the steward said it could not be opened. The water in my bath tilted deep and shallow, fore then aft, port then starboard. Later, in the dining room, the consommé in my plate moved more agitatedly than the bathwater, and the steward raised the fiddle at the table-edge closest to my lap.

Halfway from New York to Bermuda the meteorological entry in the ship's log reported 'str'g SW winds, rough sea, mod./h'vy swell, cloudy, showers'.

'Pretty bad, isn't it?' I asked a steward.

'It *is* freshening a bit,' he conceded, returning to the task of sweeping up broken china. The crashes of crockery and glass were like Wagnerian cymbals. Passengers staggered across the lounge clinging to safety ropes.

There was an eight-hour visit to Bermuda and steel-band calypso in the lighter on the way back to the ship. The next day was wild. Captain J. Crosbie Dawson, DSC, RNR, said it was the roughest day he had ever known on the North Atlantic. The language of ships' logs is generally stoically objective but the *Sylvania* recorded passage through 'NNW storm, mountainous seas, steep swell, cl'dy, fierce squalls'.

'It *is* blowing,' the steward acknowledged.

The wireless operator said the wind-speed was 80 knots, with gusts up to 105. A passenger, Mrs Alex Mackie, gave birth to a daughter three weeks before she had been expected. She weighed 6 pounds 2 ounces and was immediately named Sylvia Ann, after the ship.

'There's an enormous high-pressure area over Iceland,' Captain Dawson said. 'There's an enormous low to the south of us. I thought for a while we might end up in Cape Town. I would prefer, however, to go to Tring.' Tring is noted for its sanatorium.

What if the ship sank? Such a sad love story, I thought. I placed a radio-telephone call to New York. Before satellites, the crackle of static through the storm was very dramatic. I could just make out Diane's voice.

'Everyone at the office has been really great,' she said. 'We won't starve. They're giving me some severance pay.'

45

In London, as in Baltimore, after a certain number of 'unwinding' evening drinks, journalists often discussed the novels we were going to write, if only we had the time and the place. Now I would soon have the perfect place and unlimited time, and the companionship of a woman who was willing to read whatever I wrote and to restrict her comments to the bits she liked.

I flew from London to Guatemala City in time to meet Diane's plane from New York. I had a loyal Guatemalan friend in one Jorge Luna, who had been Guillermo Palmieri's assistant in the Tourist Office before the revolution against Arbenz. When Castillo Armas became the CIA-approved President, the American embassy urged us correspondents to name Guatemalans we suspected of Communist affiliations. Paul Kennedy of the *New York Times* named Luna, and I was able to clear him. At that time his political views were mildly socialistic; soon afterwards, as an export-import entrepreneur, he proved his soundness by playing polo on his own private polo ground. When Diane and I got in touch with him he had not as yet made his first million quetzales, but he was still grateful for my testimony on his behalf, and he enabled us to find ideal accommodation on the shore of Lake Atitlán. A New York photographer based in Beekman Place in Manhattan allowed us to stay in his lakeside house if we would feed his pets, a macaw and a spider monkey.

Lake Atitlán, a mountain lake of volcanic origin, measures 11.5 miles from east to west and 4.4 miles from north to south: big enough, but not too big – just right. The climate of the Land of Eternal Spring at 5,125 feet above sea level and not quite 15 degrees north of the equator is so balmy that our absent host's house, a large, Gauguinesque single room with three walls, was sufficient shelter. The south-west-facing side without a wall overlooked a deck, the unfathomed water of the lake (pure enough to drink), the green peaks of three inactive volcanoes and, during the happy hour of early evening, sunsets of incarnadine splendour. The house was situated close to the Cakchiquel Indian village of Santa Catarina Palopó, on the lake's north-eastern shore, and the flimsy wooden building was defenceless against intrusion; but there was no need for defences. The neighbouring fishermen, weavers and cultivators of onions were paragons of honesty, a virtue remembered only dimly in gringo communities.

In that Edenic setting it would have been easy to let time glide by while contemplating butterflies and humming-birds in the hibiscus blossoms, subsisting on fish, rice, avocado, pineapple, lime and aguardiente – an ardent sugar-cane distillate not entirely unlike vodka and very much cheaper – and floating in water of such infinite blues that Aldous Huxley, travelling *Beyond Mexique Bay*, called Lake Atitlán 'Lake Chromo'. Coming from him, the compliment was extravagant, comparing Atitlán with Italian beauty he usually considered incomparable. However, with some difficulty, I resisted the allure of total idleness. I was aware of time's wingèd chariot. James Bond swore by Jamaican Blue Mountain coffee to get the day off to an energetic start, but I found that the high coffee of Antigua, Guatemala, was even better. After breakfast and before a midday swim, I was able to spend three or four hours daily at my old Olivetti portable, on which I had typed countless thousands of words of journalistic ephemera but never before any fiction I hoped would end up between hard covers.

In some ways, the first novel proved easiest, once I had overcome inhibitions about its inevitably being read by my mother. The more formidable obstacle of self-criticism did not block me until later. In Guatemala in 1961, still under the influence of *Punch* in the days of Muggeridge and the subsequent London satire boom, I was able glibly to write the story of a rich, attractive, young American widow visiting England for the first time as the country was beginning to undergo transformation from a land of manufacturing industry into a national theme park.

The British Travel and Holidays Association was advertising to promise Americans that in Britain they would find the spirit of Shakespeare, friendly peasants in shepherds' smocks and honey still for tea. Major Warwick Charlton, the press officer who human-ised General Sir Bernard Montgomery with a Tank Corps black beret and a casual sweater so that his soldiers would love him as Monty, an informal father figure, in time for the tide-turning Battle of El Alamein, was disappointed by the anticlimactic early days of peace, with many civilian shortages and continuing rationing. The 1950s offered no immediate relief. The 1951 Festival of Britain, a woefully low-budget vision of pie in the sky, did little to alle-viate cynical grumbling. Charlton, a patriotic romantic of inde-structible optimism, felt it was time to remind the British of their heroic heritage.

He was inspired to build a replica of *Mayflower*, the seventeenth-century Pilgrim Fathers' first immigrant ship, and to sail her from Plymouth, England, to Plymouth, Massachusetts. As a correspon-dent, I was able to observe him close-up as he applied his prolific imagination to the Herculean tasks of raising the money, getting the ship built to authentic specifications in an old-fashioned Devon shipyard, and recruiting a competent and congenial captain and crew for the hazardous 53-day voyage. I enjoyed all the gallant toasts at a farewell banquet in a Plymouth wine-cellar on the eve of their departure. The venture was a great success, praised by the President of the United States, Queen Elizabeth II and other dignitaries on both sides of the Atlantic.

Soon after Charlton's return, we had a long lunch together at the Wig & Pen Club, opposite the Law Courts, at the Fleet Street end of the Strand. He had played a major role in creating the club, originally intended for lawyers and writers, and in fabricating the history of the premises, which, he alleged, had luckily escaped destruction by the Great Fire of 1666. This claim was true, as the building had not existed then. Over our umpteenth brandies, Warwick deplored Britain's lost ability to enjoy a good time.

'Enough is not as good as a feast,' he insisted. 'A feast is better. Why can't people understand that?' He proposed the establishment of Merrie England, a gigantic theme park representing the best and brightest of the nation's traditions and triumphs. There would be celebrations of successful military campaigns, and, with cosmetic adjustments, celebrations of the redeeming features of less successful ones. After all, the Charge of the Light Brigade inspired a popular poem, and Dunkirk, properly regarded, can be remembered as a sort of victory. Honour would be paid to the Industrial Revolution (without slums and smog), when the rest of the world marvelled at British railways, and letters were delivered the day they were posted. Our drinks introduced increasingly sardonic notes. There would be animated waxworks of Robin Hood, Dick Turpin, Ronald Biggs and other national heroes, orating on the benefits of free enterprise. 'Every hour on the hour,' Warwick suggested, 'Tyburn-style, the public would be cheered up by witnessing a ceremonial hanging, drawing and quartering, with choral singing.' Refreshments for sale would be cut from oxen revolving on spits. There would be no Big Macs.

Warwick actually prepared a dummy brochure for Merrie England and found a site, an abandoned quarry not far from Heathrow. However, a professional feasibility study demonstrated that the whole concept was unfeasible: there was too much competition in reality. American tourists were quite easily satisfied by doing Britain in the short time it takes to see the Crown Jewels in the Tower of London, a few dreaming spires in Oxford, Hathaway's Cottage in Stratford and the Changing of the Guard, before moving on to Paris, France.

Satire at its best implies ideal alternatives to what it deplores. Warwick was a caustic social critic, yet somehow managed to believe in the possibility of redemption. Even Peter Cook, who, after *Beyond the Fringe*, founded *Private Eye* and the Establishment Club in Soho, though his improvisations could bring blushes to the cheeks of Lenny Bruce, was a secret moralist who wished there were an orthodox Christian God. My portrayal of England in *Tourist Attraction* was relentlessly negative, perhaps excessively, as distorted as the reflection in a fun-house mirror; there were no hints of any chance of achieving a more graceful image.

I enjoyed depicting my over-privileged New World heroine's dismal fate in a love affair with a good-looking Old World con man. Their big scene was enacted on the hillside above Cerne Abbas, in Dorset, which is justly famous for the white outline in the grass of the Cerne Giant, a fertility symbol with a gigantic erection. After the daring, alfresco hedonism, my opportunistic hero fixes her up with a ticket to a Buckingham Palace garden party for nine thousand American tourists. When a characteristic English midsummer thunderstorm threatens to ruin the ladies' party hats, there is a panic stampede into the marquee. Margaret (I've really forgotten her surname), one of the first to gain shelter, is pushed by those behind her, crushed against a buffet counter and mortally scalded by a capsized tea-urn. I laughed so hard at this grim dénouement that I could hardly see the typewriter. My agent said, '*Must you kill her?*' but I was adamant.

The debut was not a financial triumph. The novel earned no more than the modest advance. Even that would have enabled us to spend many more months in Lotus-land, but we suddenly noticed that the whites of our eyes were turning the colour of marzipan. We had contracted hepatitis. We had become quite fond of the the gaudy macaw, which strutted about recording and repeating human speech with the fidelity of a tape recorder. We were not at all sorry to say goodbye to the spider monkey, which was an insatiably hungry, obscene exhibitionist.

46

Money that would have lasted many months in rural Guatemala was only enough for a few weeks in New York. However, Diane was able to persuade the occupant of her rent-controlled apartment to move out, so we had an inexpensive roof over our heads, on 84th Street between Fifth and Madison, and James M. Cannon III, who had been a good friend at the *Sun*, was now some kind of vice-president at *Newsweek* and was able, without delay, to offer me an editorial job. Nervously playing safe, the apprentice novelist reverted to journalism. I was somewhat apprehensive about the demands of high-powered magazine journalism in Manhattan, but I soon discovered that there was nothing to fear, although the most memorable events of my first week were the suicide of the publisher, Phil Graham, and the murder of one of the researchers, the pretty daughter of Phillip Wylie, the author of *A Generation of Vipers*. As I was one of several people seen in conversation with the young woman at an office party on the night of her death, I was consequently interrogated by homicide detectives, but able to establish the innocence of my whereabouts at the time.

By newspaper standars, *Newsweek* seemed luxuriously overstaffed. As students of its masthead observed, we were almost all chiefs; there were few Indians. I was one of the middle-ranking 'Associate Editors' whose principal function, I discovered, was, more often than not, like that of a newspaper rewrite man. We were required to process reports from the magazine's bureaux, located in key cities in the United States and overseas. Most of the correspondents filed too much. The hard news was usually buried in shapeless masses of 'background' and fanciful 'colour'. We hacks in the home office had to disinter the stories and do our best to translate the prose into comprehensible American English. How the contributors hated us for all the cuts! How we hated them for all the waffle!

The process was complicated by the intervention of researchers, most of them young women fresh from college. When writers admitted the nature of their assignments, the researchers inundated us with reference books and cuttings from the magazine library. Then these relentless taskmistresses assumed responsibility for the accuracy of every statement, every fact, every spelling. Even the most obvious information had to be accounted for, with sources noted in the margins. I learned that I could simplify this exercise by ascribing almost everything to 'common knowledge'. No matter how the researchers argued, they could never prove that the knowledge, though possibly new to them, was not common. But then the rigorously annotated copy had to be passed on to senior editors, who prided themselves on imposing further refinements at high speed, usually scribbling changes in the course of a first and only reading, rather than reading everything in full before considering how they might improve it. The final product was often so transmogrified and bent to fit available space that it rarely gave me any sense of achievement.

A few exceptionally disciplined staff writers had to work hard, especially on long, complex cover stories, written under intense pressure to keep up to date with breaking news. My own duties were never arduous. I soon drifted editorially to what was called 'the back of the book', pages devoted mainly to entertainment and the arts. Editors allowed a good deal of freedom where writers' opinions would not clash with the magazine's overall political policies. And at last I was permitted occasionally to venture out of the office to see performances and exhibitions and to interview various musicians, artists and writers. No other city in the world could have been intellectually more stimulating and more fun.

I met the Benny Goodman Quartet, reunited after many years for a concert at Carnegie Hall. ('How do I get to Carnegie Hall?' 'Practise, man! Practise!') Before rehearsing on the stage, Teddy Wilson, Lionel Hampton and Gene Krupa were sitting together on one side of the auditorium; Benny Goodman was sitting alone on the other side, as far away from them as possible. Why? Krupa, chewing gum as usual, laconically suggested: 'He's probably thinking.' Goodman was said to be a severe leader, not much loved by his fellow musicians. William Shawn, Harold Ross's greatest successor as editor of the *New Yorker*, was standing at the back of the hall. 'Once they're playing,' he said, 'you'd never know there are any hard feelings.'

Alan King and I had shared a fondness for Scotch when I interviewed him after his Royal Command Performance at the London Palladium. Now in New York, he invited me to his mock-Tudor mansion, once the home of Oscar Hammerstein, at King's Point, in Great Neck, Long Island. Alan arranged to have me picked up in a limousine after it had collected another guest, Dorothy Walters, the most powerful, not to say tyrannical, woman broadcaster in American television at that time. Her voice in conversation could be sweetly beguiling, even girlish in the way she failed to roll her 'r's, without quite disguising her will to dominate. As the limo crossed the East River, I observed that the hazy orange sunset was 'Turneresque'. 'Where did you get that?' Ms Walters demanded, reminding me of a *Newsweek* researcher.

Outside Alan's house, standing on a lawn near the tennis courts, I looked across the Sound at a dim green light on a distant quay, like the view that tantalised Gatsby. The house contained a White Horse pub, perhaps a replica, more likely the real thing, transported across the Atlantic like Hearstiana. At dinner, Ms Walters told me that I was holding the implement for cheese-paring upside down.

Most irritatingly, she was right. After dinner, the large room was converted into a cinema and for about 110 minutes she was silent. The following week, thanks to Alan, I was able to lunch at the Friars Club, most of whose members were foremost Jewish comedians. I sat beside Phil Silvers, who talked just like Sergeant Bilko. Another lunchtime I attended a Friars Roast at the Astor Hotel, a Razzimonial in Alan's honour. Jack E. Leonard, the principal heckler, who had his own microphone next to the main speakers, said: 'Alan, you've got a lot of polish – but it's all on your shoes.'

Then Alan took me in his Rolls up to the Concord Hotel in the Catskills, a mountainous resort area known as 'the Jewish Alps'. The Concord was so vast and prosperous that it could afford to pay Alan as much as a Las Vegas hotel paid a star for a single performance. Plenty. 'You have to get the money,' he used to say. 'It's "fuck-you money".' Sitting in the back of the chauffeur-driven car, we drank Scotch from a long flask in a hollow malacca cane. At the hotel after dinner, he showed his flair for the inverted tributes of a Razzimonial. 'Before going into my act about my wife Jeanette and suburban crabgrass,' he told the capacity audience, 'I want to introduce Pat Catling, the limey who loves kikes. Stand up, Pat, and take a bow!' Feebly waving in a dazzling spotlight, I endured the longest, least funny few seconds of my life. It has always seemed unfair that American Jews and African-Americans can publicly use offensive slang names for themselves and others which would brand WASPs as racist bigots. But, of course, like Alan at the Astor, I smiled. After all, I'm only 50 per cent WASP.

Like its older rival, Grossinger's, the Concord attracted families and younger unmarried men and women. Most of the single women were looking for husbands, while most of the men played their parts in the courtship ritual, if only for its own sake. These hotels were like the one that Woody Allen visits in *The Front*, a savage tragi-comedy about black-listed writers and performers during the McCarthy era. Woody plays a Brooklyn delicatessen cashier through whom screenwriters black-listed as Communists are able to submit their scripts. Zero Mostel plays a black-listed comedian who is desperate enough to accept derisorily low pay for a one-night stand at the hotel. The cashier, having made a lot of money as the front, believes that he, himself, is a writer. Attending a cocktail-party mixer for singles at the hotel, he wears a tweed jacket with patched elbows. When a predatory woman asks the classic initial question, 'What do you do?' he draws himself up and proudly declares that he is a writer, whereupon she turns and leaves him without another word. Having learned his lesson, he tells the next enquirer that he is a dentist, and she leans closer, enchanted. Every writer at some time must have undergone the same sort of questioning. It goes like this:

'What do you do?'

'I'm a writer.'

'Should I have heard of you?'

'Well . . .'

'What's your name?'

The name is given.

'Oh.'

Sometimes, some sort of social pressure may prolong the exchange. It gets no better:

'What do you write?'

'Novels mostly.'

'What are they about?'

'Life and death. Stuff like that.'

'Do you wait for inspiration or do you just write anyway?'

'Um.'

'Have any of your books been made into movies?'

'Not really.'

'Do you use a word processor?'

And so on, until the US Cavalry appear over the crest of the hill.

Zero Mostel was marvellous in *The Front* (he knew what it was like to be punished for left-wing sympathies), in Mel Brooks's *The Producers* (featuring 'Springtime for Hitler') and, on the stage, in *A*

Funny Thing Happened on the Way to the Forum. With quick gestures, in seconds he mimed the complete frieze on a Grecian urn. He habitually had late-morning coffee with Joseph Heller, who rented a small studio on Fourteenth Street, away from his home. Mostel took me there one morning. The author of *Catch-22* showed me some of his recent paintings. They were miniatures, all depicting apocalyptic nuclear explosions.

I spent more time than was strictly necessary wandering from bar to bar, tavern to tavern, in Greenwich Village, in a quest for the ghost of Dylan Thomas. Many ageing bohemian drunks claimed intimate familiarity with the poet, if not his poetry. They enjoyed sharing the benefits of my expense account. The excuse for the long pub-crawl was the opening on Broadway of a play called *Dylan*. Alec Guinness played the boisterous Welshman in an absurd accent and a Harpo wig. It would be difficult to imagine more unsuitable casting. After Dylan's fatal excursion from the Chelsea Hotel and the eighteen whiskies that caused his death by what was medically defined as 'a massive insult to the brain', there was a scene in the play of toe-curling embarrassment: the widow Caitlin sits by the coffin in the hold of the ship taking her husband's remains back to Britain and speaks in maudlin apostrophe to him, while a ship's officer as clean-cut as a Gillette advertisement stands stoically at attention behind her. Not even Alec Guinness could save the play. The playwright suffered waiting in Sardi's for the first reviews. The run was mercifully brief.

There were several trips down to the Five Spot, where Thelonious Monk's trio was a fixture. Gerry Mulligan and his beloved Judy Holliday were usually at a table near the stand. Monk was generally uncommunicative, except musically. When he left the piano, he slowly shambled in time with the music, with his back to the audience, like a bashful old dancing bear. I admired his pork-pie hat and bamboo-framed shades. He always passively welcomed Mulligan's late-night intrusions to join the group with his baritone sax.

Other evenings, on the way back from the office and *Newsweek*'s favourite bar, I often met Diane for nightcaps at the Madison Pub, and to play Dave Brubeck's 'Take Five' on the juke-box, again and again. Arnold Roth, an American cartoonist who contributed impartially to *Punch* and *Playboy* and played tenor sax at every opportunity, introduced me to Paul Desmond, Brubeck's alto saxophonist, who composed 'Take Five', made a quick fortune with it, and found the highest pinnacle of success intolerably vertiginous. He was a fluent and witty musician who was also adept at writing ironic words. We had a lot of laughs over lunch at the Russian Tea-Room, near his flat, but the humour was unremittingly black. I was saddened, of course, but not very surprised when I heard that he had killed himself. Suicide, it seemed, was endemic among the most talented people in big cities.

Tomi Ungerer, a native of Alsace who had arrived in New York almost destitute but soon made it in a big way as a graphic designer, the darling of chic advertising agencies, a cartoonist and the writer and illustrator of marvellously idiosyncratic children's books, was sitting quietly in a corner of a small Madison Avenue gallery when Diane and I, by chance, came upon his one-man exibition there. That morning, the gallery was deserted but for the artist. We liked his paintings' surrealist whimsy and originally stylish execution. For example, one realistically depicted a man sinking in a carpet up to his armpits as he approaches an executive at his desk. Our noisy laughter and appreciative comments gratified Ungerer sufficiently to escort us immediately to his house in the East Nineties. He showed me work in progress on a book about a Moon Man and antique dolls he was surgically torturing for fun, and introduced us to his beautiful American wife, Yvonne, whom he had met accidentally in a New York subway station.

✳   ✳   ✳

I have never liked night-clubs. I thought Fragonard's elegantly erotic ladies in the Frick Collection were much more appealing than the dancers at the Copacabana. I preferred the Museum of Modern Art's sculpture garden to El Morocco. One evening, however, a late-middle-aged editor at William Morrow, the publisher of my first children's book, invited me to accompany him to the Stork Club, where celebrities and non-celebrities pretended not to eye each other, and Walter Winchell, the execrable J. Edgar Hoover of the gossip columnists, presided nightly over his special table, receiving scandalous revelations from his toadying spies. My host was concerned with Morrow's books for grown-ups. He introduced me to Sherman Billingsley, the owner of the Stork, because his autobiography, he recognised, was 'a lousy fucking job', and he needed a new ghost-writer. As the Dom Perignon flowed, the editor's manner became increasingly sycophantic towards Billingsley. When the editor and I were left alone, he told me that all I had to do was run the script through my typewriter, as he put it, tighten the prose and smooth out the rough spots and goose it here and there to give it a little sophisticated pizzazz. For me, he promised, the chore would be a cinch and wouldn't take much of my spare time. While I was so engaged, everything at the Stork would be comped, if I knew what he meant. On the house, right? And the fee would be $5,000. In 1963 that was nice bread, I must admit, he said. My *Newsweek* salary was only $14,000, he reminded me (he had asked about that), and I had to face the fact that my allowable expenses were not all that great.

Billingsley brought the typescript over. It landed on the table with a thump. There were about eight hundred grubby pages. 'You can take it home and read it,' he said magnanimously. 'I trust you. Then come back and I'll tell you the features that have to be built up.' The editor gave me an encouraging wink behind Billingsley's back, and a waiter opened another bottle of champagne.

✢   ✢   ✢

236

At a time when every respectable establishment employed at least one token black, *Newsweek*'s liberal conscience was eased by the presence of a young reporter who looked like Harry Belafonte in his prime, in a charcoal-grey hopsack blazer of Ivy League cut, with mother-of-pearl buttons. He was a smoothie of modest charm. I was delighted to accept his invitation to meet his friend James Baldwin. The Black Power movement was bullish, and Baldwin was its angriest, most articulate literary spokesperson.

We were admitted to an apartment living room of conventional décor and indirect lighting, where the great little man was reclining against cushions on the floor, with a couple of imposing, young, attentive acolytes/lovers/bodyguards seated close by in armchairs. Baldwin had a tadpole's physique, fully compensated for by hyperthyroid eyes protuberant with intelligence, zeal and indignation. In conversation he tended to monologise in language that was both evangelical and hip. Almost immediately, he spoke to me in a manner by turns confessional and inquisitional. He had a remarkable gift for instant intimacy — indeed, he seemed to insist on it.

He told me a publisher had just offered him a million dollars, to be spread over a period of twenty years, like Howard Hughes's contracts with Jane Russell and Bob Mitchum. In return, Baldwin would have to pledge the rights to everything he wrote. 'I mean, like everything.' Fifty thousand dollars a year, almost a grand a week, would provide security that very few writers experience.

'Did you accept?' I asked.

'You gotta be kidding. I probably would never have written another word. I'd have sold my whole *self*.'

Already pretty sure of his answer, I asked what he thought of my own, humbler dilemma. Should I rewrite Sherman Billingsley's autobiography?

'There's some quite good stuff about his poverty-stricken childhood in Oklahoma,' I said. 'As a small boy, he used a toy wagon to deliver bootleg booze.'

'How adorable,' Baldwin commented. 'Don't have anything to do with it, unless you want to be a whore.'

I felt suitably chastised. 'All right,' I said, trying to save face. 'I won't ghostwrite Sherman Billingsley if you quit writing like a professional Negro.'

One of Baldwin's attendants got to his feet and moved threateningly closer to where I sat, but Baldwin waved him back. There was a reassuringly comradely clinking of glasses, and Baldwin and I both evidently agreed that our encounter was mutually beneficial. The evening was educationally my most rewarding in New York.

47

When Diane suggested that it would not be a bad idea to get married, we hired a car for the weekend and drove down to Maryland, a more picturesque venue than City Hall. Dick Kilian, an American newspaperman who had been sympathetically playful on the *Daily Express* in London and Paris, came along for the ride. When we heard Louis Armstrong sing 'Hello, Dolly!' on the car radio, it was Kilian who turned up the volume in a mood of Devil-may-care frivolity.

No preliminary arrangements having been made, we went to the Tidewater Inn, in Easton, on the Eastern Shore, where the manager informed me that I had picked the only county in the state in which a wedding could be conducted only by an ordained minister. As I had to be back at *Newsweek* on Monday morning, we did not have much time to shop around. This was before the Internet. We did what journalists usually do when confronting a tricky problem: we settled at a table in the bar. There was a telephone, and the directory's Yellow Pages listed plenty of local churches, but I discovered that an out-of-town divorcé applying by telephone for a quick wedding was up against formidable resistance. Some time back I had had to plead for special permission from the Episcopalian Bishop of Maryland, the Very Reverend Noble C. Powell, for Susan Watson and me to get married in the aptly named Church of the

Redeemer. After an uncomfortable audience, the bishop decided that my wartime marriage was merely the folly of an impetuous teenager, and really didn't count. Because of my fling with Peggy Lee, my divorce from Susan (she married Tony Crosland) and my new commitment, I no longer lamented that my officially sanctioned redemption in Baltimore had proved impermanent. On the present occasion, however, there was no opportunity to plead before a high authority; and, anyway, there was no likelihood that a plea would be considered favourably.

At the barroom telephone, I attempted, with rapidly shrinking confidence, to persuade a succession of local ministers to perform the desired ceremony – Episcopal, Presbyterian, Lutheran, Baptist, Ethiopian Charismatic, even a Roman Catholic priest, who, unsurprisingly, was astonished by my gall. My mother had had me baptised a Catholic when I was a baby. My father had been lukewarmly Church of England. We all drifted away from any church, without ever feeling happy about our lapse. Now, when I despondently returned to the table, I saw a bottle of champagne in an ice-bucket and three glasses.

'Success?' Kilian asked with a congratulatory grin.

'No such luck. I'm afraid a celebration is a bit premature.' Kilian had recently given up full-time employment, preferring the tight-rope excitement of freelancing. I did not want him to spend his money on expensive drinks.

'Why did you order it then?' he asked, frowning in perplexity. We each thought the other had been rashly extravagant.

'Well, somebody start pouring,' Diane suggested, who was often sensible. 'It might be good for morale.'

We heard a delighted chortle from a man sitting alone at the only other occupied table. Bill Veeck, the owner of the Chicago White Sox or Chicago Cubs, was in Maryland on a visit. He was an eccentric of masterful resourcefulness, famous for having enabled his baseball team to win an important game by sending properly uniformed midgets in to bat in the bottom half of the ninth inning, thus baffling the opposing pitcher, who failed to pitch accurately that low and walked in the needed runs. The strike zone between a midget's shoulders and knees is a small target. Veeck's ingenuity and sense of humour were adaptable to difficult situations. He had taken pity on us and donated the champagne.

'The bar is quiet,' he pointed out. 'I couldn't help hearing of your predicament. I went out and used the phone in the lobby for a quick call. Your worries are over. I've contacted a man I know – a nice guy, very understanding, a liberal Christian. He has a church a short walk from here. It's a pretty little church and I know he'll do a good job. His name is Archie Prevatt. Here's his number.'

Generous Bill Veeck, a providential *deus ex machina*, accepted our thanks, declined an invitation to join us, and quietly slipped away.

48

Not long after President Kennedy was murdered, Diane and I sailed back across the Atlantic, from Norfolk, Virginia, to Genoa in an Italian collier, at no cost to ourselves. As I had resigned, *Newsweek* was not obligated to pay me anything extra in farewell, but did so regardless, and invited me to return to the staff some time if I wished. The editors were so magnanimous that I felt a twinge about going out again into the cold; fortunately, however, the outside proved to be encouragingly warm.

A convivial Southerner, Bill Lashley, who was apparently something in a major railroad's public-relations department, managed to get us the voyage *gratis* with an Italian subsidiary shipping line. After coal was loaded, poured into the holds, the covers were battened down and hosed, and the collier gleamed as immaculately as a new, white yacht. We were accommodated in the owner's suite, all marble, chrome, glass and plush. We dined uproariously with the master and his half-dozen officers, on fine Italian food and wine. Although we were the only passengers, the crew set up a large, canvas swimming tank on an upper deck. And everyone was on such good terms by the time we crossed the sunny Gulf of Genoa, just before being piloted into the home port, that they laughed when I marvelled at the efficiency with which they unloaded contraband into a launch that came alongside.

On the way north we visited Jane Heaton, who was drinking pastis and chain-smoking lethally pungent French cigarettes in a converted chapel in La Garde Freinet, inland from St Tropez. The marquess's daughter was contentedly married to a retired French soldier of low rank who spoke no English, a simple man who obviously adored her. She did not miss her hectic party life in Chelsea. In the same village we called on Nicki Kaldor, the Gaitskellite Hungarian economist, who was staying in a holiday villa and missed his hectic party life a lot. Having lived in voluntary exile in Guatemala, we thought we knew how Jane and Nicki felt. Exile is sometimes simultaneously both good and bad.

After a brief detour to look at Gaudí's vegetable-form cathedral and his apartment house with balconies resembling breaking waves, we flew from Barcelona to London. The woman who ran the press office at the Savoy, in response to a cry from the heart, had been able to secure for us the Charlie Chaplin Suite, overlooking the river, for one night, on the house. Journalism can sometimes gain access to benefits that otherwise might be difficult to afford.

I could already imagine the inconvenience of running out of money. I made some Fleet Street telephone calls. As my Aunt Alys was temporarily abroad, we were able to move into her flat in Edinburgh and use her car, while we awaited developments, if any. I had no idea for a second novel, traditionally reputed to be the most difficult of all.

Alys was almost due back when Michael Hogg, the Deputy Editor of the *Telegraph Magazine*, offered me a retainer; if there were even one article a month the earnings would be considerably more. At the same time, a sporadic income would continue from *Punch*, though that publication was noticeably in decline. Warwick Charlton, who tended to show up at times of need, said he knew of a nice little flat in his block in Hampstead Way, on the edge of Hampstead Heath. The flats gave onto a rose garden. Diane was pregnant and did not seem to mind my inevitable absences. John Anstey, the Editor of the *Telegraph Magazine*, gave me many picturesque feature assignments, some requiring foreign travel and all requiring lavish expenditure. Anstey did not only tolerate flamboyant expenses, he insisted on them; he felt they were good conditioning for the accountants – after all, he had expenses of his own.

There was a preposterous fashion shoot among icebergs in the fjords of Greenland. In those days, models were being posed more and more bizarrely in juxtaposition with primitive natives in outlandish locales. There was a Bacchus robot that gave a vinological spiel in various languages in the cellar of La Tour d'Argent. Claude Terail, the proprietor, provided pressed duck at a window table with a view of the Seine. There was a long excursion with Christopher Moorsom in the Bahamas, surveying estates for sale. Anstey was always interested in luxurious bargains. Shortly before we left Nassau, Christopher and I gave a thank-you party in a borrowed beach-house for local socialites whose families had not spoken to each other since differences of opinion over the murder of Sir Harry Oakes. We had a barman and waiters in white jackets, a large quantity of drink on sale or return, and the venerable Blind Blake, the Calypsonian, still shocking but disarmingly funny. There were some reconciliations.

Research for a profile of the British Ambassador to Romania gave me an opportunity to interview Dr Anna Aslan at her gerontological clinic in Bucharest. She claimed that daily injections of a procaine cocktail with amphetamines (shades of Dr Feelgood) was greatly prolonging the lives of her inmates. She exhibited a couple she said were 102 and 108 years of age who had just got married at the institute, 'and' she added, nudge, nudge, wink, wink, 'it's a *real* marriage.' She also indiscreetly revealed a dossier of testimonial letters from celebrities thanking her for rejuvenation by courses of KH-3 capsules (later available in Britain). The satisfied clientele included Chancellor Adenauer, Maurice Chevalier, the so-called Red Dean of Canterbury, and others previously thought to be far past their prime. Perhaps her laboratory dissertation on sexuality helped to inspire Novel Number Two.

Diane had our first baby, called Charlotte. John Gale, of the *Observer*, said she must be spiritually advanced: at one week of age, she looked 'like a Tibetan monk'. The flat suddenly became too small. I got in touch with Gerald Nabarro, a Member of Parliament, rumoured to be heir to an Armenian carpet fortune, who lived in high style in Broadway, Worcestershire, close to the Cotswolds. Did he know of any houses for rent? Thanks to his good offices, we soon moved into Mary's Acre, a lovely old house in Broad Campden, near Chipping Campden, Gloucestershire. There were an orchard, a flower garden and a kitchen garden and, part of the package, a cottage housing a gardener rejoicing in the name Hector Hathaway. He spoke broad mangel-wurzel, a dialect obscure to townsfolk, in which, perhaps, he deplored greenfly. While performing his arcane horticultural rites he kept repeatedly singing, in a slow, liturgical bass, 'We All Live in a Yellow Submarine'.

The owner of the house was English, a member of Boodles who had lived for many years in Brazil. Luckily for us, he must have been unaware of rising costs in England or he simply didn't care about them. The rent was low. But that was all that was low. As I sat in my study at my cobwebbed typewriter, gazing through the leaded panes of the mullioned windows, I was enthralled by a never-ending procession of tradesmen's vans, from Campden's modest grocery, from a gourmet delicatessen in Broadway, from Harrods and Fortnum & Mason – and from El Vino; even there, I had an account. Frank Bower regularly delivered cases of Fleurie and Traminer, our current favourites. Immediately outside the front gates, there was a tiny chapel; however, to flee from contemplation of our dissipating finances, I usually passed it for the more profoundly oneiric sanctuary of the Baker's Arms.

The Muse of Fiction answered my 4 a.m. whimpers after I read Masters and Johnson's work of best-selling popular science, *Human Sexual Response*. Carrying on from where Kinsey had left off, they reported in graphic detail on subjects' sexual behaviour appraised, measured and statistically collated in a lab. Never was a medical treatise offered more temptingly for burlesque. I jumped at it.

As most browsers in bookshops are believed to judge the readability of a novel by the first paragraph, I devoted careful consideration to the opening of Chapter One. The very first word I eventually chose was intended to give potential readers a representative sample of what was to come: '"Orgasm?"'

I took the magic word and a one-page synopsis to Anthony Blond, an unapologetically wicked Old Etonian who was glad to publish salacious fiction as long as it made him laugh. The publishing house over which he presided was his own and he could publish anything he liked. His star novelist was Simon Raven, a classicist whose own amorous predilections and fantasies would have made Catullus cringe. Anthony paid Raven a weekly subsistence allowance while writing, on condition that he stayed away from London. He was easily lured by flesh-pots and gambling hells. This strict regimen significantly helped Raven to produce his *chef d'oeuvre*, his novel-sequence *Alms for Oblivion*.

Blond read what I gave him while he sat at the desk in his office and I stayed in the room. He did not take long.

'Mmm,' he commented with a judicious nod and a crafty smile. 'This smells of money.' Coming from him, that was the most devoutly to-be-wished-for tribute. Right from the start, we understood one another perfectly. His office was an elegant terrace-house in Doughty Street, until he sold it to the *Spectator*. I named my hero Doughty in honour of the street, for he was 'able, strong, brave', in accordance with the Chambers definition, although also vulnerably naïf. Blond had once been a literary agent. As a publisher he preferred to eliminate the middle-man. The preference should have put me on my guard. The instant contract might have been devised by Groucho Marx. But I was very happy to sign it, and Anthony is still a friend.

Blond advised me to take the next train home and get cracking. The trouble with topicality, he explained, is that there may be a race with unexpected rivals. Before I hurried from his office, he conferred upon the novel its title, *The Experiment*.

Creamy erotica gushed from the typewriter, without let or hindrance, at the rate of almost two thousand words a day. I wrote in a state of feverish tumescence, more as a satyr than a satirist. But this isn't pornography, I told myself; it's Swiftian social commentary. Then I cackled like Hyde after gulping the elixir and sloped off into the thunderous night of my imagination.

Blond's impatience was supportive. Telephone calls, he soon decided, were not enough. His long, shiny, black Lincoln filled the drive. He seized the work-in-progress and devoured it with snarls of gratification. 'More! More!' was the cry. Home-made parsnip wine at the Baker's Arms stimulated further hilarity for a while, then tranquillity, and finally a condition like rigor mortis. The next day was a non-writing day. Anthony came downstairs at noon, with several shaving cuts stanched with scraps of Kleenex. Over tall glasses of brandy, ginger ale and lemon peel, we recapitulated the essentials of the editorial conference. His enthusiasm, though some-what muted, was undiminished. What a publisher!

And what a salesman! On the Sunday after publication day, London's principal three 'quality broadsheets', as they called them-selves, the *Observer*, the *Sunday Times* and the *Sunday Telegraph*, devoted their lead fiction reviews to *The Experiment*. There are novelists who say they never read reviews of their books; others who say they sometimes glance at reviews but never take them seriously. They lie. I read my reviews over and over again, and Diane read them aloud, marvelling at the reviewers' sublime judgment and eloquence. The book immediately became a bestseller – Number One for two delirious weeks – and continued to sell like hash cookies.

In New York, Simon & Schuster bought *The Experiment* for Trident, the imprint that was created to move the works of Harold Robbins in vast numbers. Herb Alexander, my publisher there, passed me to his friend Paul Gitlin, a New York agent who out-hustled Swifty Lazar – and was literate. A former employee of Warner Brothers who wanted to be an independent producer took an option on the screen rights to the novel. A quotation from the

syndicated Kirkus review service, 'The Experiment is the most sensational book of the year,' was displayed prominently in a half-page
advertisement in the New York Times. My Trident editor with a name
of astronautical promise, Buck Moon, toasted success in martinis
at 21. For a while, I floated on a pink cloud. For a while, though
Diane and I did our utmost, we were unable to spend the money
as fast as it was coming in. For a while . . . Aesthetically, that
triumphant, dizzy period might have been the right time to die.

But then Desmond would not have been born, my one and only
son. I would not have written ten more novels and seven more
children's books, got to know P. G. Wodehouse, Graham Greene
and Diana Laing, flown in Concorde and spent winters in Grenada,
the fairest island in the Caribbean.

And learned to play better golf.

49

While still buoyantly confident, we used some of *The Experiment*'s faerie gold to move back across the Atlantic, to Antigua, Guatemala, the sixteenth-century Spanish colonial capital, a ghostly city of massive stone churches half-ruined by earthquakes. I thought we would prefer the mustiness of the haunted remains and secluded courtyards of antiquity to the modern capital. We leased an unnecessarily large, gloomy house, behind which there was a low, truncated pyramid, which, according to the owner, the Mayans had built for esoteric rituals on a small scale. I used this relic of questionable legend for alfresco dining and for launching rockets into the night sky. Unaccustomed to literary commercial success and unable to imagine its fragile ephemerality, I enjoyed the make-belief that life was a continuous fiesta. I disregarded the ominous rasp of saws and the banging of hammers in a nearby workshop whose sign proclaimed, in Spanish, 'The Sweet Sleep'. Carpenters were busy making coffins of all sizes, including tiny ones to fit the new-born.

When John Anstey asked me to write a piece for the *Telegraph Magazine* on Saba, in the Leeward Islands, a Dutch possession of absolutely no importance, I accepted the commission with a blithe shrug. All I remember of that venture is that I went on a two-man iguana hunt – really a one-man hunt; I was only a squeamish observer. The hunter, a migrant from Anguilla who looked as if he would soon resemble Uncle Remus, swung a machete vigorously enough to force our way through tangled undergrowth. At last, scratched by thorns and tormented by the whine of insects, I sighted the quarry, a miniature dragon, a lizard about three feet long, with scaly armour and spikes on its spine, of appearance so grimly primitive that its descendants could well have been live models for one of Spielberg's Jurassic nightmares. At a range of twenty yards or so, three rifle-shots had no apparent effect, but it was not entirely bullet-proof: it succumbed to a fourth shot, point-blank, through a small, red eye. I declined the hunter's offer to share this wretched creature, which, until then, had defied Darwinism, although I was assured that "guana good eating! Just like chicken, man!'

There were further brief interruptions of the Guatemalan sojourn: *Telegraph* junkets to Belize, which was still the capital of British Honduras; to Georgetown, British Guiana, which was no more fragrant than when I had sometimes refuelled at Atkinson Field, many years before; and to the Bay Islands, in the Gulf of Honduras. The Bay Islanders, like the iguana, had survived in spite of obvious unfitness. Descendants of maritime human jetsam, the failed freebooters and other riff-raff of ancient colonial conflicts, for generations they had lived as castaways, degeneratively inbreeding to the point of lethargic cretinism. They were simpletons with the straw-coloured hair, pale eyes and hectic complexions of the poor whites called red-necks in some backward parts of the United States. The Bay Islanders were clumsily hospitable, stupidly grinning, unless a stranger's skin was black. On the small island of Utila locals concerned with maintaining the purity of their genetic heritage, like the denizens of some God-forsaken shanty-town in rural Mississippi, threateningly made it clear that black visitors must leave by sunset.

Why did I undertake these inconsequential, out-of-the-way assignments? Apart from being beguiled by their otiose weirdness, I was probably subconsciously aware that it would be foolhardy not to retain at least a tenuous connection with somebody in Fleet Street as kindly disposed as Anstey. My wife did not complain about being repeatedly left alone with our very young daughter in a place where there were mysterious amoebic infections and most people did not speak English: however, though there were no overt complaints, there were increasingly frequent intimations that my hobby of exotic journalism was for her a pain in the neck. Perhaps it was time to try to write another novel.

50

I t is strange that a city as powerful, exciting and beautiful as New York keeps yearning for love. The lyricists in the Brill Building do their maudlin best to supply singers in the Sinatra mode with passionately sentimental civic eulogies. I like New York in June and all the other months but August. When we found a house with a big garden at a moderate rent near enough to the beach at Westhampton, I thought I should write a New York novel.

Westhampton, the first of the Hamptons to be reached on the Atlantic shore of Long Island, is socially not as chic as Southampton and intellectually and artistically not as smart as East Hampton, but, partly because of its generally perceived inferior status, it is the most relaxed of the three, and I like it best. There is an architectural gaudiness about many of the villas along Westhampton Beach, and an extravagant, Runyonesque verve about many of the people who occupy them during the Summer Season, tycoons of the garment industry, as they call the rag trade, and the only slightly more dignified senior executives of the Mafia. Their siliconed ladies gleam. Only about two hours by train from Manhattan, Westhampton is close enough to the city for frequent incursions, and yet sufficiently distant from it for a pseudo-anthropologist to gain an illusion of objectivity. At the time, I did not consider the advantage of a long perspective, but it is nice now to pretend that our choice of a temporary lodging was based on common sense.

Inspired by municipal roamings for *Newsweek* and an old article I had written in London on Britain's foremost company of pest exterminators, I made the principal character of *The Exterminator* an innocent young man new to marriage, new to New York and new to employment by Sanikill as a killer of rats. He was helped by Sam Rathbone, a rich dilettante whom I found helpful as a plot-fixer in this novel and in other novels afterwards.

What I liked best about Westhampton was that we lived less than ten minutes' drive from P. G. Wodehouse's home in the neighbouring village of Remsenburg. I got to know him as soon as I could. His friends called him Plum (Pelham, his first name, said fast), and he soon awarded me the privilege of calling him that. He was certainly the most amiable writer I have ever met. He was a literary phenomenon: in a notoriously anxious occupation, he seemed always to be tranquilly content. Many writers, both in and out of their cups, often complain that writing is hell and there is no more terrible sight than a blank sheet of paper. Plum, however, actually enjoyed writing. 'After all,' he wrote, 'there's nothing else to do in this world.' In his nineties he signed a contract with his American publisher for three novels – and delivered four. He continued to write until 1975, the year of his death, when he was ninety-four.

He was universally popular. His work was highly esteemed by discerning peers such as Evelyn Waugh and Hilaire Belloc, who called Wodehouse 'the best writer of our time: the best living writer of English'. His stories are said, perhaps apocryphally, to have persuaded German wartime spymasters that their agents could best operate undetected in England if they wore monocles and spats and kept saying 'What-ho!'. He regarded himself as a 'historical novelist' whose 'stuff has been out of date since 1914', yet his opinions on plotting, characterisation, dialogue, plagiarism and other literary matters remain pertinent always.

Popularity made him a millionaire and he continued to be interested in making more money, though he did not live extravagantly. But his contentment was evidently founded on his satisfaction with orderly work for its own sake and, more profoundly, on his blessedly sanguine nature.

Malcolm Muggeridge, as a British Army intelligence officer, got to know Wodehouse and his wife Ethel in France at the end of World War II, where they had been living when it broke out. The Germans interned him until he reached the age of sixty. While the war was still being waged, he indiscreetly recorded five flippant talks on his experiences in an internment camp, where, astonishingly, he continued to write novels and short stories in a communal recreation room, in spite of the noise of ping-pong. His fellow prisoners appreciated his humour, but at the time it did not travel well. The Germans transmitted the talks to Britain and America. William Connor, who wrote a sometimes vitriolic column as Cassandra in the London *Daily Mirror*, made a BBC broadcast reviling Wodehouse as a Nazi stooge, a propagandist for the enemy.

Muggeridge was among the first to recognise that Wodehouse was an innocent, living in a world of his own, whose German radio talks had been foolish rather than wicked. Wodehouse expressed his regret after the war, and characteristically befriended Connor. Several years later, Connor told me he regretted the intemperance of his wartime attacks against Wodehouse. Waugh actively campaigned for Wodehouse's rehabilitation, and millions of readers effectively demonstrated their loyalty by buying his books. When Muggeridge became the editor of *Punch* he invited Wodehouse to contribute to the magazine. He gladly wrote letters from America, commenting cheerfully on bizarre items in the American press. He said he felt that being paid to write these casual, 1,000-word pieces was very much like taking candy from a baby. Muggeridge, an expert on regrets, having changed colours as often as a chameleon, visited Wodehouse in Remsenburg to interview him for BBC Television. Muggeridge probed assiduously, yet failed to discover in Wodehouse any unhappy memories and opinions. Unlike so many other English writers who say they loathed their schooldays, Wodehouse remembered his time at Dulwich College most fondly. He followed the fortunes of his old school's cricket elevens and rugger fifteens with unwavering devotion until the end of his life.

'We are toying with a scheme for going round the world in December on the *Empress of Britain*,' he wrote from Hollywood to his friend William Townsend. 'Sometimes we feel we should like it, and then we ask ourselves if we really want to see the world. I'm darned if I know. I have never seen any spectacular spot that didn't disappoint me. Notably the Grand Canyon. Personally, I've always liked wandering around in the background.' During a professional stay in Hollywood, in 1937, he wrote to Townsend: 'I get so bored by the people I have to meet, especially at big parties. I would like to be an absolute hermit.'

In a 1954 letter to a fellow novelist, Denis Mackail, Wodehouse quoted what he candidly called 'a good line in my forthcoming Jeeves novel about Bertie's Uncle Tom. "His face wore the strained, haggard look it wears when he hears that guests are expected for the weekend,"' and he added: 'Don't you hate having people about the place?'

Fortunately for him, Ethel, his wife for sixty-one years, subordinated herself to Plum's needs and wishes and fully supported his withdrawal to the hermitage at Remsenburg, where he could write undisturbed in simple luxury. She was his perfect chatelaine, companion, secretary and nurse, and she made excellent dry martinis. Though reclusive, he was no misanthropist. His friendships, maintained mainly by correspondence, were warm and long-enduring. He rarely made the journey to Manhattan, where once he had lived in an apartment on Park Avenue, but he was able frequently to see Guy Bolton, his beloved collaborator on hit musical comedies, who lived in Remsenburg and had persuaded Plum to settle there. Ethel drove him in their plum-red Buick once a week to a supermarket in nearby Westhampton; Remsenburg was not marred by commercialism. Like some other married couples without children, the Wodehouses used to lavish affection on pets. They acquired a succession of dogs and cats deliberately, and hospitably accepted all others that applied for accommodation. He gave $35,000 to a local institution now called the P. G. Wodehouse Bide-a-Wee Shelter for strays. Ethel used to enjoy feeding the animals there, until a new manager foolishly ruled that only the staff were allowed to do so — a mistake that lost the shelter $300,000 that Plum had intended to leave it.

Plum was flourishing in his early eighties when I was his neighbour. With his encouragement I found that the best time to visit him was at 5.59, for his Happy Hour began punctually. Ethel concocted two large martinis apiece at the bar in the drawing room, never fewer, never more. Serenely smoking a pipe, with a dachshund recumbent at this feet, he spoke of his invariable, carefully structured, daily routine.

Before an early breakfast, he spent 30 minutes doing the Royal Canadian Air Force exercises. After breakfast, he wrote until noon, which was time to watch *Love of Life*, a sentimental TV soap opera, in which, he said, he was 'absorbed'. From two till three, he took their dog for a walk, which included a visit to the post office. Then he would 'brood on work' till five, have a bath and dress for cocktails, dinner and a game of two-handed bridge with Ethel. The routine was always basically the same, 'and somehow', he once wrote, 'it never gets monotonous.'

Like two other successful though very different novelists I have met, Arthur Hailey and Graham Greene, Wodehouse used to write 600 words a day. 'Six hundred words are not very many,' he told me. 'But if you write 600 words *every* day, the pages pile up, and every now and then you have a book.'

He was generous. When he visited my family in one of his infrequent deviations from routine, he brought a bouquet big enough for a Mafia wedding and an enormous box of Belgian chocolates. Charlotte entertained Plum by chasing rabbits in the garden. She was good at that. Some years later, she became a good architect. He was also generous in praise of other writers. I never heard him utter a word that could have been interpreted as bitchy. When I wrote an article about Wodehouse past and present for the *Telegraph* the subeditor's headline said, 'Come Home, Plum – All Is Forgiven'. But he had been irremediably wounded by the hostile criticism of his Berlin broadcasts. He never returned to England, even when, belatedly, shortly before his death, the Queen knighted him.

I did not show Plum any of *The Exterminator* while we stayed in Westhampton, and I didn't suggest to anyone at my London publishing house, the Bodley Head, that they should ask him for a comment suitable to improve the book's jacket. However, somebody did ask, and Plum responded typically with the best and most succinct review I have ever got: 'Brilliant! – It makes you laugh and it makes you think.'

P. G. Wodehouse was a paragon of writers. His advice was perfectly sound. If only I could have written 600 words a day ever since . . .

51

September is an idyllic month in Westhampton. The sunshine is still golden but slightly milder, with amber hints of autumn. After Labor Day 'the summer people' suddenly vanish; the beach reverts to pristine purity; the tradespeople count their takings. P. G. Wodehouse, having just finished a novel, immediately began a new one. I wondered idly whether I would ever have another idea. It was the beginning of the academic year, the beginning of the New York theatre season. But Charlotte was not old enough for school, and we stayed away from Broadway. The days drifted by until James Michie, a director of the Bodley Head, on a business trip to the United States, came to see us. Over lobster and white Burgundy, he expressed the view that I should end my Long Island holiday, return to England and get back to work. He himself was not indolent: in the taxi from his house in Eaton Terrace to his editorial office in Bow Street he customarily finished most, if not all, of the *Times* crossword puzzle.

On this occasion Cunard gave me only a discount rather than a free passage. I bought Cabin-Class tickets, and Public Relations kindly permitted us to pass the barriers to the ship's First-Class facilities. The *Queen Elizabeth* was making her final voyage. There were Scottish pipers on the quay. Diane's brother Douglas was so moved by their valedictory lament that he elected to stay with us as a stowaway and shared some more champagne. As soon as disembarkation was impossible I introduced him to the Purser, who was sufficiently amused to sell him a cabin.

Edward Montagu, Lord Montagu of Beaulieu, was aboard, displaying a vintage car to lure passengers to his Motor Museum. On the eve of his Jazz Festival he entertained the media at one end of a reception hall with beer and his friends at the other end with wine and spirits. I was promoted to gin and tonic only when he noticed that I already knew his star performer, Anita O'Day, whose faithful drummer and minder had successfully kept her on vodka, instead of less predictable mind-transformers.

Another passenger in the *Elizabeth*, Frankie Howerd, was working his way across the Atlantic by doing his act just once, for a First-Class gala cabaret on the last night but one. Having dinner with me the night before that, he morosely confided that the ship's senior officers were treating him like a servant. He managed to tell his audience what he thought of the Captain. 'He sent for me,' Howerd said. 'Oh, yes. He did, *really*. I was *summoned* to his quarters. He has lovely quarters. He came to the door himself, in *person*. He smiled. He seemed so friendly as he chatted. For a moment I thought *hello*, he's going to invite me in!'

Our car accompanied us to England, a white Chevrolet that seemed ordinary enough in Suffolk County, Long Island, but inordinately bulky in the country lanes of Gloucestershire. The steering wheel was on the left, of course, making solo navigation hazardous, especially when overtaking. Luckily, we had been able to return to Mary's Acre. Unluckily, on the way home after a long, solitary lunch, with plenty of claret and two or three glasses of port in a restaurant in Chipping Campden, I failed to avoid a lamppost a few yards from our gateway. The Darby and Joan couple who lived in Beehive Cottage, beside the dented lamppost, telephoned the police. The police, possibly sharing my wife's opinion that the car would be safer off the road, rushed to the scene with astonishing speed. A humbling appearance in the local magistrates' court brought about the inevitable fine and a twelve-month suspension of my driving licence.

Diane had a car of her own, a small Riley. There was another compensation. John Oldrey, a retired Royal Navy commander and stockbroker, a bon vivant who ran the Redesdale Arms Hotel in Moreton-in-Marsh, had jokingly persuaded me, just before the accident, to pay seven guineas for membership in the St Christopher's Association, providing insurance coverage particularly for drink-drivers. I joined for the fun of wearing the members' colourful tie, bile-green with stripes of blood-red. My reward was twelve months' taxi-service, up to £20 a week of it, which went a long way in those days. One month, not having used my full quota, a taxi took me from Broad Campden to London for a *Spectator* party. I was then the weekly's television critic.

James Michie is a poet, temperamentally as lugubrious as Larkin, yet much funnier, and a more fastidious classicist than Raven, but also stimulated by the eroticism of Latin poetry. Michie has translated it stylishly, rendering its bawdiness in metres and rhymes of exquisite precision. Auden said he had considered translating Horace, but, on reading Michie's version, had decided not to try, because he acknowledged that he could do no better. Conditioned by Horace and Catullus and emboldened further by the *Zeitgeist* of London in the latter years of the Swinging Sixties, Michie was quite enthusiastic when I followed *The Exterminator* with a modern inversion of *Fanny Hill*. *Freddy Hill* is the satirically moral tale of a Westhampton Beach lifeguard, 'the handsomest man in America, though he didn't know it yet', and the libidinous women who exploit him as they lead him down the Primrose Path.

Herb Alexander, who exerted a decisive influence over Pocket Books, also welcomed what he called my '*jeu d'esprit*'. 'You can write a commercially viable novel', he rationalised, 'without obviating the possibility of making a cultural gesture.' We walked along Fifth Avenue, towards the Plaza, but he dispensed his valuable advice over blackcurrant cheesecake at a more appropriate venue, Reuben's

Delicatessen. With no additional editorial guidance from New York, I awaited Michie's reaction to my first few chapters with white knuckles. It was only slightly reproachful. 'You have written forty-five pages,' he pointed out, 'and still haven't taken down Freddy's Y-fronts.' I was then quick to take them down, repeatedly, and Michie accepted the finished typescript with gratifying complaisance.

The carefree days lasted a bit longer. An excellent son, Desmond James, was born in the cottage hospital in Shipston-on-Stour. The clientele of the Baker's Arms, like Orientals, heartily helped me to celebrate the birth: after siring three daughters, I had finally proved, in their estimation, my virility. Desmond was born in November. By Guy Fawkes Day, I gathered enough high explosives for my biggest ever display of fireworks.

52

An international congress of distinguished medical scientists met in Edinburgh to discuss sleep. There was an institute of sleep research at the university. Through my aunt, by chance, I became acquainted with one of the researchers, who was able to arrange my admittance to the congress, though I did not propose to cover it for a newspaper. Like most other people, I spend about a third of my life in bed, usually asleep, and sleep is obviously important: during sleep the subconscious mind is dominant.

The convention programme included the presentation of papers on the function of dreams. When sleepers are dreaming, rapid eye movements (REM) are discernible beneath their closed eyelids. Researchers repeatedly woke volunteers at the beginning of REM episodes to prevent them from dreaming and discovered that dreamlessness soon causes severe psychological disturbances. Dreams are necessary for mental health: they clear the mind of psychic garbage, information not worth retaining; without them, the overload of sensory input (I picked up some jargon) can become intolerable. Normal people dream several times a night, but often forget having done so. Keeping a dream diary immediately on awakening can improve recall and provide data for analysis. That Edinburgh visit gave me ideas for two novels that I found especially interesting to write, *The Catalogue*, about a sort of clinical casting directory with photographs and biographies that enabled a single woman to dream about a variety of men whose semen was available for Artificial Insemination by Donor, and *Bliss Incorporated*, about programming dreams by inserting probes into the brain.

Ogden Nash came to our house for roast lamb, Stilton and fruit on our medieval refectory table. The evening was a jolly one: in the early stages, we exchanged Baltimore reminiscences; we both liked Maryland rye whiskey; and the jollity was only a little diminished when Ogden tumbled into the inglenook, where logs still smouldered. He was an Anglophile and considered the evening very Olde Cotswold and just as it should have been.

Wolf Mankowitz, an East End Londoner who became a Cambridge Leavisite and then a prolific author of short stories, novels, screenplays, a West End musical (*Expresso Bongo*) and the definitive work on Wedgwood china, was directing Richard Burton and Elizabeth Taylor in a little-theatre production in Oxford when he read *The Experiment* and decided it could be filmable. He wrote a script and made a tentative offer, but nothing came of it, except that our getting to know each other resulted in the next major change in my life.

Once again, Diane and I were running through our funds as if, as the saying goes, money were going out of fashion. That, of course, was when the Inland Revenue Service suddenly became pressingly importunate. When a writer starts showing symptoms of hubris, nemesis is almost sure to be represented by the tax-man. Wolf experienced his own difficulties in this respect. When I told him that my accountant's letters were becoming more urgent yet longer and more difficult to understand, Wolf suggested that I follow his example and take my family to Ireland. English authorities give the impression that they despise writers, unless they are supported by regular gainful employment. Freelances are treated as pariahs. The Republic of Ireland is different.

53

Philip Hope-Wallace of the *Guardian*, Patrick O'Donovan of the *Observer* and Kingsley Amis of the Garrick Club wrote testimonial letters enabling the Revenue Commissioners in Dublin to classify me as a 'creative artist', thus exempt from liability to taxation of my literary earnings. When the law was enacted, the Commissioners were instructed to interpret it liberally: they were not to serve as art critics, nor did they wish to. All sorts of writers, sculptors, painters and composers moved to Ireland, adding nothing to the tax coffers but reminding the world that Ireland is a civilised country that honours all artists, even those of meagre ability. In the age of television, Ireland still thinks of itself as the island of saints and scholars.

Closely following Wolf's footsteps, we went first to stay with Desmond Leslie, a wildly imaginative grandee in reduced circumstances, who was doing his utmost to preserve his inherited estate at Glaslough, in County Monaghan close to the border with Armagh, Ireland's seat of ecclesiastical authority, both Catholic and Protestant, and home of Northern Ireland's most zealous IRA activists. Patrick O'Donovan, when briefing me, had said: 'Behave as if you were going to live in a foreign country – because you are.' Desmond let me rent a flat on the top floor of Castle Leslie, an enormous granite refrigerator. In the severe frost of a Monaghan winter we went to bed wearing sweaters over our pyjamas, augmented by socks and woollen hats. Desmond told me which pub I could safely patronise in the town of Monaghan, and which one I should stay well clear of, because of the intensity of its anti-British virulence. My accent would betray me, he warned. I pointed out that my mother's maiden name was Houlihan and that her mother's maiden name was Blake. I was motivated by powerful Celtic genes from Skibbereen and Galway. 'You might not have enough time to explain,' Desmond said. 'They would only notice that you are your father's son.' The Leslie family, though Protestant, had been allowed immunity from arson since they had fed the local populace during the Famine. Inside the stone wall that encircled the extensive demesne, Castle Leslie felt stable, except for Desmond's theories on intergalactic travel. He was the co-author of *Flying Saucers Have Landed*.

We enjoyed the company of Desmond and his buxom wife Helen, but we were glad to follow Wolf again, on his recommendation. He had gone as far from County Monaghan as it is possible to go in the Republic, only a few miles short of the country's south-western extremity. He had restored a house beside a small road-bridge over a stream in the village of Ahakista, on the Sheep's Head Peninsula on Dunmanus Bay in County Cork. According to the sort of legend that Wolf found peculiarly attractive, his Bridge House was situated near the place where a fortune in gold had been secretly buried by the Man Who Broke the Bank at Monte Carlo. Wolf fixed us up with the absentee owner of a cottage which Wolf had finished with. The rent for the cottage and fourteen acres of barren, rocky hillside was £5 a week. Even back in the 1970s, that was as close to a peppercorn as a rent could be.

Cotton's Cottage was a far cry from Mary's Acre, but we quickly felt at home, even without daily renditions of 'We All Live in a Yellow Submarine'. The cottage was rudimentary, consisting of one long room on the ground floor, a kitchen with a dining table at one end and a large stone fireplace with a sofa and armchairs at the other, and three very small bedrooms and a bathroom on the floor above. A local carpenter, after lengthy consultations, put up some bookshelves. The total effect was a hygienic, well-furnished version of the cabin in Flann O'Brien's novella *The Poor Mouth*, which was so well illustrated by Ralph Steadman. Even without *The Poor Mouth*'s resident pig, our cottage was *cosy*.

The Gulf Stream, bearing warm water from the Gulf of Mexico, first touches Ireland on the Atlantic coast of County Cork. Palm trees flourish and daffodils bloom in February. Donald Grant, formerly of the *St Louis Post-Dispatch*, who seemed to feel he was doing rural Ireland a big favour by retiring there and keeping goats and bees, provoked native opprobrium when he published a book about the people of Kilcrohane. He portrayed them as quaint, old-fashioned peasants. To avoid that abysmal pitfall, I will refrain from describing the local publicans, farmers, doctors and teachers, except to say that they were friendly and amiable individualists, loyally integrated within a flexible but unbreakable communal web.

In theory, aided by all the new communication technology, writers are free to live anywhere in the world. Why is it then that so many elect to stay in their big cities in bad climates, as if by moving they would somehow lose the essence of their personalities? In one of the remotest outposts of Western Europe, I felt that there would be nothing to distract me from writing. However, there were days when I felt there was what a new friend in nearby Ballydehob called 'stimlack', a lack of stimulation. Sometimes Diane and I missed the very things we were glad to have escaped from, the noise of heavy traffic, the jostle and babble of crowds. When it seemed that relaxation was turning into lethargy, I found immediate relief in hit-and-run visits to Dublin, London and New York; travel required only money.

David Hanly, a publicist of Bord Fáilte, the Irish Tourist Board, was able to facilitate travel within the Republic, sometimes as members of media junkets which he made wonderfully festive. The first time I met him, in Dublin, he was wearing a three-piece suit of ginger tweed and an orange beard, which, as I confided to readers of the *Sunday Telegraph*, had the appearance of a leprechaun's ambush. Although I had stayed in the Algonquin several times before, it was Hanly who added another dimension of pleasure to my relationship with the hotel by putting me in touch with Andrew Anspach, its managing director, who proved to be an infallible guide to the theatre. And it was Hanly who cited the aphorism which many writers sometimes live by: 'I drink to forget that I cannot afford to drink.' He is a talented, original manipulator of the pen, the typewriter and the mouse. He flirted with the notion of himself as a novelist and, indeed, published an Irish novel with the traditional scenes of hangover and funeral and some untraditional interracial sex. Richard Condon, who was living in Ireland at that time, read the novel before publication and gave it his rhapsodic imprimatur. But the pram in the hall forced Hanly into a more careful way of life. He left the Tourist Board and became a broadcaster, on RTE Radio and Television, the esteemed anchorman of the morning news on radio, and a sympathetic TV interviewer of novelists who had remained stuck in their self-imprisonment.

Superagent Paul Gitlin magically produced another contract. It gave me an excuse to spend a few days in New York. He took me to lunch at a sumptuous expense-account restaurant. I think its name was the Forum of the Twelve Caesars. If there had been a forum of more numerous caesars, I'm sure he would have taken me there. He was a believer in the morale-boosting benefits of first class. We drank large measures of Chivas Regal slightly diluted with Perrier (Manhattan tap-water tastes abominable). After a certain amount of preliminary conviviality, we sat at our reserved table – the best table, of course – and, after some teasingly irrelevant small-talk, Paul instructed me to 'look under the matzo'. I lifted the wafer of unleavened bread on my side-plate and revealed a cheque for $25,000. I can recall very few joys in life that surpass the joy of eating and drinking with a good friend in a luxurious restaurant and being given a substantial advance for a novel that would be easy to write.

The novel in this case, according to my one-page outline, was to be entitled *Best Summer Job* and would concern the adventures of a young male graduate student researching articles for a newspaper resembling the *New York Times*. His subject was New York sexual mores, especially those of delegates to the United Nations, who, he discovered, enjoyed a private, bacchanalian club of their own called 'Jollies'. There was a subplot about an unhappily married police officer who sought consolation at the annual 'Gay Fuzz Drag Ball'. Imagine my chagrin when, much later, I found the novel in a branch of the New York Public Library on a shelf of books on 'Occupational Guidance'. Much thought should be devoted to the composition of novels' titles.

After lunch at the Forum, I went to Abercrombie & Fitch on Madison Avenue, and came out of the store wearing white buckskin shoes with red soles, a seersucker suit and a Panama hat with an unusually wide brim. The ensemble made me feel like a prosperous riverboat gambler, almost as up-beat as Tom Wolfe. Juleps in the Blue Bar at the Algonquin enhanced the illusion. I'm pretty sure I continued the celebration at the Carlysle. Bobbie Short's performances of sophisticated show songs, as if by James P. Johnson accompanying Hutch, could always be relied on to inflate a great, pink bubble of euphoria.

In Dublin, I paused to buy a Danish record-player and twin speakers. A puzzled Dublin taxi driver, unaccustomed to venturing far beyond the suburbs, drove me all the way across Ireland, from the Shelbourne Hotel to Cotton's Cottage, stopping en route only for us to dine at the Bishop's Palace, a restaurant in Cashel. I got home very late. Diane and the children remained asleep until I set up the speakers on opposite sides of the fireplace and played the test record. With the highest imaginable fidelity and the volume turned up high, it announced my return in an express train roaring through the cottage.

As Graham Greene said more than once, writers brag about money because they know that their success is only failure deferred.

I hurled the Gitlin bonanza about like confetti. As might have been predicted, the euphoria did not last long. After a few happy months, autumn came, and winter. The same Paul Gitlin telephoned for the first time with news of a disaster. Simon & Schuster had awarded me yet another contract, for a novel about an idealistic chef; two thirds of the advance had been paid, and about one third of the book had been written, when S & S were taken over by the vast company which Mel Brooks, in *Silent Movie*, caricatured as 'Engulf and Devour'. The faceless bosses of the conglomerate did what reorganised publishing houses often do with new brooms. Some contracts were unilaterally annulled. My contract for *Secret Ingredients* was one of them. It was published in London, but never in New York, though the best scenes take place in the Algonquin during the era of the Round Table, in a Hollywood producer's mansion, and in General Eisenhower's trailer on the eve of D-Day. Only Wolf Mankowitz, a calloused pessimist, was unsurprised. I was devastated.

54

Would-be novelists, novelists and ex-novelists pose more or less severe tests of women's faith, hope and charity. Writers of fiction, inevitably, it seems, spend many of their waking hours in a self-indulgent, narcissistic fantasy, in which, even in the early stages of amorous enthusiasm, women of intelligence and sensitivity can only pretend to find a comfortable place. Over the years, writers' moods characteristically range from nervous aspiration to arrogance to resentment and despair. Their companions' only good chance of finding something like shared happiness occurs during that fleeting period when ambitions first approach close to fulfilment. Like manic-depressives in some other occupations (banking, farming, driving trains), writers are equally awkward to live with whether up or down; at either extreme they are just about impossible. The stronger and more idealistic the woman, the smaller the likelihood of a permanent relationship. Anyway, that is what I have been given to understand, more than once. My comments, of course, come from a masculine point of view. Are writers more balanced, reasonable, unselfish and lovable if they are women?

In the valley of the shadow of debt, my despondency made writing increasingly difficult; and the less I wrote, the more profoundly despondent I became. A gloomy state of mind cannot be accommodated conveniently with a wife and two young children in a small cottage in rustic seclusion. All four of us, in our different ways, got on each others' nerves. If such melancholy situations can be assessed statistically, I am bound to concede that the fault was about 90 per cent mine. Perhaps a bit more.

I lived then whole-heartedly by the Hanly maxim. I drank to forget that I could not afford to drink. At the time, I believed the people's poet in Flann O'Brien's exemplary novel, *At Swim-Two-Birds*, the public-house bard who declaimed: 'A pint of plain is your only man.' Flann O'Brien understood the twisted psyche of thwarted literary drinkers, because he, himself, was one of them/us. Although he had published several novels of scintillating originality, including a frightening simulacrum of hell, *The Third Policeman*, and though he had written Myles of unsurpassably misanthropic wit for the *Irish Times*, at the forefront of his brain there was a nagging awareness that dramaturgically he was a disappointing commercial flop. He was never satisfied.

So Diane politely demanded out. I drove the three of them up to Shannon Airport. As they walked away to board their plane to New York, Desmond, at the latest possible moment, ran back and quickly kissed me goodbye. Then I was *really* sorry.

55

The world continued to revolve about its axis and around the sun, not that I immediately cared. At a certain low level of wallowing, it is possible actually to derive morbid pleasure from solitude, even among friends, until aloneness becomes loneliness. For a short time, I dressed very casually indeed and gave up shaving, but I have never been able to endure the itch of stubble for more than a few days. When I unenthusiastically took up my razor and addressed the bathroom looking-glass, I noticed that my face was swollen at the edges below the ears. An amiable horseplayer who habitually drank 'one-and-ones' (whiskey and ale) in the neighbourhood shebeen offered the opinion that my condition was 'probably mumps'. As, in his spare time, he was a general practitioner of medicine, I responded to the diagnosis by drinking a few more pints for the road and retiring to my bed. Maybe the malady was mostly in the mind. I suppose there could be such an affliction as psychosomatic mumps.

Two days after my withdrawal from society, there was a gentle knock at the door, and then further knocks. Ignoring them had no deterrent effect.

'I thought this might help,' said an encouragingly attractive, petite blonde (dress size 10) who was ten years younger and much better turned out than I. We had recently met. She offered a lonely widow's sympathetic smile and a covered dish of custard, a goyish equivalent of chicken soup. My cure was instantaneous. I was so moved that we have spent the next thirty years together, with hardly any interruptions. She has forbidden mention of her name in this text, perhaps because of fear of association with my past matrimonial failures. She apparently regards them with superstitious dread rather than disdain. It is not that I have a bad track record; there has been no advance whatsoever along anything as orderly as a track; before I encountered the present incumbent consort, I was a zig-zag jogger of limited endurance. There were joys on the way, for which I am grateful, but we don't talk about them.

There is no place I know more tranquilly charming than the green shore of Dunmanus Bay, with easy access to one of the loveliest of all golf courses, on Bantry Bay, and yet the anonymous she and I have travelled inordinately.

We visited Baltimore, where my mother spent the terminal years of her second widowhood and my brothers happily prospered. Duncan, the younger one, who was good at writing but eschewed it as a career, served in the Peace Corps in Malaya and the South Pacific and then taught in Baltimore public schools and collected Japanese prints, until his untimely death. Timothy made enterprising and systematic progress in his own public-relations company, with sufficient success to buy a town house with a large, heated swimming pool and a farm with horses.

We took Greyhound buses to Las Vegas, for a reunion with Alan King, though a friend pointed out that buses were what losers *left* Vegas in.

We spent two months in Taos, admiring New Mexico's red sunsets and making the trip (not a pilgrimage) to the remote ranch-house where D. H. Lawrence and Frieda had some of their last jealous rows. His ashes are immured, actually mixed in the concrete of the miniature altar, in the shrine erected there in his memory. In Taos, a Greek-American hotelier showed us his collection of Lawrence's clumsy paintings of nudes, which London's police censors had seized from a gallery in the late 1920s and released on condition they were removed from Britain. On seeing the paintings, Rebecca West said: 'I didn't know he had such pink friends.'

We spent three months in Nassau in an apartment supplied by the Ministry of Tourism. I began a novel, which I proposed, sardonically, of course, to call 'It's Better in the Bahamas', the Ministry's advertising slogan. I still have the tee-shirt. We enjoyed the midwinter Junkanoo carnival and the swimming, but I found that the former colony's highly developed tourist industry and the Bahamians' highly developed xenophobia made the place less lovely than it had been during World War II. The Ministry said I could use their slogan as a title only if the publisher gave them ten thousand free copies to use as promotional gifts to rich potential clients. The unacceptable bargain was the excuse I needed to abandon an increasingly distasteful project.

Another time, Arthur Hailey, the author of *Airport* and other tremendous bestsellers, let us stay in his Lyford Quay guest house for a couple of weeks, while I profiled him for the *Telegraph*. He was methodical about everything he did. He kept his large collection of vintage wines in a thermostatically controlled 'cellar' above ground. In his study, he received daily reports from New York, London and Zurich on the state of his investments. His principal interest, he said, was in gold, which was then worth close to a thousand dollars an ounce. He solemnly advised me to 'get into gold'. However, on my freelance financial roller coaster I had nothing available to invest – and just as well, as the price of gold later plummeted.

We spent a month in Australia, collecting material for a *Telegraph* travel piece. British Airways and the Australian Tourist Board enabled my partner to accompany me when someone on another London newspaper commissioned her to write an article for them, which I then had to write for her. On the summit of Ayers Rock there was a massive visitors' book on a pedestal for all climbers to sign. As I knew we were soon to be followed by a journalist from the *Sunday Times*, I wrote a note asking him, 'What kept you so long?' It isn't easy to rise above the taunts of rivalry in the tradition of El Vino. We called on Morris West, the Australian millionaire novelist, who had recently returned from Italy to an ultra-modern mansion overlooking his swimming pool, jetty and yacht about an hour's drive north of Sydney. He was such an expert interviewee that my notes on our conversation amounted to a smoothly readable, instant article. After a Lucullan feast in an Italian restaurant on a clifftop, he provided a large, white Rolls for our journey back to Sydney. Since then I have admired the technical virtuosity of his prose, and have forgiven him for having caused my heart temporarily to shrivel with envy.

We spent a couple of months in New Orleans, while I did the research for a novel that Anthony Blond eventually published as *Jazz Jazz Jazz*. Thanks to Hibernian camaraderie, the Irish-American manager of the hotel near Canal Street, where we stayed for the expensive first twenty-four hours, made some telephone calls, and the next day we moved into an air-conditioned three-room apartment with a pool in the patio, in the middle of the old French Quarter. The rent for the apartment each month was the same as the hotel rate for a single day. Ben Bradlee, the legendary editor of the *Washington Post*, covered the first month's rent by accepting a feature that focused on a trade fair in the Dome. There was a big exhibition of state-of-the-art garbage trucks, and many opportunities to make what Herb Alexander had called cultural gestures. In Preservation Hall, we listened to brave old men playing old music for tourists. For only one dollar, the musicians would respond to any reasonable request; for five dollars, they would somehow overcome their boredom and play 'When the Saints Go Marching In'. Sated by Dixieland classics, I interviewed dancers in a company of transsexuals. One gorgeous creature somewhat weakened the glamorous illusion by complaining that inflation had made vaginas so outrageously costly that she hadn't yet been able to pay to have her vocal cords surgically adjusted and she was stuck with a voice as deep as Tallulah's. I was reminded of *Conundrum* and the delicacy with which James Morris, once a colleague on the *Manchester Guardian*, told about the experience of becoming Jan.

We visited Gregory's, a very pleasant little *boîte* on the Upper East Side of New York. Brooks Kerr, a blind, young, white pianist, was playing Duke Ellington music, with the help of two ex-Ellingtonians, Russell Procope, clarinet and sax, and Sonny Greer on drums. Brooks had a phenomenal musical memory: he remembered every note of everything that Ellington ever wrote, a monumental body of work. I dredged obscure titles from the depths of my memory, compositions I had not heard for many years, such as 'Misty Morning', 'Saturday Night Function' and 'In a Jam'. No matter what I asked for, Brooks would tilt his head to one side, as though listening, and say: 'You mean the one that goes like this?'

Sonny Greer, who was in his eighties, enchanted us with the suavity of his wire brushes and the good humour of his showmanship and verbal asides. He was Ellington's first and longest-serving drummer, starting in the Washingtonians, in Duke's home-town, then accompanying him to the Cotton Club, in Harlem, and around the world. 'When we went to London, back there early in the thirties,' Sonny recalled, 'we were invited to a party where the guest of honour was the Prince of Wales. He asked to play my drums, so of course I had to let him. He got champagne and a bottle of brandy just for him and me. He wasn't a great drummer – he could keep a sort of slow fox-trot tempo – but, man! Could he drink! After that I called him "The Whale". We got on fine.'

Sonny accepted my invitation to lunch at the United Nations the day after our first meeting. He picked us up at the Algonquin. His car was driven by a trumpet player called Tasty Parker. Why 'Tasty'? 'When they ask for two choruses,' he explained, 'I only give them the one – just a taste.' Sonny, a neat, diminutive fellow with hair as black and shiny as patent leather, was wearing a light-brown suit of consummate dapperness and highly polished, pointed orange shoes. 'You're looking mighty sharp today, Sonny!'

Tasty admiringly exclaimed. Sonny raised his eyebrows, as if the compliment surprised him. 'Going to the United Nations, Tasty,' he replied, 'you *got* to look sharp.'

Raymond Carroll, a friend who was *Newsweek*'s UN correspondent, met us at the entrance to the Secretariat and we were cordially greeted by the uniformed black guard at the door. 'Mr Greer!' he acknowledged with a broad smile. '*Sonny* Greer! This is an honour.' The guard and Sonny heartily shook hands. By the time we were settled around a coffee table by the long bar of the Delegates' Lounge, word of Sonny's visit had somehow already circulated. Dutch, Swedish and Indian delegates separately came up to declare their allegiance to the music of Duke Ellington. Sonny received their eulogies with diplomatic aplomb.

The occasion was a very happy one. In the Delegates' Dining Room, lunch was preceded by the cocktail of the day, 'El Presidente', a sort of daiquiri with secret complications. After lunch, there was some sightseeing. In a corridor, by chance, we encountered the Liberian lady who was then the President of the General Assembly. Raymond effected the introductions. The General Assembly were not in session, so she led us to the platform of the great, empty chamber. Sonny stepped up to the speakers' lectern and made an eloquent, impromptu speech.

'This place isn't empty,' he said. 'I see friends from all over the world.' Addressing the imaginary international gathering with passionate conviction, Sonny quoted the basis of his benign philosophy: 'Cast your bread upon the waters and it will come back buttered toast.' At Gregory's that evening almost everyone was drinking El Presidentes.

56

My publicity-shy partner and I spent most of the time at home and on Bantry Bay Golf Course. In between games and slumping in my old-folk posture in a Lazy Boy armchair, watching *Dad's Army*, *Keeping Up Appearances*, *The Simpsons* and documentaries on wars far away and long ago, I wrote book reviews for the *Spectator* and the *Irish Times* and seven more books for children.

Children allow unlimited imaginative freedom. I depicted fantastic situations as realistically as possible, involving, for examples, time-travel into the Australian aborigines' Dreamtime, Transylvanian vampires, a pterodactyl hatched from a supermarket egg, and even an intelligent pop musician. I found that children are tolerant readers, if you don't bore them with sermons. However, they do favour a basis of implicit morality. The fan-mail kept coming. I noticed that many letters were composed on personal computers, with elaborately ornate, multicoloured graphics, which, alas, failed to conceal the fact that not all children between the ages of seven and eleven have quite achieved literacy. I urged them to read E. B. White.

Although rustication became increasingly habituating, and the impulse to fly to page-one trouble-spots finally ceased to disturb me, there were occasions when I ventured abroad on my own.

Never having regarded myself as an 'investigative reporter' of the ingenuity that did so much to glorify the *Sunday Times* 'Insight Team', I was surprised when John Anstey said he wanted me to go to the Turks and Caicos Islands, in the Caribbean (goodie!) to find out about drug-smuggling (not so good). At first, I thought uneasily that I would have to operate as a detective and secret agent, a combination of Sherlock Holmes and James Bond. The scope of the assignment seemed immense; the briefing was vague.

In Miami, a spokesman for the Drug Enforcement Administration of the US Department of Justice, Cornelius Dougherty, of Irish descent, estimated that the drugs entering Florida from Latin America via the Caribbean annually amounted to the equivalent of about five and a half billion pounds in street-sale value. The DEA estimated that that was approximately an eighth of the annual US consumption. In Fort Lauderdale, Gene Francar, a DEA criminal investigator with special knowledge of the Turks and Caicos, criticised the Foreign and Commonwealth Office for not ordering an effective crack-down on the Crown Colony's illicit suppliers of aviation fuel to smugglers.

According to Francar, the usual bribe for refuelling a plane carrying narcotics was $25,000. 'There are people on South Caicos Island taking in at least $250,000 a *week*,' he said. 'That kind of money is hard to beat. We know who the people are and who's in charge, but we can't take overt action in a foreign country. Those people down there have gone from extreme poverty to great, illegitimate affluence in a very short time. The narcotics money is so influential that it is rapidly bringing about the creation of a completely new kind of power structure in the Turks, a whole new political system. They ought to think about *that* in London.'

I arrived in Cockburn Town, which was founded in the seventeenth century to produce salt. It was still a pleasantly drowsy little capital. I was there, ostensibly, to write a travel article, but my cover became immediately transparent. I spent most of the first day in the company of a man recommended by the DEA, Detective Inspector W. John Dagley, a brawny and shrewd forty-nine-year-old veteran of the West Midlands Police, Special Branch, the Prevention of Terrorism Unit and the Central Drugs Intelligence Unit. Even the simplest-minded observer, seeing us drinking beer and talking together for hours in a hotel garden, surely must have thought it unlikely that we were primarily concerned with improving the islands' facilities for tourists.

The inspector told me all about the Piper Cubs and Cessnas, the Beechcraft and Dakotas and the four-engined DC4s and DC6s he had seen taking on fuel at Caicos Air Services, all of them 'practically bursting with marijuana and cocaine'. There was plenty of easily observable evidence of what was going on. 'Absurdly conspicuous' was the way Francar described it; 'flagrant,' said Dagley. He said his function as an adviser was strictly circumscribed. 'The police and Customs officers, the tower operators and the people who paid them to co-operate with the traffickers have all got away with it. Their names are well known. The Americans have had the principal under surveillance for two years. He makes frequent trips to the US, where he has a large bank account. There have been no arrests . . .'

The Foreign and Commonwealth Office did not want to embarrass the local government, because the Chief Minister, Norman B. Saunders, was trusted by foreign investors. He personally guaranteed the confidentiality of bank accounts in Cockburn Town, which, according to the government-approved *Investor's Guide*, were protected by 'strict secrecy laws'. Dagley said the colony's eight-man police drug squad was ineffective. After two years advising the local police, he was disgusted by inaction and was looking forward to returning to the relative innocence of the West Midlands. He said he carried a gun in the Turks and Caicos, and when he visited Miami he checked into one hotel and stayed in another.

As well as being the Chief Minister, Saunders was the Minister of Tourism. When I interviewed him in his office, tourism was all we talked about. He suggested I go and have a look at Providenciales Island, where major touristic developments were taking place. He would provide me with a private plane, he said — an offer I couldn't refuse.

The small Cessna had a passenger seat to the right of the pilot. Beside each of us there was a large, open window. The visibility was excellent. At two thousand feet above the sea, it suddenly occurred to me that it would very easy for the pilot to shoot me and tip me out. The body would never be recovered. 'Too bad,' the pilot could say. 'He didn't fasten his seat-belt properly. When I banked to starboard, he just kind of fell.' There really wouldn't have been any point in the Chief Minister's having me murdered, though my nosiness might have irritated him, but all the talk about smuggling made me feel like a potential victim in a B-movie. A ridiculous thought. Saunders was so friendly. He invited me to accompany him and his family to church. On the other hand, weren't the most powerful gangsters famous for loving kittens and flowers?

A few days later Saunders and I sat side by side on an Air Florida afternoon flight from Grand Turk to Miami. We drank whisky, the sodium pentathol of journalism, but he only regaled me with stories of royal visits to his islands. Before we parted at the passenger terminal, however, I asked him who owned Caicos Air Services. I knew the answer but wanted to hear it from him. 'I do,' he said. I noticed that he carried his single piece of luggage, an attaché case, through Customs without inspection. After all, he was a Chief Minister.

The *Telegraph Sunday Magazine* did the story proud. On the cover, there was a photograph of a smartly uniformed police corporal standing at ease in front of Grand Turk Police Station. The traditional colonial solar topee with its silver spike looked unsuitable for a drugs war. The caption read: 'CARIBBEAN DRUGS SCANDAL. Is a British colony a stop-over for smugglers? Patrick Skene Catling investigates.' Six pages of text and pictures made the question mark seem redundant. I had not actually had to do much investigating. The DEA and the West Midlands Police had handed me the facts on a platter.

A short time after the article appeared there was a classic sting operation in a Miami hotel. Gene Francar told me on the telephone that a Florida court sentenced Chief Minister Saunders to eight years, 'but,' Francar added, 'he won't serve that long.' In any event, the DEA was gratified. Perhaps the FCO had decided that Saunders should no longer be protected. The *Telegraph* must be read carefully at the FCO.

57

In need of a postage stamp when walking from Albany along Piccadilly one fine Saturday morning, I dropped into the Ritz to seek help from the concierge. In the foyer, I saw Graham Greene coming my way. We had never met; but, of course, I knew the face well. Who didn't? It exactly resembled the famous, grey portrait by Karsh of Ottawa, those bags under the eyes, those vertical creases that harrowed the cheeks, emblems of a life of intellectual anguish and pleasures. That time I had seen Aldous Huxley browsing in a Beverly Hills bookshop I had not dared to accost him. Now, three decades later, I was determined not to let formality inhibit me.

'Mr Greene,' I said.

He paused with an interrogative frown, as if mildly curious rather than shocked. I got straight to the point.

'I wonder', I blurted out, 'whether there's any chance of our having a drink?'

The timing was fortunate: it was five minutes or so before opening time. He was a man able quickly to make up his mind.

'What a good idea,' he said.

'But not here,' I boldly added.

'No,' he agreed. 'I know just the place.'

Tall and lean and evidently energetic, he briskly led the way in silence down St James's Street and off the street into a small, hidden pub that I later recognised at the beginning of *The Human Factor*. He used real places in his fiction. Once he had written about them, they became mythical: Haiti, to his readers, is now little more than the setting for *The Comedians* and *Travels with My Aunt*: he had an extraordinary ability to fictionalise reality.

Recognising the well-known patron, the barman nodded a deferential greeting, and, without instruction, quickly filled a pint mug with beer and a second one for me. Still refraining from conversation, we took tentative sips. Greene spoke: 'I don't think this is doing it, is it?'

It was true that the flat, watery bitter was rather uninvigorating. With revived decisiveness, he ordered two pink gins. Without having to be told, the barman constructed large ones, very pale. Talk soon ensued. Greene had been a director of the Bodley Head when they published three of my novels. When, having requested the next round, I diffidently identified myself, he accepted the information without condescension. He even revealed that he was not unfamiliar with my repeatedly relied-upon *deus ex machina*, Sam Rathbone. An exhilarating moment, cherished ever after.

Greene was so impregnably established that he felt free to speak with candour astonishing in a casual first encounter. When I asked him what he thought of a London publisher we both knew, Greene said: 'He's a thief and a fool, a dangerous combination.' When Greene and I eventually went our different ways we were both cheerful.

The following year, I reviewed his novel *Monsignor Quixote*, the one I enjoyed most of all. Greene's version of the Cervantes romance presents an innocent priest as Quixote and a deposed Communist mayor as Sancho Panza, in modern Spain. Their affectionate, strongly felt, closely argued dialogue, between confrontations with the secret police, were perhaps the ultimate expression of the dichotomy of thought of many Greene protagonists and of Greene himself since *The Power and the Glory*. His serious work was always a battleground for doctrinaire faith against sceptical reason. Though reason seemed harder and sharper, faith finally prevailed. After the *Sunday Telegraph* published my respectful praise, I was surprised to receive a note from the author, thanking me for my 'encouraging review', which, he said, gave him 'a lot of pleasure'. This friendly acknowledgement led to the exchange of a few letters over the next several years.

His letter that meant the most to me was written in response to one of mine confessing that the more I considered Christianity the more I was confused by doubts. Could he offer any advice based on his own experience? In spite of the immensity of my request, his reply was patient and careful. Inscribed in his tiny hand-writing from La Résidence des Fleurs, his home in the South of France, the three-page letter said:

> Your letter arrives at a time when I find it most difficult to reply. I have always had reservations as a Catholic, even when I became one in 1927, especially as regards contraception. I find myself more and more opposed to the present Pope [John Paul II], the most political Pope from whom the world has suffered, for nearly 100 years. In age too I find myself more and more agnostic – I cling to the idea that I am wrong.
>
> I accepted Catholicism in 1927 as intellectually the most probable – or rather probably the nearest to an unknown truth. I discovered an emotional allegiance in 1938 during the persecution in Mexico. In John xxiii I felt reinforced. Today I pray without much hope to find again the intellectual conviction that the likelihood of the Christian faith is more reason-able than the denial.
>
> You see my difficulty in answering your letter. I have to go back nearly 50 years.
>
> I was impressed in those first years by Karl Adams' *The Spirit of Catholicism* – but I haven't read it since, and I mightn't be impressed today. Of late years *The Agony of Christianity* of Unamuno (a doubter too – doubt seems to me an essential

shadow cast by faith). *The Phenomenon of Man*, Pierre de Chardin. Newman's *A Grammar of Assent* (difficult reading to me now).

My own experience is that now I wouldn't perhaps have become a Catholic. I began the road too intellectually, and I am trying to find the road back – to a faith full of doubts. I would advise what I never practised – the leap – and not be too much concerned about doubts. A faith without doubts seems to me inhuman. There must be doubts about a mystery.

I'm writing rather late in the evening and my writing is very illegible. Do jump!

His writing, in fact, was crystal-clear, and so was his advice. In another letter, written in 1990, he gave me some literary advice, which was equally clear, and equally difficult to follow.

'I look forward to reading your new book,' he wrote. 'I suggest you are more honest even than you dare to be.'

58

There are many ways of escape from inconclusive theological self-questioning. I made two visits to the United States by Concorde, which moves faster than a bullet, at twice the height of Mount Everest, without any sensation of moving at all. At 58,000 feet, well above the weather, there were no ripples in the surface of the champagne.

On the first flight, the captain permitted me to visit the flight deck. I marvelled at the gadgets, such as the machmeter, which indicated that we were flying at 1,340 m.p.h. The Baltimore attack bombers I had helped to ferry across the Atlantic used to cruise at only a little more than 200 m.p.h. The captain smiled politely when I said I used to need about twenty minutes to take three sextant shots, work them out and plot a fix. I complimented him on his inertial navigation system, with its continuous read-out of the plane's exact position.

'Well,' he said, assuming a cockney accent to avoid any danger of seeming pretentious, 'it's just as well we've got it. At twice the speed of sound you couldn't 'alf get lost.'

Warwick Charlton, who was engaged in an abstruse propaganda exercise on behalf of the Victoria Sporting Club, a London casino, took me in Concorde to Washington to try to plant a story in the *Washington Post*, to give the report respectable credibility when it was played back in London. After Buck's Fizzes in the Concorde departure lounge at Heathrow, we left at 11 a.m. and spent most of the three hours and twenty minutes of the journey eating and drinking (the Lobster Newburg was good, but the pheasant, sad to say, was a little bit overdone), and arrived an hour and forty minutes before we started. Concorde passengers are provided with chauffeur-driven limousines to anywhere in the city of destination, so we got ours to go to the Madison Hotel, where Ben Bradlee customarily took refreshments; it was conveniently close to his office. Warwick and I completed our business in time to leave Washington before lunch. So much easier than *Mayflower II* . . .

My only other Concorde trip was arranged by John Anstey, who was in a hurry to get an interview with Miles Davis, the cool trumpet player, in time to go with some photographs the *Telegraph* had somehow acquired. This was at a time when Miles was deep into heroin, wasn't playing any music, and never, never gave interviews. I had to return to London without having got anywhere near the great recluse, but Anstey and I were able to put together something that looked like a new appraisal of the man. The photographs were excellent. And the flights, as usual, were enjoyed at no expense to me or the paper.

Those frivolous ventures inspired a frivolous book in which honesty seemed irrelevant. Bloomsbury commissioned *The Joy of Freeloading*, which they published as non-fiction, elegantly illustrated by Nicholas Garland, narrated in the first person, and discussed as non-fiction with Pat Kenny in his Saturday-night chat-show on Irish television. Most of the book was extravagantly fictional, but the TV appearance won me unprecedented prestige in the streets of Bantry. I discovered that when people say 'I saw you on television!' they mean the observation as a compliment, not an accusation.

But Graham Greene's exhortations were never long out of my mind. I went up to Roscrea, in County Tipperary, to Mount St Joseph Abbey. The Guest-Master of this warmly receptive

Cistercian monastery, Father Gabriel McCarthy, a Cork man, got me permission to use the library inside the enclosure, ordinarily barred to lay visitors. I visited the monastery several times. The librarian was very helpful. I read the books Greene had recommended, and many more, and was able to contemplate their tantalising concepts in spiritually salubrious surroundings. In the guest house, I was regularly assigned Room 12a.

One weekend, a group of seventeen- and eighteen-year-old sixth formers from Blackrock College, known as 'the Eton of Ireland', were making a retreat in Roscrea. The Abbot granted them and me an audience at the same time. After welcoming us with a conventional homily, he invited questions. One of the senior schoolboys asked with a wise-guy sneer: 'Do you ever have doubts?'

The Abbot cordially smiled. 'Oh, yes,' he said. 'Every day.'

59

Winter in West Cork can be boringly wet. It is never too cold, but sometimes there are fierce gales off the Atlantic. February is the dreariest month: the days still begin late; the nights begin early; in between, there is blue-grey melancholy. It is a month when many old people give up, a month of funerals, and my birthday.

Now, in the winter of 2003, I am seventy-eight, and this case history approaches close to date of publication. My companion and I have escaped from northern winter weather. We are spending three months on the tropical island of Grenada, the Spice Island, in the Eastern Caribbean, at 12 degrees north, quite near Venezuela and Trinidad. Grenada is a small, volcanic island (21 miles by 12), with dense rain-forest on the upper slopes and soft, white sand all around the coast. The population is about 100,000. Farming and fishing are still important (nutmeg, cinnamon, cocoa, bananas; tuna, swordfish, dolphin, etc.), but tourism is a seductive employer. Cruise ships call at St George's the capital on one-day visits, and there are new hotels along nearby Grand Anse Beach.

Since flying in Chapter One from Nassau, south-east across the Caribbean, I have visited several islands in this turquoise sea. Grenada is the most beautiful one I've seen, and is inhabited by some of the friendliest, most cheerful people I have ever met. They don't seem to resent that most of their early ancestors were brought over from Africa and enslaved on colonial sugar plantations. Grenada is where film-makers shot the best bits of Alec Waugh's *Island in the Sun*. It seemed the ideal place for the Harry Belafonte character to commit interracial adultery in, when that sort of activity was considered excitingly scandalous. The film was made long ago, but the beauty and friendliness endure. Patrick Leigh Fermor's description of Grenada in his Caribbean masterpiece, *The Traveller's Tree*, is still valid. Here today it is still possible, off the beaten track, to sense the exquisite languor of Ronald Firbank. And Nabokov/Humbert Humbert would have appreciated all the dark Lolitas in their teenage nubility in immaculately innocent school uniforms.

Our first Grenadian winter, we explored from a base at the Flamboyant. The hotel is poised on a steep hillside, descending terrace by terrace through gardens gaudy with flame trees and bougainvillaea, the national flower, to a swimming pool, a bar and restaurant breezily open to Grand Anse Beach, aquamarine-to-indigo sea and cobalt-blue sky. The Matisse intensity makes watercolours inadequate. I should have brought acrylics, but a camera is much easier. Grenada is a wonderful place for writing – an even better place for not writing. The proprietor of the hotel, Lawrence Lambert, MBE for charity, dispenses rum punch and presides over crab races on the restaurant floor. On one good night, I plumped for the calypso eroticism of Big Bamboo, an easy winner at 6 to 1, and hoped that my success was observed by the ghost of Jeffrey Bernard, who often had bad luck with horses.

Then we moved to a house in Calivigny, up a corkscrew road served by kamikaze buses with names such as Final Assassin. Though only four miles from the capital, this district is pleasantly rural. Here, under coconut palms, goats graze. At sunset, tree frogs sound like small, rusty wheels squeakily revolving. Anachronistic cocks, endemic in the tropics, crow vehemently almost all the time, except when they are exhausted, just before dawn. We became fond of a waterfront restaurant called Tout Bagay, which, according to a waitress, means 'everything is possible'. The creole sauce is enlivening.

A huge, lumpish, white cruise liner, like a Miami hotel adrift under a Liberian flag, ties up in the harbour. A horde of passengers, landlubbers for a few hours, trundle their fatness from souvenir shop to shop, buying baseball caps and tee-shirts to show the next port of call that they have already been somewhere else.

This year, thanks to Dermot Nolan, an Irish priest, we are settled in one of Hilda Milne's villas in Morne Rouge, a district only three minutes' walk from the beach. 'Why don't you live here all the time?' people ask. Like Odysseus lingering on the way home, I ask myself that question, and find it difficult to answer.

During three months without television, we read a lot. A couple of times a week, we visit the National Library, where there's a section of books about the West Indies. I have been reading about Grenada's turbulent history. The Caribs killed the Arawaks; the French killed the Caribs; the English took the island from the French; the French took it back, with the aid of a private army commanded by Count Dillon, an Irish Wild Goose; and the English finally occupied the island again, until Grenada gained independence in 1974. There was that terrible period in the early 1980s when Maurice Bishop and others seized power and were murdered by their more militantly Marxist conspirators in 1983. President Reagan, with some 6,000 troops and a few Eastern Caribbean policemen, restored Grenadian parliamentary democracy, much to the chagrin of Mrs Thatcher, it is said, who must have thought it was very rude of her friend Ronald to invade without prior consultation. The Grenada Post Office sells a set of stamps depicting Reagan beaming after the success of Operation Urgent Fury. Though the traumas were so recent, Grenadians seem politically carefree. The only traces of past dissidence are a few fading graffiti in support of Maurice Bishop and Fidel Castro. Grenada may have been caught like a fly in the World Wide Web, yet it is an island of smiles.

My helpmeet is swimming while I lounge in the shade of a palm-thatch umbrella outside the Coconut Beach Restaurant. This beach is a prime site for sunset-watching. I have just put aside Anthony Burgess's almost unbearably clever novel *Earthly Powers*. I am grateful that I can read all sorts of novels here, good, bad and indifferent, enjoying the luxury of not having to review them.

Slowly sipping rum and passionfruit juice through a straw, I review instead my own long past and consider my short future. I have done many of the things I originally hoped to do, and some that I should have tried harder not to do. My occupation as a sort of writer has certainly been better than working, though I sometimes envy men such as ditch-diggers, who probably rarely awake at 4 o'clock in the morning wondering what they are going to do next day. Is there such an occupational distress as ditch-digger's block?

Warwick Charlton died last year at the age of eighty-four. He spent the last two years of his life devising what he called his 'last hurrah', the ultimate theme park. He developed a concept for a 'Spacetime Centre', with the co-operation of none other than Stephen Hawking, Companion of Honour, Lucasian Professor of Mathematics at Cambridge University, who is widely considered to be the greatest scientific thinker since Newton and Einstein. As promised in Charlton's prospectus, the Hawking Spacetime Centre will combine 'the most successful elements of the theme park, inter-active multimedia, together with creative, compelling and educational entertainment'. Visitors to the centre will be able to go on simulated voyages through space and time to the farthest reaches of the cosmos. Travelling from the Big Bang to the end of time will be 'an exploration of man's struggle to see better, farther, bigger and smaller'.

Charlton said he was inspired by Hawking's first phenomenal international bestseller, *A Brief History of Time*, which was first published in 1988. In that book, which more than 20 million people have bought, and perhaps half a dozen people have fully under-stood, Hawking, according to Carl Sagan's foreword, was 'attempting to . . . understand the mind of God'. Hawking's heroic efforts to achieve the grand synthesis of a unified field theory, the 'answer to everything', have added further significance to my visits to Roscrea and memories of the infinity dreams of my early childhood. So, of course, I am very glad that, God willing, if there is a God, I will be allowed to write the Hawking Spacetime Centre's official history.

Writing is an addiction I do not wish to be cured of.

Ahakista – St George's

2003